Lillian Birnbaum

PETER HANDKE

QUIET PLACES

Translated by Krishna Winston and Ralph Manheim

Peter Handke was born in Griffen, Austria, in 1942. His many novels include *The Goalie's Anxiety at the Penalty Kick*, *A Sorrow Beyond Dreams*, *My Year in the No-Man's-Bay*, and *Crossing the Sierra de Gredos*, all published by FSG. Handke's dramatic works include *Kaspar* and the screenplay for Wim Wenders's *Wings of Desire*. Handke is the recipient of many major literary awards, including the Georg Büchner, Franz Kafka, and Thomas Mann Prizes and the International Ibsen Award. In 2019, he was awarded the Nobel Prize in Literature "for an influential work that with linguistic ingenuity has explored the periphery and the specificity of human experience."

Krishna Winston, now retired from teaching German literature and environmental studies at Wesleyan University, has been translating the work of Peter Handke since 1993. She has translated the work of many other authors, including Johann Wolfgang von Goethe, Günter Grass, Christoph Hein, and Werner Herzog.

Ralph Manheim (1907–1992) was an American translator of German and French literature. He translated the work of many notable authors, including Bertolt Brecht, Louis-Ferdinand Céline, Günter Grass, Hermann Hesse, and Peter Handke. The PEN/Ralph Manheim Award for Translation, inaugurated in his name, is a major lifetime achievement award in the field of translation.

ALSO BY PETER HANDKE

The Goalie's Anxiety at the Penalty Kick

Short Letter, Long Farewell

A Sorrow Beyond Dreams

The Ride Across Lake Constance and Other Plays

A Moment of True Feeling

The Left-Handed Woman

The Weight of the World

Slow Homecoming

Across

Repetition

The Afternoon of a Writer

Absence

Kaspar and Other Plays

The Jukebox and Other Essays on Storytelling

Once Again for Thucydides

My Year in the No-Man's-Bay

On a Dark Night I Left My Silent House

Crossing the Sierra de Gredos

Don Juan

The Moravian Night

The Fruit Thief

QUIET PLACES

Picador
FARRAR,
STRAUS
AND
GIROUX
New York

QUIET PLACES

COLLECTED ESSAYS

PETER HANDKE

Translated from the German
by Krishna Winston and
Ralph Manheim

Picador
120 Broadway, New York 10271

Originally published in German as *Versuch über die Müdigkeit*, *Versuch über die Jukebox*, and *Versuch über den geglückten Tag* in 1989, 1990, and 1991 by Suhrkamp Verlag, Frankfurt am Main, and as *Versuch über den Stillen Ort* and *Versuch über den Pilznarren* in 2012 and 2013 by Suhrkamp Verlag, Berlin
"Essay on Tiredness," "Essay on the Jukebox," and "Essay on the Successful Day" were originally published in 1994 by Farrar, Straus and Giroux as *The Jukebox and Other Essays on Storytelling*
Originally published in 2022 by Farrar, Straus and Giroux
First paperback edition, 2023

The Library of Congress has cataloged the Farrar, Straus and Giroux hardcover edition as follows:
Names: Handke, Peter, author. | Winston, Krishna, translator. | Manheim, Ralph, 1907–1992, translator.
Title: Quiet places : collected essays / Peter Handke ; translated from the German by Krishna Winston and Ralph Manheim.
Description: First edition. | New York : Farrar, Straus and Giroux, 2022.
Identifiers: LCCN 2021050322 | ISBN 9780374125592 (hardcover)
Subjects: LCGFT: Essays.
Classification: LCC PT2668.A5 Q54 2022 | DDC 834/.914—dc23/eng/20211029
LC record available at https://lccn.loc.gov/2021050322

Designed by Janet Evans-Scanlon

Paperback ISBN: 978-1-250-86296-9

P1

CONTENTS

ESSAY ON QUIET PLACES

Translated by Krishna Winston

Stilles Örtchen, "quiet little place,"
a German euphemism = privy, outhouse, WC,
restroom, bathroom, toilet, ladies'/men's room,
washroom, lavatory, comfort station . . .

LONG, LONG AGO I READ A NOVEL BY THE ENGLISH WRITER A. J.—Archibald Joseph, if I'm not mistaken—Cronin, in a German translation, whose English title was *The Stars Look Down*. It was a fairly thick book, but it's not the fault of the author or his story, which at the time captivated and filled me with enthusiasm, that I remember very few of the details. What has stayed with me, in addition to those stars, always looking down: an English mining district and the chronicle of a hard-up miner's family, juxtaposed with the story of the well-heeled mine owners ("if I'm not mistaken"). Much later, when I saw John Ford's film *How Green Was My Valley*, the faces and landscapes fooled me, in a good sense, into thinking, though I knew better, that I was seeing the film version not of the novel by Richard Llewellyn but of Cronin's *The Stars Look Down*. Yet I did retain one detail from the tale of the stars that look down, and this detail haunts me to this day and provides the starting point for my almost lifelong circling and encircling of the Quiet Place and quiet places, and accordingly that's where I mean to begin my essay on the subject.

The detail to which I'm referring conveys the following, whether in my memory or in my imagination: one of the heroes in *The Stars Look Down*—I think there are two, children who grow up as the story progresses, one from the wealthy family, the other from the poor family—anyway, one of them makes a habit of taking refuge in the toilet, lavatory, privy, not when he needs to go but whenever the company of others—adults, family members—gets on his nerves and becomes too much for him, a burden and a torment. He locks himself in the water closet ("as the name suggests") so as not to have to listen to the incessant jabber, and stays there longer than usual.

The story—or is this now my version?—says it has to be the scion of the wealthy family who feels driven to the Quiet Place, and it wants this place to be located far from the parlors and chambers in the manor house, and decrees that the boy does nothing there but listen to the silence. And I'm fairly sure it's not so much the original story, the novel, as my own version that wants it to be in that out-of-the-way place, away from the family, that the youthful hero conceives the idea and the sensation to which the book owes its title: that when he's there, the stars look down on him. His Quiet Place had no roof, was open to the heavens.

For me, too, the Quiet Place has a story, different in some ways, but analogous to the one I've just summarized, and a lively and varied one, too, considering the place itself, which is really not "monotonous." Now I'd like to try to trace the outlines of that story, not filling in the specifics, but parallel and in counterpoint to suggestions for stories and images that several people have sent my way.

It was on the threshold between childhood and adolescence that the Quiet Place began to take on a meaning for me over and above the ordinary and customary. As I sit here at my writing table, far from the sites of my childhood and from childhood itself, and try to remember what toilets were like after the Second World War in East Berlin—in Niederschönhausen, part of Pankow, and later the privy on my grandfather's farm in southern Carinthia, only sketchy images come to me—not a single one from the city—and besides, and above all, I don't figure in them, not as a child and not as a living being; those images lack any subject that could say "I," are disembodied.

Just the usual: thick or less thick packets of newspaper cut into conveniently sized pieces, with a hole punched through them so they could be hung on a string from a nail driven into the board wall, the variant being that the words on most of the pieces were in Slovenian, from the newspaper my grandfather subscribed to, the weekly *Vestnik* (The Courier). The vertical shaft under the drain hole ran down toward the manure pile outside the cow stalls, or didn't it continue on to a kind of dry well?—the distinguishing feature being that the shaft was unusually long, or at least seemed so to me as a child, because the privy was located on the second floor of a farmhouse built into a steep slope in the middle of the village, at the end of a long wooden gallery, where the house and barn came together, and it formed a part or corner of the barn as well as of the gallery, completely unobtrusive, its board walls the same weathered gray as the planks of the gallery and the siding of the hayloft, easy to miss, hardly recognizable as a distinct place, even as a shed, let alone as a privy, since the heart shape traditionally cut into privy doors throughout the region was absent, and the door not even recognizable as such—all you saw was a slight bump-out in the wall where the gallery met the hayloft, which a stranger to the village might well have mistaken for a cubby where my grandfather kept his carpentry tools. Visitors rarely came to the house, however, and the regional agent for the insurance company, Assicurazioni Generale, stopped by at most once a year, and to him, should damage caused by fire or lightning have occurred, a room that small would hardly have counted. What I find striking in any case is the distance between that peasant privy and the main part of the house, whether for everyday use or special occasions; hard to picture, in the Slovenian village of Stara Vas, unlike in the more middle-class market towns down on the plain, someone peeing in a public place as portrayed in a number of seventeenth-century Dutch genre paintings.

But now another special thing about that Quiet Place comes back to me: the light in that little enclosure, which had two sources (without electricity, of course, and I wonder now how the members of the extended family found their way there at night along the dark gallery: with a kerosene lantern? a flashlight? a candle? by feel?). The first kind of light came from above, in the place itself, so to speak—shining through cracks in the board walls? No, my grandfather was competent enough as a carpenter not to have left a single crack—rather the light came through the wooden walls, through the boards themselves, as if filtered, also through dot-sized holes, hardly as big as the eye of a needle, in the knots, more or less round, where branches had once grown out of the tree trunk; over time these knots had perhaps shrunk more than the rest of the sawn trunk. A strange indirect lighting, found nowhere else in the house; indirect meaning without windows, but all the more substantial; light that surrounded one, by which one found oneself surrounded in the privy—one?—me; so there was already an "I" there after all?

And the second source of light? The light that shone into the long vertical shaft from the open-air manure pile below, in the depths, as it were. That light comes up the shaft—please don't expect me to say "along with the stench"; having no memory of that, I won't mention it. This light doesn't reach the person, "me," peering down through the hole, but at most comes halfway up the shaft, no, not even that, hardly a wrist-to-elbow's length up, and remaining pooled down below, a substantial shimmer completely different from the one surrounding the person peering down from above, a shimmering probably reinforced by all the yellow from the straw mixed with the cow manure way down there, which makes the inner walls of the shaft visible by following its form, the circle: living geometry, entirely natural. And why does a local anecdote I heard from my mother come back to me now, in which a child presents a basket of well-shaped, gleaming pears to the local clergyman, announcing, "Pastor, I'm supposed to bring you greetings from my parents and these pears from the shithouse tree!"?

For whatever reason: unlike the young hero in *The Stars Look Down*, in my childhood I didn't need the Quiet Place as a retreat, not even once. From that time, I remember the Quiet Place or Places, if at all, only from the perspective of an observer, an eye-er, as a kind of medium. I didn't even experience the place as quiet—either as quiet or secret or in any other way: sounds of whatever kind had, and have, nothing to do with it. (Nor do smells—strange though that may be, or not so strange.) Eye-er? A way station? A minor character, bodiless, invisible, the place empty, nothing but a sight, then as now.

The first time I see myself in such a Quiet Place as the main character, in flesh and blood, the scene takes place far from my native village—yes, that's the term that was used once upon a time. I'm thinking of my years in boarding school. And the experience that left the strongest impression occurred at the very beginning, on the evening of the day I entered (or what word should I use?). It was a day in early September in the nineteen fifties; rain was coming down hard and darkness came on early. In those days daylight saving time hadn't yet been introduced in our area. Before the three hundred or so pupils could sit down to our first communal meal in the enormous dining hall—I'd never eaten in a hall, indeed had never been in a hall of any kind other than the gym in my elementary school—all of us had to stand and repeat the blessing offered by the spiritual prefect.

The prayer went on and on, or so it seemed to me, probably also because since arriving at the school in early afternoon I'd had an urgent need to relieve myself but had no idea how to find the toilets in the rambling and bewildering building, a former castle; in fact, I hadn't even looked for them. What about asking? How did they expect us to behave? So we newbies, a ragtag crew from the most remote corners of the country, stood and stood and repeated and repeated, wishing we could take our seats on the benches at the long, long refectory tables, while outside the closed doors of the dining hall the cold evening rain beat down harder and harder on the gravel paths in the castle's courtyard, where—or am I deluding myself?—the fountain continued to patter. But no: we had to keep on standing and praying, and when we finally sat down, a flood of something I thought no one could help noticing, eyed by all the other adolescents at the table, trickled onto the handsome old stone pavers, lit by many chandeliers, wound its way for all to see from bench leg to bench leg and then from table leg to table leg, leaving my own legs and my new trousers, purchased for the beginning of this next phase in my life, clammy from the crotch down, and soaking into my more or less brand-new shoes.

So until the evening meal ended I remained seated in this condition, not daring to move, pretending to eat, acting as if nothing were amiss. The minute we streamed out of the hall, however, I slipped away from the crowd and made my way to the darkest corner of the arcade that surrounded the courtyard. In my memory I see myself finally (!) leaning against a column in the dark, completely lost, in the true sense of the word, in this unfamiliar environment, I who had often had to adjust to unfamiliar environments of various sorts since I was little. Escaping into the open was out of the question, and not only because of the locked gates and the rain pelting down, but so was rejoining the others, my age-mates, in the study halls and later the dormitories: my reputation with them was done for.

The sound of running water, noticeably different from that of the rain, made itself heard somewhere behind the new pupil. It seemed to be coming from the other side of a door, and this door turned out to be unlocked, the door to the most secluded, most secret restroom in the boarding school, perhaps meant for visitors, or the groundskeepers, or workmen brought in from the outside, and usually locked, but by chance open on this particular evening. Upon entering I didn't turn on the light, didn't hunt for a switch, just stood there in total darkness, with the sound of running water all around me, coming both from the urinals and from one or two stalls in which the toilets hadn't shut off. For a long time I didn't budge. I'd already relieved myself elsewhere, for better or worse. But this place now met a very different need, and in the course of the hour or so I spent there, it assuaged that need, at least for the present—for my introduction to the school. Here for the first time I became the main character, in person, in a Quiet Place. And for the first time it got me to listen in a way typical of such a place, which would come into play later on, and left a lasting influence. What could be heard was not limited to the various kinds of running water, both inside and outside the unvaryingly cold stone walls, but also the noises or whatever, muted by the sound of the water and by distance, made by my fellow pupils on the upper floors of the building, which accordingly reached my ears not as yelling and hollering but rather, for moments at a time, as something almost homey, almost. The sound of running water in that unlit

Quiet Place as the undertone. But the tone that counted, way off in the background, was the other one.

During the years I spent at that Catholic boarding school, the restroom, and not only this one off the arcade, provided a possible haven, even though I hardly ever sought refuge there again. I'm not sure why my far more prevalent penchant for seeking out the confessional during Mass comes to mind now as similar, albeit only to a certain degree. Similar in what sense? In this sense: without having any sins to confess to the invisible "Father Confessor," and certainly no specific ones, instead rattling off a few generic ones from the catechism's catalogue of sins, I felt impelled to get away from the others, my fellow pupils in the pews and the rest, away from the whole ceremony, to an out-of-the-way place, and the confessional, the confession booth, was indeed out of the way, far back in the nave, as I recall, and simply making my way there did me good. Upon my return to my classmates and the service, my heart usually felt free, or at least freer, almost bouncy, but not because I'd unburdened my conscience in the darkness of the confessional into the dimly glimpsed ear of the otherwise invisible confessor—and by the way, what did *conscience* mean to me in those days?

These two places, the quiet one and the sin booth, aren't really similar; in fact, they're altogether different in view of what I have in mind, at once vaguely and urgently, as the main concern or main theme of this essay (yes, it's hovering before my mind's eye, and may it continue to do so, unresolved), and on which I want to remain focused: getting up in the middle of the service, with my fellow pupils all around me in the pews, and slipping away, all by myself, to the confessional: neither action came from a compulsion, and certainly not from a pressing need. Every time it resulted purely from boredom. Of course boredom can also turn or develop into a kind of need, and a powerful one. But that kind of boredom, boredom as a form of suffering, as the opposite of being pressed for time, was something I hadn't experienced yet in those early years, or am I merely imagining that now, or acting as if that were the case, now that I'm working on this essay about the Quiet Place.

There were times when I loved school ("love of learning" still applies), but there I also went through periods, not that seldom, when I wished that I could retreat to the infirmary, leaving the study hall and my desk in the classroom behind, not with a serious illness but maybe with a fairly high temperature, and especially that I'd be allowed to stay there to convalesce for a few days after it went down, with nothing to reflect on and puzzle over from morning to night but the geometric or other patterns woven into the exceptionally white and soft sickroom bedsheets. Such wishes hardly ever came true during those years. On the rare occasions when I did have a fever, it never got that high, and rubbing the thermometer, as others advised me to do, wouldn't have helped: from an early age I had no talent for pulling off a good scam, except as a game, when nothing was at stake. The moment it turned serious, with something to be gained or someone to be defrauded, I invariably got caught, often when I was completely innocent—the actual perpetrator was sitting in front of, next to, or behind me.

One time I was in luck, however—allowed to spend several days in the infirmary, don't ask me why, as the only patient there, nursed solicitously by a nun, and as I lay there from early to late, the tall, wide window gave me a view from my bed in a direction and of a landscape entirely different from what could be glimpsed through the classroom transoms or from the study hall, whose rows of desks were bolted down far from any windows: I saw an area that, with its woods and cow pastures, was at once familiar and novel, with no school buildings or other barriers between the landscape and my sickroom, itself quite small, in contrast to all the halls in the former castle: study halls, dining halls, and dormitories.

If only I could stay in this cozy room! But one morning there was no help for it: I had to get up, dress, and make my way back to life and the company of the hale and hearty. Away from the boredom of snow-white sheets, cud-chewing or dozing cattle outside my window, the uniform crests of spruce trees forming an even horizon. (Yet during those days in my sickroom, just as much later, in a hospital, with all kinds of electronic thingamajigs on my chest and a view from the window of a densely occupied cemetery, I never once felt bored, and if I did after all, my memory, which has the last word here, says: no.) While I was away and alone, I may have missed one of my friends or another, or, more likely, certain teachers. But now, after leaving the infirmary, I hadn't the slightest desire to rejoin them. I should have reported to class immediately, up in one of the schoolrooms under the castle's eaves. Instead I sneaked along the corridors and the galleries that surrounded the castle's courtyard, deserted during these early-morning hours, and hid or rather slipped into one of the restrooms, likewise deserted. The next recess was quite far off, and I was in luck again, free to stay there undisturbed for a good long time. But after my warm infirmary room my various refuges felt freezing cold, and the constant sound of running or rushing water on all sides seemed to make the cold more intense. I was chilled through and through. Could it also be that my temperature was below normal after days of being elevated? And this freezing, shivering, and shaking suited me just fine. I'd stay in the restroom till the fever returned, maybe even higher. I locked myself into the stall closest to the half-open window and stood there till the next recess passed, and the one after that. No one came looking for me—not yet. I just had to keep my teeth from chattering. Do your work, cold place, bring back my fever. But the fever refused to return, even after that ice-cold morning.

Later on I had only one more extended stay in a Quiet Place like that. It happened in the monthslong period I had free after graduating from secondary school. I'd transferred for my last two years to a public school, enjoying the social scene thoroughly but glad to see it end, the boarding-school experience faded by then as if it had never been, even as a figment of my imagination. My new classmates, boys and girls, had coalesced into a congenial group, and I, or "the person I was then," was accepted into it, if not as the cock of the roost, then at least wishing I could be that at certain moments, as did the few other boys, some more, some less, in our class, which was unusually small—which perhaps accounted for our solidarity.

And now, with our school years behind us, the others, the members of the group, my group, all of them but me, set out to travel through Yugoslavia and Greece. They'd all wanted me to come along—and I'm not just imagining that—and I was the one who'd weaseled out of the trip. Weaseled out with various excuses and evasions: my mother couldn't give me money for the trip. That was true, but it was also an excuse. I also explained that as a stateless person, I had no passport. That was likewise a fact, but according to the authorities there would have been a way around it, and in rejecting that possibility, as I had the earlier suggestion that a collection be taken up for me, I was in essence using the obstacle to get out of going.

To this day I don't know why something in me resisted so strenuously taking that trip with a group for whom I actually felt considerable affection. Be that as it might, one fine summer day in the early sixties I found myself alone in my village, done with school, separated from my friends, and frantically idle after all the intense times we'd enjoyed together.

So I set out by myself, alone, with the duffel bag popular at the time, stuffed with clothes, etc., on my shoulder, which was supposed to make me look like a boy who'd be on the road for a good long time.

In the end I didn't get far, and certainly wasn't on the road very long. True, I headed west, but even in that direction Carinthia doesn't extend very far, and I didn't even make it past the western border. On the first day I got as far as Villach, I no longer recall how, a distance (as in a Western) of about fifty miles from home, and there I spent the night, I no longer recall where. On the second day I made less progress—only to the market town of Radenthein, near Lake Millstatt, where I dropped in unannounced on a classmate's family and spent the night there in my thick sleeping bag, whether on a bed, a sofa, or where or how, I no longer remember.

I do recall, however, where I spent the third night, and especially how. It was in the town of Spittal on the Drau, only a short distance from Radenthein and an even shorter distance from Lake Millstatt. Nowadays the town no longer mentions the river, referring instead to the lake: Spittal on Lake Millstadt.

Got through the night—"spent the night" wouldn't be the right way to phrase it—in the railroad station's restroom. I'd run out of money, or at any rate didn't have enough for a hotel room or even a bed in a youth hostel, which the town of Spittal didn't have at the time—and perhaps still doesn't? But in those days railway stations didn't close at a certain hour of the night, so I could hang out till midnight and maybe even later, in the building and the surrounding area.

For a while it remained almost warm; it was summer, after all. Except that in those days at least it usually cooled off rapidly on summer nights; as I recall, we regarded a summer night that stayed mild all the way through as very unusual, very special: rather than go inside one wanted to stay out no matter what, sitting together, yes, with others, not talking, the occasional words and the sounds of nature forming part of the stillness, and even though no scent of honeysuckle wafted through the summer night, only the night breeze, that breeze meant as much as the honeysuckle in Mississippi and other southern states in the books of William Faulkner.

At and in the railway station in Spittal on the Drau it wasn't that kind of night. Long before midnight the air turned chilly, and soon the cold spread through the building, which might as well have been open on all sides. First I tramped all around outside, passing the railroad workers' gardens and going down into the meadows along the river, out of range of the station lights, then gradually making smaller and smaller circuits.

For a while I managed to pass the time, keeping my blood flowing, so to speak, and distracting myself from my tiredness by watching the trains from the various platforms, especially the long-distance trains bound for Athens, Belgrade, Sofia, Bucharest, Munich, Cologne, Copenhagen, and Ostende—all of which made stops, by the way. But then fewer and fewer of them came through, and from a certain moment on tiredness got the better of me. It became so overwhelming that I didn't know what to do. Or rather I did know: I locked myself into one of the stalls in the station's restroom, which, though out of the way, was somewhere inside the complex.

The door to the stall had to be opened with a one-schilling coin, and when I locked it from the inside, at first I felt somewhat protected or sheltered. Without more ado I lay down on the tiled floor, using my duffel bag as a pillow. The stall was so small, however, that stretching out was impossible, so I braced my head on the back wall and coiled my body around the toilet in a sort of semicircle. The lighting in the rather large restroom, quite bright and white, stayed on all night and shone only slightly subdued into the stall, which was open at the top and also at the bottom, though there only by about as much as a child's foot was long. Using a few articles of clothing from my duffel bag as covers, I tried to read Thomas Mann's *Buddenbrooks*, which for a long time hadn't appealed to me but the day before in Radenthein had proved unexpectedly fascinating when, toward the end, with death approaching, the doomed Thomas Buddenbrook almost jauntily begins to reflect on the meaning of life.

But in this position, curled around the white toilet bowl, I discovered that reading was also impossible. Besides, after the initial excitement of bedding down in a place like this, I found my tiredness returning with a vengeance. (Today, as I'm writing this, I feel my head and eyes growing heavy, and I have to fight the temptation to lie down and go to sleep, just as back then all I could picture was a bed.)

My eyes did close. But sleeping in the bathroom stall was out of the question. Though I'd paid the price of admission, as the night progressed I felt more and more like a lawbreaker. I had no right to be lying on the floor in that restroom, let alone to sleep there. Nonetheless I didn't unlock the door and step outside. There was no other place for me to spend the night. This was my place, including the spectral reflection of my face in the porcelain toilet bowl, which I lay facing until after the sky first began to turn gray, and including the lubricating oil, or whatever it was, pooled around the bolts that fastened the toilet to the floor, along with wisps of hair, or fluff, or mulch, or whatever it was, stuck to the oil, along with the sleeping flies—"ah, sleep!"—or spiders, or daddy longlegs, or whatever they were, on the walls of the stall.

In my position as a lawbreaker I heard the sounds of the outside world that reached me in my Quiet Place entirely differently, not as distant or even disembodied but rather at close range, eardrum-close. For one thing, maybe that kind of hearing was perfectly normal, since those hours of the night belonged mostly to the freight trains, racing through the railyard without stopping in an iron Wild Hunt. For another thing, during the longer and longer periods of silence, the young man lying there without permission heard the distant hooting of owls in the meadows down by the river as if it were also right by his ear: "There he is—lying there—catch him—grab him—hold him!" Even the summery concert of crickets chirping in the railway workers' gardens (so the night can't have been that cold after all) startled him when he'd almost dozed off with a burst of screeches or trills seemingly aimed straight into his ear canal; and likewise the faintest swish from one of the trees around the station. Though some hours of the night were completely silent, that Quiet Place was anything but.

Nonetheless no other place called to me. After a while I even stopped wishing I were in a bed. I was determined to stick it out till dawn—which, to be sure, would come early, it being the beginning of July—curled around the toilet bowl in a half- or almost complete circle, in which connection it now occurs to me that when the legendary Wild Hunt stormed through the air, panting for the kill, those in its path would seek protection from the ground, lying down in a wagon-wheel formation. But what if one was alone? All by myself I created a wheel, almost, but gradually that felt like a haven, if not a very safe one.

Not for anything in the world would I have wanted to change places with the rest of my group, who, while I lay curled up awkwardly on the hard stone floor, were outdoors in their sleeping bags somewhere under the southern sky, and here and there two of them would be holding hands or such as they slept or lay awake. Of course they, too, might have some stories to share afterward, but those would be nothing compared with what I had to tell, though not the following day, and not the following year either—the situation in and of itself and at the time wasn't sufficiently meaningful—and I had no one to share it with, whether a special someone or someone else close to me: any such person would have looked at me, picturing me curled around the toilet bowl, and shaken his or her head.

Not until years later did the moment arrive when I could recapitulate some features of that night, not orally but in writing, transforming it, though not intentionally; the transformation just happened as I was writing.

In my first longer story, written toward the end of my time at the university, when I wasn't a real student anymore, the blind narrator imagines his brother, whose return from the war he waits for in vain to the end, spending a night on his way home in just such a railroad restroom and with just such a duffel bag, and having nothing before his eyes all night long but the white reflective surface of the toilet bowl.

And twenty years later, Filip Kobal, the "I" in the story *Repetition*, sets out after graduating from secondary school, while all his classmates are bound for Delphi and Epidaurus, and likewise spends his first night on the ground with his duffel bag. He beds down, however, not in a public restroom but rather in an alcove in the who-knows-how-many-miles-long railway tunnel between Rosenbach in Carinthia and Jesenice in Yugoslavia, and it turns out to be a perilous night in the pitch-black tunnel, with freight trains stampeding by at unpredictable intervals, just inches away from where Kobal is curled up in his alcove. The following day Filip Kobal starts out on his epic hike, lasting an entire season, through Slovenia, in those days still part of Yugoslavia, seeking, likewise in vain, the brother who went missing during the war, and the encounter with a different landscape and language opens Filip's eyes, whereas "I," after that night in the station of Spittal on the Drau, just roamed around the area a bit more and then: home as fast as I could go, back to my village. Only much later did I get to Slovenia in Yugoslavia, including Jesenice, and even later to the Karst, without which there would have been no *Repetition*.

During my years at the university, the WC lost its meaning as a refuge. Increasingly other venues, buildings, locales came to take its place. And these I didn't have to seek out in person. Usually it was enough to catch sight of one of these "requisite objects." It could be a toolshed somewhere, a shelter at a streetcar stop, a bus parked for the night, a partially collapsed underground bunker from who knows which war. Equally good were spaces not intended to serve as such: the mere sight of the hollow area under a ramp—the loading dock of a dairy or a shipping company, or some other ramp—could suggest the possibility of sheltering or hiding out, and occasionally a pile of A-frame advertising or political-campaign placards could offer a teepee-like space, which, if not suitable for habitation, could at least offer a person temporary shelter, imagined as dry and warm, or somewhat warmer and more homey than being out in the open.

At times these moments of feeling hidden or protected could result from a simple glance at the ground, at streetcar tracks and the sand and leaves accumulated between them. That would become a Quiet Place, even if, at the same time, the streetcar's bell broke the silence and, as the car rounded the nearby bend, its wheels screeched more harshly than the thickest piece of chalk on a blackboard. One could feel one's way into this quiet set of tracks, deserted except for the sand and leaves, and in one's mind be transported to an entirely different place (here the use of "one" is appropriate, for a change), without specifically wanting to crawl into a rolled-up dry leaf, like the "I" in a poem by Hermann Lenz.

Remarkable, too, that again and again the mere image of one of the quiet places from my childhood back in the village came to represent the place itself, that this memory, at a remove of place and time, could make the place appear more vividly than when I was actually there. Such sites of homecoming or turning in/off could now be represented for instance by the rural cattle scales—used less and less, by the way—installed in the ground, either bare earth or asphalt, on grade: flexible wooden planks with room for the longest bulls and the fattest cows, the weighing mechanism located in a hollow under the planks, from which the animal's weight would be transmitted, accurately one hoped, to the gauge in the hut right behind the scale; as a child, and also later, one could get onto the scale and rock and rock on the flexible planks, and at a certain point the planks would go on rocking by themselves, which offered a kind of swinging and being swung.

And it goes without saying that during my student years in the city certain places experienced in the past as quiet took on, at a distance, a greatly magnified role in radiating the quiet I yearned for more and more: platforms on the side of country roads where farmers left their milk cans for pickup, hayricks and hayracks in meadows, and especially tiny wooden huts out in the middle of cultivated fields.

It wasn't homesickness. These sites didn't call out to be visited. The milk stands, even if they hadn't been used in a long time and were rotting and falling down, the hayricks, even if the hay from the year before the year before the year before last had turned moldy and decayed, the field huts, even if the last cider jugs inside had cracked in the winter's cold and split apart, and the stone-hard bread crusts and leather-tough bacon strips could no longer give field mice the smallest spurt of energy: all those Quiet Places were present, inside me and with me and especially around me, and though they might not be as graspable, tangible, "knowable" as earlier, that made them perhaps better able to withstand the present—all the more capable of resistance, and actually resisting.

Even more remarkable that from case to case, without intending to or even planning to, one could generate Quiet Places from one's own inner resources, in the midst of a hubbub (precisely in a hubbub), in the midst of the kind of jabber that sometimes proved even more soul-deadening. Such places could spring up and shelter one if, during a professor's lecture, one read the great books and even some less great ones—yes, literature. One time I experienced the same effect without actually reading but simply from remembering that kind of reading; it happened in the cafeteria, which, overcrowded from morning to evening, was often the only place available for passing the time.

One evening, on the television screen far from the corner where I was sitting, there appeared, at the end of the news broadcast, which the constant uproar in the room made it difficult or impossible to hear, the face of William Faulkner, looking out of place and noble, and it immediately became clear to me, I don't know why, that this writer, who for years had been a sort of father to me, had died that day. A powerful, painful, yet gentle stillness spread through me and around me, and accompanied me that night—it must have been in July 1962—as I biked to my room on the edge of town: a stillness that spread over the entire city.

Creating Quiet Places through reading (which obviously, or not so obviously, has little or nothing to do with reading in a Quiet Place): almost a cliché. But something else that's remarkable, perhaps most remarkable of all: that a Quiet Place could emerge, independent of a book or childhood refuges, simply from certain physical actions or positions, unplanned and unintended. These might include stopping in the middle of something, turning back, walking backward, or merely holding one's breath. The most reliable of these physical actions—or does it seem so only now that I'm writing this?—I borrowed from Thomas Wolfe's *Look Homeward, Angel*, in which Ben, the hero's older brother, old and wise even at a young age, develops a technique for dealing with ceaseless blather, quarreling, nonsense, conflict, etc., in the family or elsewhere: when he can't take it anymore, he turns his head and looks over his shoulder to an unoccupied corner of the house or such, and says to his "angel" there: "Listen to that, won't you?" In similar situations I still follow Ben's example, looking over my shoulder in a direction where there's nothing to be seen, the only difference being that I say the angel sentence quietly to myself, and the nonsense that the angel's supposed to listen to in the Quiet Place is usually of my own making.

The moment has come to clarify something: the Quiet Places, of one kind or another, haven't served me merely as refuges, shelters, hiding places, retreats, screens, and hermitages. In part they certainly have had that function, from the outset. But from the outset they also meant something altogether different, and more, much more. It was the altogether different feature, the much-more-ness, that's motivated me to attempt, by writing about it, to achieve some clarity, by its very nature rather fragmentary.

Yet another remarkable or noteworthy feature: that at least during the time in question the places recognized officially or by consensus as quiet hardly deserved that designation, as far as I was concerned. To be sure, I repeatedly felt drawn, precisely in my time as a student, to the city's empty churches and cemeteries. But my memory tells me that the houses of God most shielded from noise never gave off the slightest light or warmth; at most, when I was in luck, a welcome flickering and a fleeting, comforting puff might come from the sacristies, from behind their locked grilles. It felt almost liberating to be back on the street again, drifting along amid the din.

All the unfamiliar cemeteries, even more unfamiliar when the graves were decorated for All Hallows' and All Souls': All Souls' was more likely to bestir itself and wave to and waft over one in response to a glance over one's shoulder into the void, in response to the image of the cattle scale swinging horizontally beneath one's feet, in response to the image of the drafty field hut where the shaft of my grandfather's or someone else's rubber boot is rotting away in a corner.

The first cemetery to embrace me as a Quiet Place, and a very special one, became that thanks to the public comfort station in the middle; I happened upon it much later, in Japan. Yes, back from quiet places to Quiet Places. While I've been jotting down notes for this essay, I've also realized that during my student years, contrary to what I asserted above, at least one Quiet Place in the city of Graz deserved the name, so to speak. It wasn't one of the public restrooms, whether the one by the Hauptplatz or the one by the main railway station, probably also because of the homosexuals, or whatever they were, who loitered in the vicinity or stood motionless for minutes on end, perhaps even hours, in the pissoirs, at most glancing over their shoulders now and then, not like Ben in *Look Homeward, Angel* (but who knows?).

I'm thinking of the restroom in the university building that housed the faculty of law. During my four years as a student, that restroom twice became a Quiet Place for me. Both times it happened at night, when the lecture halls and corridors had emptied out. I didn't feel welcome in the small villa on the edge of town where I rented a room, nor did I relish being shut up there in the cold from late afternoon on, so I developed the habit, when I got sick of hanging out in the cafeteria or riding the streetcars to their various last stops and back, and when there was no movie I cared to see, of staying in my building as long as I could. I no longer recall whether I studied or read in the lecture halls that were still open—it seems to me now that I just sat there in the dim light. What I am sure of is that from time to time I made my way to the large, brightly lit restroom, which in my memory is always warm and hospitable, and there I would use one of the sinks, located somewhat away from the stalls, to wash my hair. (The bathroom in the villa was often locked, and in general . . .) I always hurried, because someone, another student, might still be on the floor and catch me in the restroom with my hair soaking wet, which would probably be even more awkward for him than for me.

One evening I actually was caught washing my hair, not by a student but by a professor. This professor had conducted one of my public examinations the previous year, and I, confident in my knowledge of the material and also acutely interested in it, had contradicted him once or twice (I can still hear the general murmur of the crowd in the auditorium at the brashness I'd shown in challenging a *Herr Professor*). The professor had shown hardly any reaction, just stared at me coldly, as he'd done on previous occasions that year in the lecture hall, and though he was standing below me in the amphitheater, he'd continued the examination as if gazing down from a great height, the epitome of coolness and authority, and after that incident, despite the near-intimacy and intensity with which we'd clashed, looked past me even more magisterially than before. From then on I'd viewed him as my enemy, feeling, precisely because he made a point of ignoring me, persecuted by this man who had so much power over me.

On the evening in question, when he came into the restroom, probably from his office across the hall, he at first acted as though he didn't see me standing there with my head in the sink filled with water, and with water splashed all over the floor around me. He washed his hands, not at the sink right next to mine, but also not at the one farthest from me—at a remove but still close. My professor took a while washing his hands, scrubbing one finger after another, while I dried my hair on the towel I'd brought in my briefcase for that purpose. Not a word was spoken, not a look exchanged. Then he surprised me by washing his face as well, first just with his fingertips, then, abruptly leaning deep into the sink, cupping both hands and pouring water repeatedly over his forehead and cheeks, as if after a march or a ride across prairies and deserts in a Western. Next he combed his dampened hair, including the brilliantine on his—of course—graying temples, again taking a long, long time, and changed his tie in front of the restroom mirror: instead of the dark silk tie he wore in the lecture hall and in his law office, a light-colored crepe one with a floral design, which he pulled out of his inner jacket pocket. And finally he took out miniature scissors and snipped some fine hairs from his ears and nostrils, then with tweezers shaped his noticeably thick, dark eyebrows. Then he was off, without glancing at me or saying good-bye, to join the woman who'd asked him to meet her at the Thalia, a café with dance music, who'd just parked her car in front and was powdering her nose in her car's rearview mirror and licking the lipstick off her teeth.

After that he continued to look past me in the lecture hall and elsewhere, but now we both knew it had become a game, our game. He was no longer my enemy. Since that incident in the restroom we shared a little secret, and I'm sure that if we ran into each other today, after almost half a century, we'd promptly strike up a conversation, for the first time, and swap stories, not about the university or current events, but about the unpredictable, surprising moments we'd experienced in that Quiet Place.

The other incident that counts for this essay also involves a time when I went, at an even later hour, to that same restroom to wash my hair. Night had already settled in, and I thought no one else would be in the building, with only my familiar, more or less secret, refuge accessible. When I pushed open the door to the washroom, the glaring lights were switched on—or still "turned on" in those days?—and at my usual sink someone had stuck his head in water and was washing his hair. As I entered, he squinted up at me and greeted me, a complete stranger, as cordially as if the situation were perfectly normal.

I didn't know the man, had never run into him, not at the university, in the department store where I sometimes worked in the shipping department before the holidays, or anywhere else. And yet this stranger wasn't strange to me at all, or strange in a way that almost radiated familiarity. No, not familiarity, but a kind of fright. Though the man had taken off his shirt to wash his hair, something I'd never felt I needed to do, and was also old enough to be my father or someone of that generation, I saw, and at first glance, myself standing at the sink. Here in the washroom I'd stumbled on my double, who, I'd known since childhood, was somewhere beyond the horizon and bound to cross my path someday, or I his.

Unexpectedly—the image in my imagination rather faded already—there he was in the middle of the night, in that bright light, hunched over, with long, wet strands of hair covering his face, his suspenders off his shoulders and dangling down to the backs of his knees. And like me, he had a towel with him, one with a pattern of large checks (different from mine).

Without missing a beat I began to wash my own hair, two or three sinks over from his. Wordlessly, and as if it were perfectly ordinary, we performed our ablutions next to each other: he went on to shave, using shaving cream and a brush, while I, as I rubbed and scrubbed my hair, eyed my double from the side, not surreptitiously but openly, at once reflective and lost in thought, again as if it were perfectly normal, in a way I'd never experienced when observing another person, with the exception of a sleeper, a newborn, or a dead person. So that man was me. And one day I'd be like him?

And who was I? Not nearly as much of a loner and outsider as I'd always thought. A bit odd, but others were more odd. And who else was I? A member of an expedition, or no, someone who'd been on an expedition all by himself, and after forging his way through all sorts of difficulties, had come back here to civilization to freshen up, for the time being, before his next one-man venture. And who else? At first sight a disturbed person, who, when you got to know him, seemed much more normal, indeed the only normal person among a thousand, while the other nine hundred and ninety-nine eventually turned out to be as mad as hatters.

And who else was I? (As if, having seen my double, I suddenly couldn't find out enough about myself—couldn't get enough of myself.) Let me be someone else as well, play someone else: a pioneer, a deserter, a soccer referee or at least a linesman.

And what was I like, considering my double there in the restroom's white neon glare? Not special. Not that bad. Maybe somewhat deficient in that certain something, but not entirely deficient either. Far from being a star, but if an idiot, a village idiot, not a provincial or city idiot. And what else was I like?

And in what way? And in what other way? Well, what d'you know! Yes, just look at that! You didn't expect that, did you? Look, just look! Yes, just look. Look!

Almost two decades passed before I stumbled on another Quiet Place—in the Japanese cemetery's restroom in the early eighties—or at least one I'd feel like writing about, for myself or anyone else.

In the meantime blood flowed in and out of toilets—movie blood; and an acquaintance of mine, not in a film but in a privy, whose door he couldn't get open, suffered a stroke; and another acquaintance, in a different country, bent over to vomit into an old-fashioned privy's pit, tipped forward, and, fortunately for him, got stuck in the seat, since he had broad shoulders (and still has), and remained there, facedown, all night, almost suffocating; and I myself still have the voice of an old attendant ringing in my ears from the restroom at the last stop on a streetcar line, where I, for the first and (thus far) last time in my life, drunk to the very roots of my hair and my eyeballs from a bottle of whiskey that yet another acquaintance and I had drained, stuck my head under the faucet to let the ice-cold wintry water run over it, and as I staggered out into the night heard her screeching, "Lord have mercy, what an ugly sight!"

If this essay on the Quiet Place were a film, telling a story, the sequence of those decades without proper Quiet Places would be punctuated by repeated shots of crisscrossing railroad tracks glimpsed through the drain holes of train toilets, and by startling aquamarine flushes to nowhere in windowless airplane restrooms.

But what made me think the Quiet Place in Japan was located in a cemetery? Today, before sitting down to write, I opened Tanizaki's *In Praise of Shadows* (or of Dim Light), more or less by chance, because the book happened to be lying there, and came upon his description of Japanese temple restrooms, which he praises for their architecture and for the silence in them, where "one's spirit finds peace and quiet in the truest sense," an experience Tanizaki prizes even above that provided by teahouses. When I read that, I realized that the restroom I had in mind didn't belong to a cemetery after all but formed part of a temple complex. I hardly remember the temple, except for a flock of sparrows high in the pagoda's wood-shingled roof, the little birds the same gray as the shingles and distinguishable from them only because they moved, puffing up their feathers and playing hide-and-seek with one another in the gaps between shingles. And it seems to me now that I registered that only thanks to the time I'd just spent in the temple's restroom.

That temple, Ryoanji, was located in Nara, the former residence of Japanese emperors. I'd arrived in the country two or three weeks earlier, and after a couple of days in Tokyo had been on the move a good deal. Actually it was more like wandering around lost. Although that often suited me, after a while this experience of constantly losing my way and my bearings produced a disorientation that bordered on confusion and eventually even inner disintegration. After zigzagging across Kyoto in one wrong direction after another and finally reaching the temple garden, when I'd come upon a sight familiar from thousands of photographs—the expanse of gravel punctuated by random boulders thought to suggest the islands in the Sea of Japan, while the gravel raked in undulating rows represented the sea, or whatever, or nothing at all—I'd asked myself, "What am I doing here?" and I'd asked myself the same question in Kamakura, when, after a great deal of frenzied rushing hither and thither in the cemetery there, I'd finally found the grave of Yasujiro Ozu, whose films had thrilled me and filled me with peace and quiet, and still do so today when I think of them: "What am I here for?" And the character *mu* on Ozu's block of granite—meaning the equivalent of "nothingness"—which had had a kind of glowing aura when I looked at photos of it back home in Europe: there in Kamakura, with it before my eyes: nothing, really, less than nothing.

Not until the morning when I stepped inside the temple restroom in Nara did Japan begin to feel like home to me; did I arrive on the island; did the country, the whole country, take me in. In his praise of Japanese temple restrooms, Tanizaki makes special mention of the fine graining in the wooden walls and especially of the sliding door, whose wooden latticework is filled with light-colored paper that lets in air but only dim light from the outside: I'd be lying if I said I could see these details distinctly as I'm describing them. All I know is that the dim light Tanizaki invokes filled that space, and that after all those weeks of wandering around lost, I felt embraced and welcomed with an inimitable delicacy, yet also substantiality, and that promptly whisked me magically back into existence, into the here-and-now, into life, as its guest. (Yet outside, in the city of Nara itself, and not just in the temple precinct, it had already been an overcast, gloomy morning. So it couldn't have been only the light in the remote cabin that had this effect.)

A sense of arrival, of being taken in, of here-and-now? The Quiet Place of Nara was also a site of liberation. It was not a mere refuge, not a shelter, not an out-of-the-way place. In that morning hour it was the essence of a place, such as perhaps had never existed, pure placeness. There I became—what word did people use at one time?—*ebullient*, filled with an invigorating, unfocused energy. The place awakened enthusiasm. Yes, a "spirit" was at work in that Quiet Place that, to paraphrase Tanizaki, provided "peace and quiet" and at the same time got one moving—a spirit of restlessness, of ebullience, of magical invulnerability. Again according to Tanizaki, the only drawback to such temple restrooms, "in case one insists on mentioning a drawback," is that they're located quite far from the main structure, "which puts one at risk of catching cold, especially in winter." But I felt as though nothing could get to me, not even Siberian cold, and if the wood cabin, "fine graining" and all, had suddenly burst into flames with me inside, I would have escaped without a single hair on my head singed—a pretty illusion? And does it fit with that spirit of invulnerability that Jun'ichiro Tanizaki declares that no place is more suitable for letting "the chirping of insects, birdsong, a moonlit night, and altogether the transitory beauty of things have their way with you in all four seasons," and presumably the old haiku poets "discovered an infinite number of motifs" in such a Quiet Place?

Be that as it may: since that morning in the temple garden's comfort station in Nara—now more than twenty years ago—the Quiet Place accompanies me, above and beyond the thing itself and its location, as an idea. In other words, since then it's been a project for me, or, going back to the ancient Greek, πρόβλημα, a problem, an intriguing one—in its original meaning of "promontory," something that must be navigated around, sailed around, with the ship, or the boat, or the skiff, consisting in this case of language, circling or circumscribing the phenomenon to be narrated.

And it's also true that the dim light there motivated me above all. (Not the "shadow": the sun wasn't shining, and the place had no artificial lighting.) It felt as though that little space consisted of nothing but dimness, as clear as it was substantial. This kind of clear, luminous dimness had always stirred me to the depths of my being, stirred me to bestir myself and do something. Do what? Nothing specific or purposeful, simply to become active, to set out for who knows where, to go who knows how far, or to remain in place and do something without delay. Do what? Something lovely; something amazing; something equal to the substantiality and intimacy of that dim light. And in the tiny Quiet Place in Nara I found that kind of light concentrated into an essence.

At first it seemed as though the sight I'd experienced in train toilets when looking down through the drain hole during my earlier back-and-forth years, the sight of tracks, ties, and blackish crushed rock receding rapidly into the distance, had suddenly been brought to a halt, and I now had an entirely different sight beneath me: instead of the tracks et cetera, bare ground, reddish yellow clay, giving off an inimitable glow.

Then this dimness made something else occur to me—no, it occurs to me now—that I did airplane toilets an injustice earlier: there was a time when one of them actually had a little window, high up in the wall, and through that window I could see, above my head, the moon and even a couple of stars looking down, an image I could gaze up at for a good part of my flight on the smallest of the Ilyushin passenger planes, since I was, again actually, the only passenger on that flight from Moscow to what was then East Berlin: wonder of wonders.

I owe it solely to the Quiet Place in Nara that I finally experienced Japan after all, and can say today, "I've been to the Far East." A large part of that was what I experienced when I first crossed the threshold, which I picture now as light-colored knotty pine: the anxiety that had plagued me during the previous weeks of the trip promptly evaporated. The dense twilight glow transformed me into a person free of cares. And I sensed that this absence of cares would endure beyond the moments I spent in the temple restroom; it would have a certain staying power, at least for the foreseeable future.

What a sense of lightness that transformation brought with it! Ah, lightness and freedom from cares, so lovely. And it was no contradiction that I also felt a desire to promise something to the place that had lifted my spirits that way. To make a vow to the temple toilet, but what? That if I met the woman with whom I could spend my life—who, I had no doubt, existed somewhere, so filled was I with lightness and freedom from cares—I would spend my honeymoon with her in Nara (in those days I still harbored such fantasies).

And now the actual sight of that reddish yellow clay through a knothole in the restroom's plank floor. But why is the ground so far down, why does its gleam come from so far below, from such a depth? Because it's not the clay under the Quiet Place in Nara but the ground glimpsed elsewhere in Japan, also through a knothole, but from a gallery, also wooden, around the outside of the second floor of a *ryokan*, a guesthouse, an inn, let's say in Mitsushima (town of pines), on the northern sea, where weeks later I, still somewhat carefree, spent days, time and again lying prone on that balcony, gazing down at the clay through a particular knothole, fixing my eye on pebbles, grains of sand, pine needles, a beer-bottle cap, all rimmed from that vantage point with a glow; and at the same time, yes, the same time, I'm lying, yes, let's say six decades ago, facedown on the gallery on my grandfather's farm—that long gallery leading from the living quarters to the privy—and gazing, or staring, through the cracks between the boards down into the chicken yard, at the concrete slab, from which no glow rises, but instead, yellow on yellow, the corn kernels strewn there glow, and from time to time a beak, of a different yellow, descends among the kernels, scattering them, the sight accompanied by a peck-peck-pecking on the concrete. Not a human soul to be heard far and wide; the courtyard deserted, the rooms empty, the courtyard broom nothing but a stump.

As I've been writing this, I've sometimes secretly asked myself something, and now I'm going to put my question in writing: Did my lifelong search for Quiet Places all over the world, time and again without a specific necessity, express, if not a flight from society, perhaps a revulsion against society, an aversion to society? When I'd get up in the middle of a gathering and walk out, trying to put as much distance and more than nine times thirty-nine steps between myself and the others: an asocial, an antisocial act? Yes, that was, and is, undeniably the case in some situations. But it was true only of the first few moments, when I brusquely got up and vacated the premises. On my way to the Quiet Place, taking a roundabout route if at all possible, I'd be thinking, "Just let me get there!" and already my attitude could change; what had seemed unambiguous could be transformed into something more complex. And it was also true that my locking of the toilet door would be accompanied by a great sigh of relief: "Alone at last!"

But how to explain, on the other hand, that soothing though the quietness of the place was, it proved even more effective when accompanied by sounds from the world outside—wind, a river right outside the window, passing trains, tractor trailers, streetcars, even police and ambulance sirens? And perhaps most effective when grounded from a distance by sounds of social interaction and indeed from the very space I'd just got up and left? Almost every time—though not always—the noise audible in out-of-the-way Quiet Places—laughter, the jumble of voices, entering the space through inner and outer walls and doors, became not exactly euphonious but cozy and familiar, and I felt drawn—though not always—after a certain time, which I regularly dragged out and tried to savor—away from the particular Quiet Place and, thanks to and by virtue of my time there, back to the others, to my people, even if they weren't really my people, to the noise, the racket, to the, God willing, ceaseless din of those spaces.

In the course of the years and decades after my visit to Japan, I even used that specific time in Quiet Places, which I "dragged out"—in soccer we call it "running down the clock"—for "sociological studies." I'm not referring to the graffiti, drawings, and the like on walls in public restrooms. Now and then I did read them—how could you not?—and took note of them. But to analyze them and think deep thoughts about them wasn't, and isn't, something I care to do. Nonetheless in Quiet Places—not private ones, with all their more or less self-indulgent cutenesses and sillinesses, but rather the public or semipublic ones—I've always been stimulated anew to reflect, observe, and, last but not least, ponder, and indulge in fantasies and imaginings.

In France, the country where I've lived for a long time, several years ago smoking was banned in public buildings, cafés, and bars. As a result, various things one can observe in restrooms that hark back to the smoking era have become subject matter for archaeological research, so to speak. In certain places, on the top of the once pure-white enamel of toilet tanks, and likewise on the perhaps originally white metal flap, or whatever it's called, over the toilet paper roll, users of those toilets in bars and cafés would rest their cigarettes, and the heat would leave a kind of pattern on the surface. At any rate, when I come upon such places from the time before the smoking ban—they're more and more rare, by the way—I see the burn marks as a pattern, and in my role as a member of society, I feel obligated to reflect on them as deeply as I can.

From one Quiet Place to another, those patterns seem to me to vary quite a bit. Not that I'm inclined to interpret them. Out in nature I'm always tempted to read the tracks and traces of both animals and humans, and that seems perfectly natural. While I also see the burn marks in toilets as traces, sometimes epic, sometimes dramatic, I don't read anything into them—as I might when I come upon tracks in mud in the woods or on a riverbank, seeing them as traces of those who've lost their way, traces of a struggle, or the traces of a person suddenly at a complete loss, or perhaps traces of a person or an animal at war with itself. The scorches on toilet tanks and metal flaps, whether single or multiple, whether pale or so distinct they can't be missed, with blackened singe rings, don't want to be read. Instead they awaken my imagination, which, however, remains unspecific, without even a glimmer of a story—unspecific and free, patterns for a different story; and if contemplation of these patterns suggests anything, it has nothing to do with what really went on at one time in these Quiet Places: rather, as I explore these epic-dramatic patterns, they bring on other images, which in turn bring on yet others, possible ones, passing before what would once have been called my inner eye, equally epic and similarly dramatic. A strange researcher, I am. A strange member of society. But wasn't that always the case?

I became a member of society like that, imagining I had a role to play that would be useful and of service to the community at large, when, almost at the moment I stepped inside and closed the door of a Quiet Place behind me, I turned into a space surveyor. In almost all toilets I immediately discerned a system of forms, a geometric one to be precise, a system I hadn't noticed on the other side of that door. Once inside, I acquired the eye of a discoverer. Each object in there revealed its geometric form: circle, oval, cylinder, cone, ellipse, pyramid, truncated pyramid, truncated cone, rectangle, tangent, segment, or trapeze. The Quiet Place was itself a geometric space and wanted to be perceived and reported as such. And I, taking its measure, was its geometer, and as such charged in no uncertain terms with fulfilling this duty. If that duty wasn't useful to the community, what else was it, right? But that's enough irony; as I recognize not for the first time, being ironic is not my cup of tea, at least not when it comes to writing.

Seriously: the purpose of that place was self-evident, and not merely as the geometric site of the toilet seat, the base, the water tank, the flush buttons, the pipes, the sink, the faucets, and so on, but also as the site of all the other cubic forms, useful in a different way, indispensable, convenient, and beneficial, outside of this *petit coin*, this nook, outside of this *mustarâch* (Arab.), this place of peace and quiet, on the great sphere once known as the earthly orb. "ἀεὶ ὁ θεὸς γεωμετρεῖ": this assertion, attributed by Plutarch to Plato, that I saw once on the triangular gable of an old house haunts me, so I translate it as follows for myself: "God always plays the geometer" (measures the earth). Or, for anyone who'd rather leave "God" and also that strange foreign term out of it, and even the idea of "always": The world takes shape.

Yes, to my mind the Quiet Places, with their concentrated geometry, are where, among other places, the world takes shape, and more measurably so than in most others: quiet bowers, hermits' desert caves, vow-of-silence cells, bunkers hardened (at least nowadays) against bombardment by electrons, neutrons, or what have you, and, with their natural utility to the community, different in that utility from that of Silicon or any other Valley. And there you have the public-utility seal of approval for the geometer of Quiet Places, certified herewith by himself!? (The exclamation point followed by a question mark, so this story can continue, and continue in a different way, and with a different ending.)

In preparation for writing this essay on the Quiet Place, I've read not a few books and looked at not a few photos.

But hardly anything from those sources has found its way into these pages. Historical and ethnological studies on shifts in the cultural significance of—what is it called? relieving oneself—from more public to more private, and vice versa, from uninhibited to shameful, from shameful to a social game, and varying from country to country, from people to people, from era to era: they offer plenty of reading material. But what put me on the trail of these places long ago was something fundamentally different, and the historical, anthropological, sociological disquisitions threatened to obliterate those traces.

Similarly, the photos in the coffee-table book *Toilets of the World* (including outer space: see the facilities for astronauts), however amusing, astonishing, also often disturbing they might be (see the facilities in impoverished neighborhoods, dungeons, and death-row cells), hardly proved stimulating to the imagination, at least in my case. Ah, yes, the wooden toilets that an indigenous tribe in Panama or somewhere builds out over the ocean, to be reached by way of footbridges, with the water beneath them not recognized by the tourists swimming there as "sewers": a photo of a clueless swimmer's hand below, viewed from above through the poop hole. And, oh dear, the colored photos of curtainless concrete-block cubicles, for boys and girls alike, in Africa's Zambezi territory, in Namibia, and elsewhere. And, ah, still in Africa, the cabin that otherwise seems far from any outpost of civilization, but by way of compensation has a view of one of the world's largest, most beautiful wandering dunes, complete with the golden gleam of the sand in morning or evening light. And, oh, perhaps last but not least, those photos from New Zealand, which almost make one want to go there just to experience the Quiet Place: the public restroom complex that the painter and architect Friedensreich Hundertwasser designed for a small town, painted in a thousand and one colors and, as was also his way or his whim, avoiding right angles at any cost—but not, if it was his way, at least to judge by the pictures, to have this community project impel his critics to ask forgiveness for their not at all positive judgments on his other, earlier community projects in various parts of the world. Am I contradicting myself now, after what I said about geometry? So be it. The design for those public toilets in New Zealand was Hundertwasser's last project before his death, by the way.

Once on their trail, I've photographed with a disposable camera almost every Quiet Place I've encountered far and near (photos that now convey very little to me). Among them were odd places, picturesque ones, worldly ones, snobbish ones, primitive ones, pathetic ones, desolate ones. Some occupied the top floor of skyscrapers or broadcast towers, their panoramic windows providing views from Central Park to the Statue of Liberty, from Copacabana to the statue of the Redeemer to the last corrugated tin huts in the favelas, or from an inn in Alaska to a glacier in the process of calving, and from another, through the window screen, to the Yukon River on a midsummer's night, with swallows flitting back and forth all night long, the entire river seeming to drone or pound under the giant wooden Indian fish wheels, turning slowly and then suddenly much faster as if snapping shut. Not to mention some Balkan toilets or privies, though not because not one of them was found worthy of inclusion in *Toilets of the World*—just one point about them: strange that all the spiderwebs, daddy longlegs, and flies, along with the straw broom as a substitute for a toilet brush, and the like, never disturbed me, on the contrary.

The strangest Quiet Places of all are the ones meant to be luxurious, located far, far from hustle and bustle and everyday sounds, usually in a spacious, even labyrinthine, basement, one or two stories beneath restaurants, conference venues, or meeting rooms. You go through door after door, accompanied by a kind of music of the spheres, and still haven't reached the place you've been making your way toward for ages, and when you finally get there, it's in the middle of nowhere, with not even a distant echo of the crowd or the familiar setting where only a little while ago you were in the midst of daily life.

Those catacomb-like Quiet Places remind me of the suites of rooms I've periodically encountered all my life in dreams: under the house or apartment where I actually live, day in, day out, in the dream I come upon quiet, yet brightly lit, luxuriously appointed rooms, one after the other, each larger and more splendid than the one before, and every one deserted, at my disposal as the master of the house, for whom these palatial suites of rooms have been waiting half an eternity, waiting for me to put them to use at long last and make them fruitful.

But the Quiet Places I have in mind and wanted primarily to write about here are completely independent of their particular location and any other particular external features or oddities. The kind of thing I'm interested in could manifest itself just as well, or maybe better, in Quiet Places that are otherwise unremarkable, even standardized, with only the event staying with me, not one detail connected with the premises, let alone its geometry, and I'm tempted to apply "Ideal Standard"—not the brand name but the term—to the problem I've undertaken to explore.

A small example: one time I was leaving just such a faceless toilet in another country when I happened to run into someone who was "my reader," someone from yet another country, who, regardless of the location, seemed very happy to see me, and I felt the same about him, and even more so, given where we'd met.

Only a few weeks ago I was in Cascais, on the Atlantic in

Portugal; I was sitting on a park bench by a path that led to the public toilets, for the sake of research, if you will, but mostly to let the place and the surroundings sink in. As time passed, and probably due in part to my observing, a kind of procession formed among those coming and going at random, the sort of procession I hadn't experienced in the streets and elsewhere in a long time, and had sorely missed. You see, I, as such and such a person, or as the person I happen to be, need that kind of procession, a human procession, and I don't mean it to sound blasphemous when I admit that as I'm writing this, it occurs to me that elsewhere I've experienced a similar procession at most in church, during Mass, when the faithful go forward to receive the body of the Lord and return to their pews or wherever. Yes, there in Cascais it was that kind of procession to the Quiet Place and back, and it was associated neither with urgency nor with a sense of relief afterward, and also not with my role as a spectator. For when I finally got up from the bench and inserted myself among those coming and going, I became, for moments, which, however, weren't negligible, part of the procession of very old folks and children playing hooky, of cripples and the frail, of natives and foreigners, of widows and the indigent, of housewives in hairnets and slackers with slicked-back hair. And in distinction to Communion, this was a procession in which those coming greeted those going, in various ways—in words or silently, only with their eyes, without ulterior motives for those few moments, and if there were some such motives after all: unlike in church, they were appropriate and quite all right. It was a friendly little procession we strange birds formed, and is.

"For the sake of my research" I also asked a few people for their thoughts on the Quiet Place, no, didn't ask them, just mentioned my "problem." The tales they told, or hinted at—I never pressed them for details—reinforced what I was after.

Leaning one's forehead against the cool tiled wall of a restroom when one was feeling lonely and abandoned in a strange place. Hiding in the restroom as a schoolboy to smoke, but more to carry out a secret mission, because from the window one could see the house where one's first love lived. Looking out a similar window in the house of one's disagreeable grandparents, who'd taken one in as an orphan or half-orphan, and keeping one's eyes for hours on a hotel called the Sun until it filled up with guests, their silhouettes visible in the far-off rooms. And it strikes me now that all these fragmentary anecdotes about Quiet Places take place in the distant past, less in childhood than in youth, in adolescence. No such accounts from later in life, not a peep, at least not from my informants. At most someone might tell me about his elderly mother, who, whenever she crouched down outdoors to relieve herself, always chose a particularly beautiful spot, with a view, if possible. It wasn't supposed to be only a Quiet Place but also an appealing one. But that's another story.

All the time I've been writing, an image has been nagging me, one that runs entirely counter to what I hoped to accomplish with this essay on the Quiet Place, and that image involves the little girl who, in the spring of nineteen ninety-nine, during the West European bombing war against the Federal Republic of Yugoslavia, made her way late one evening to the toilet in her apartment house in Batajnica, northwest of Belgrade, and there—while all the other occupants of the house and the town remained unscathed, at least during the night in question—was killed by shrapnel that smashed through the wall.

And another image, contrary to that one or perhaps not, has preoccupied me during the writing: in an enormous convention center somewhere a man mistakenly wanders into the ladies' room and there meets a beautiful stranger—or was it the other way around, and the woman wanders into the men's room? In any case, they don't end up having sex (or what should it be called?), but the encounter in the Quiet Place develops, slowly and with many obstacles, into the Great Love. But that's an image from a film, a film set in the future, a dark one otherwise, if not hopeless.

I sat down to write this essay on the Quiet Place in a rather deserted part of France, somewhere between the Île-de-France, with Paris as its hub, and Normandy, in an in-between area, almost equally far from the great metropolis and the ocean. The writing took place during a period commonly described as the darkest of the year, from the second week in December to December thirty-first, two thousand and eleven, in other words today. Before and after my writing sessions I roamed day after day through the leafless forests, across harvested fields that stretched for miles—this area was once the breadbasket for the royal court—and along roads that seldom saw traffic. True: it got dark early, and even in the daytime the wavy expanses of countryside were shrouded in profoundly dim light. But whenever the sun came out, even for just an hour, I could hardly imagine a more hearty glow than this December light, the rays almost horizontal: no more all-encompassing, animating glow, bringing out blues and greens, no more fervent gleam than that of the grassy strips down the middle of the dirt roads. "A bit of sun," as the weather forecasts in the *Parisien*, the only daily newspaper available, put it morosely—but there's no such thing; any moment of sun meant so much. And the urban paper pitied the country folk for the fact that from early to late nothing but clouds formed the "horizon."

The chronic rain that invariably followed these moments turned the roads as well as the fields and pastures into sheets of mud, but wading through knee-high pools in rubber boots or cutting across fields always produced a pleasure all its own, even in the dark, when all that could be seen of the path—if it was one—was an irregular succession of puddles. For the first time since those childhood days as a cowherd, one stomped along in those boots and was tempted to strike up a song in praise of them.

The rain came down with particular force during the nights between the old year and the new, in the period once known in the southern German-speaking regions as the *Rauhnächte* (Rough Nights). And in that connection, back to "boots": as the water sloshed around the remote house where I was working, it seemed as if the rain itself had boots on: first it tiptoed, then it strode, and finally it marched, all night long. There was no snow, and for once I didn't miss the snow.

As I ranged over the countryside, which was greening up—precisely in the dim glow, colors, and with them forms, shone forth with special clarity—I felt like a one-man infantry unit. In that couple of weeks I hardly ever ran into anyone other than hunters, always at least three of them together, wearing yellow reflective vests, grouped like wardens or other officials on the plowed blackish brown soil, their rifles at the ready. But those don't count as encounters, and the constant banging and popping around the woods had nothing welcoming about it.

In the widely scattered villages, I saw hardly anyone outdoors. Looking in a window once, I glimpsed an old woman, standing motionless, leaning on her walker. In a village bar that could be reached only on foot, the single guest was a retired long-distance truck driver, to whom the bartender suggested that he get a TV for his apartment to keep him company, whereupon the other man replied that he'd spent his life sitting behind the wheel, and "je vais pas me mettre maintenant dans un fauteuil devant la télévision."

During my writing phase I hardly saw people, but instead not a few other things. When I unexpectedly spotted a thousand-year-old church tower sticking up above the seemingly uninhabited area, I involuntarily raised my arm to salute it.

The skylarks above the fallow fields, peeping rather than trilling or warbling, built ladders in the air as they soared vertically, rung after rung, while the swarms of sparrows, popping up from the furrows, whizzed back and forth through the air like trapeze artists. The pheasant that sashayed back and forth in front of the house, as if, especially with his long, brilliantly colored bobbing tailfeathers, he were the house rooster in charge. The family of wild boars, which, having survived another day of hunting, grunted at nightfall in a chorus from the underbrush along the road, where no hunter thought to look for them, then heaved their many backs out of the near-darkness and, no, didn't grunt, but whispered, whispered and humped their backs. The owls that flew here in broad daylight from their hollows in the abandoned limestone quarries, silent as only owls can be, with their flat faces, their feathers chalk-white like the limestone they flapped past. Then other owls hooting all night on one note, a lasso missing its loop (and not after all), which toward morning, as if responding to the roosters' first crowing, became a two- or three-note hooting, in antiphony to the roosters, with the owls not infrequently getting the last word. Added to that the cackling of hens, the mooing of cattle, the groaning or silence of donkeys, the squawking of the pheasant, the bawling or muteness of ravens, and, as an undertone to all that, the cooing of wild doves, anticipating that of cuckoos, as well as the screeching of falcons in this prevernal time of year. A hopeless cacophony? Hopeful, for long moments. The hedgehog I found one morning, after I'd stepped outside to sharpen my pencils, huddled under the desk when I came back to my ground-floor writing room—and staying there through my entire writing day, now and then raising its quills and curling into a ball, but most of the time showing its large nose—or snout?—freely. This animal, too, I involuntarily greeted, whereupon it pricked up its round ears and gave me a black-eyed stare. On one especially dark night, as I was crossing a fallow field, suddenly, more felt than seen, two enormous owls, circling overhead in a pair—and was it, or did it become, more and more of them?—again in complete silence, closer and closer to the walker's head, not to be scared off by any shouts, and also hardly deterred by my flashlight, until I waved it frantically—what did they want? What were these nocturnal birds after? And the following day, as I waded across a quietly flowing brook, in the middle I suddenly felt myself sinking, deeper and deeper, into the mud, nearly up to my hips, saved "at the last minute" by an almost desperate leap to catch a limb hanging over the brook from the opposite bank—this story here, waiting on my table back in the house to be continued, would otherwise have been left unfinished—which it also is, though in a different sense.

And this very morning, as I was walking along a slope in the steppe, a deer in full flight, and at the same moment the crack of a gunshot on this last day of the year, the deer saving itself and, as it gallops away, its white flag creating the image of a horse and rider, conjuring up Indian country. On that same steppe, whitish prehistoric seashells, snails, and ammonites scattered over this largely uncultivated in-between space, these fossils remarkably heavy in one's hand by comparison with modern-day snail, mussel, and oyster shells. The hunting traps in the woods: cylindrical, square, truncated cones, pointed like pyramids. In the clearing night sky the Charioteer as an irregular four- or five-angled figure, Cassiopeia as an incomplete double triangle, the Pleiades—my failing eyesight—thickened into an ellipse, and of course, over there, the hunter Orion, the premier winter constellation, guarding and ruling over the night sky, though without a rifle at the ready, with nothing but an arrow or no weapon at all in his belt, the shoulder and knee stars almost parallel to each other.

A mental image of parallelism also during the day at those moments of turning off from roads and wagon tracks and heading straight across fields and through patches of forest: parallelism with what? With standing up and peeling off to Quiet Places over the course of a lifetime. And then, while on such missions, pausing and standing still at the midpoint of the earth. Nothing but the little white balls on the snowberry bushes. Underneath, the teeny-tiny ellipses of rabbit droppings. Here and there blossoms: those of the silvery clematis vines growing along the edge of the woods, their twisty forms evocative of Arabic script. Poking up now and then from muddy fields, small yellow petals: the first, or last remaining rapeseed blossoms, swaths of which will appear all over Europe come summer. Among the only flowers to be seen: daisies along the roads, *pâquerettes* in French, the name perhaps derived from *Pâques*, Easter? (Or perhaps not after all?)

And another edge of the woods, with a jagged border created by the pointy triangular forms of spruces, not common in this in-between space—do they signal the proximity of the little cemetery, Cimetière à Têtu, which, according to the detailed local map, should be here somewhere? But where in the patch of woods is that cemetery? A rabbit springs up, and as it zigzags away draws my eye in the right direction: aha, here's the cemetery—nothing but two stones, the third, a truncated pyramid, toppled over, covered with a tangle of vines and rendered almost invisible, but the inscriptions on the other two stones clearly legible, the larger monument marking the double grave of a husband and wife who died in the mid-nineteenth century (the wife "a good spouse and gentle mother"), the other, much smaller one dedicated to the man from whom, to judge by the map, the scrubby stand of trees got its name, Arthur Têtu (died, *décedé*, in 1919), with the postscript, the same on the stone next to it: DE PROFUNDIS. So Têtu is a family name, and the cemetery is named after Monsieur Têtu, first name Arthur, and not, as my imagination had pictured it, inducing me to strike out in search of this place, designating a cemetery for a *têtu*, a headstrong person.

And only now, late in the game, do I notice that I forgot to mention the most compelling and powerful motivation for this essay on the Quiet Place: namely, those unexpected transitions from wordlessness, from being stricken with silence, to having language and speech return—transitions experienced time and again, ever more powerfully in the course of my life, in the moment of my closing and locking that certain door, alone at last with the place and its geometry, away from other people.

Outside: falling silent. Silenced. Losing the power of speech. Speechlessness. Losing language. Loss of language. Rendered monosyllabic by the wordiness and words of others, reduced to silence by them—worn out by them—hollowed out by them. Not a word crosses my lips, or worse still, sparks anything in my heart, lungs, blood. At most a soundless, inaudible, "Excuse me, back in a minute!"

But no sooner have I withdrawn to the Quiet Place than the source of language and words begins to well up anew, perhaps fresher than ever before, even if the writer who seemed to have fallen silent once and for all doesn't make himself heard to those around him. Down the stairs, usually steep, and worn in a homelike way, door closed, bolt slid vertically or horizontally, and already words begin to flow in the obdurate writer's mind, de profundis, in the tone of the psalms, with tongues of fire, in exclamations, several in quick succession, bringing an entirely different, unheard of, kind of relief, even if it only takes the form of "Yes, look at that. How is that possible? When the need is greatest. Take pity on us. Root and branch. Ashes to ashes. Child, child. Auld lang syne. Well, if that's how it is. And now? Tonight or never. Sound and fury. Why hast thou deserted me? New words! Wake up to new words. No more aching breast. Continue living word for word. Man and woman. And woman and man. I'll never be a singer. Good Golly, Miss Molly. Wonder is all. Take: this is my body."

The bellowing, yelling, raving, and screeching outside: transformed into the murmur of the crowd and the buzz of the world. Shake a leg, back to the others, multisyllabic, raring to speak.

—MARQUEMONT/VEXIN,
DECEMBER 2011

ESSAY ON A MUSHROOM MANIAC

A STORY ALL ITS OWN

Translated by Krishna Winston

"UH-OH, IT'S GETTING SERIOUS AGAIN!" I BLURTED OUT TO myself a few minutes ago, before setting out for my desk, where I'm sitting now, hoping to achieve a certain—or more likely uncertain—clarity about the story of my friend the mushroom maniac, who's vanished without a trace. And then I exclaimed, "That can't be true! That it gets serious just as a result of my broaching and writing about a subject that probably has nothing earthshaking about it; a story that in the run-up (an expression that's appropriate, for a change, in this context) to this essay brought to mind the title of an Italian film made decades ago, *Tragedy of a Ridiculous Man*, with Ugo Tognazzi in the title role—just the title, not the film itself."

Yet the story of my old friend isn't a tragedy, really, and whether he was, or is, ridiculous, that's not clear to me, and stubbornly refuses to become clear; and now I find myself exclaiming and writing: "May that continue to be so!"

Before I set out for my desk, another film came to mind. This time it wasn't the title but one of the opening scenes, if not the very first scene, that passed before my eyes. It was another Western, directed by—you guessed it—John Ford, and as the story begins, Jimmy Stewart, as the famous sheriff Wyatt Earp, long, long after his now-legendary Tombstone adventures, is sitting in dreamy idleness, as only Jimmy Stewart can, on the porch of his sheriff's office in the south Texas (?) sun, just letting time go by, seeming at once peaceful and decisive, with the brim of his ten-gallon hat drawn halfway down over his eyes, his relaxed attitude at once enviable and seductive. But then, because it wouldn't be a Wild West tale otherwise, he gets roped into a new adventure, initially reluctant and—am I remembering this correctly?—seduced only by the reward money, and this time he heads north rather than west. Eventually, however, and especially at the end of the story: his intervening, no questions asked, his gentle attentiveness, his quietly helpful presence of mind, again qualities only Jimmy Stewart could project—and still can. Not only two rode together, to borrow the title of a different film, in which Richard Widmark is the second rider: by the end of this one, more rode together, many more, if not (almost) all. Why, when I was about to, yes, set out for my desk, would this particular scene of all things, at the beginning of this particular film, come to me, with the sheriff's pair of legs in boots stretched out as he lounged there, so tantalizingly indolent, not lifting a finger, self-assuredly exposing the so-called marshal to liberating laughter?

I was sitting there with my own legs outstretched, also in boots, though not on a porch but indoors on the window seat in a house several hundred years old, with walls almost a meter thick, and also not in the Deep South but in the gloomy north, far from any southern sun, with gusts of late-autumn rain outdoors and a cold wind sweeping in from the already denuded beech forests on the plateau and whistling through cracks around the windows, and the boots were rubber boots, without which it was nearly impossible to walk anywhere outside, let alone strike out across fields or through forests, and when I got up to go to my desk, I removed these boots, pulled them off outside the front door with the help of something that used to be known as a bootjack, in my case an old-fashioned device of heavy cast iron in the shape of an enormous snail, whose metal antennae jimmied and shimmied my boots off my heels before I took the couple of steps through the door into the addition, the small shed, the annex, I call it, to the desk where I'm sitting now, writing.

What? Describing these couple of steps outside and then in to my desk as "making my way"? "setting out"? That's what it seemed like. That's what it felt like. That's how it was. And meanwhile a Novemberish dusk is settling over the plain below, which extends in a northerly direction from the foot of the plateau, on whose steep edge I'm sitting, to the great horizons, and my desk lamp is switched on. "So let it get serious."

My friend was already a mushroom maniac at a young age, though not in the same way as in his later or even late years. Not until then, as he was approaching old age, did a story about him as a maniac make sense. Quite a few stories have been written about mushroom maniacs, usually—or perhaps without exception?—by the maniacs themselves, who speak of themselves as "hunters," or at least as trackers, collectors, or naturalists. It seems that only in more recent times, perhaps only since the two world wars of the last century, we've had not just a literature about mushrooms, mushroom books, but also a literature in which an author connects mushrooms with his own life. In nineteenth-century world literature mushrooms hardly play a role, and if they do, only a minor role, in passing, and without reference to a hero of any kind, mentioned simply for their own sake, as in the works of Russians such as Dostoyevsky or Chekhov.

I can think of just one story in which someone gets mixed up in the world of mushrooms, if only in one episode, involuntarily, against her will even, and that's the novel *Far from the Madding Crowd*, by Thomas Hardy—England, late nineteenth century—in which the beautiful young heroine, lost somewhere in the countryside at night, loses her footing and falls into a ditch full of enormous mushrooms, and then, surrounded by these sinister forms, which seem to be growing and multiplying before her eyes, remains trapped in this mushroom pit till daybreak (at least that's my vague recollection).

And now, in this entirely new, in—what's it called?—"our" time, we seem to have an increasing number of stories in which mushrooms for the most part play a conventional role in the imaginings of the general public, either as murder instruments or as agents of—what's the term?—"consciousness expansion."

Nothing like that will be the subject of this essay on the mushroom maniac: not the mushroom hunter as hero, or as a person dreaming of the perfect murder, or as the pioneer of an altered consciousness. Or perhaps some aspects of all three after all? Be that as it may: a story like his, in the way it played out and as I shared the experience, at times from close up, has never been committed to paper.

It all began with money, a long time ago, when the future mushroom maniac was still a child, began with the money the child was obsessed with obtaining, even in his sleep, when all night long he'd see coins glittering everywhere he went, which turned out not to be what he thought, began with the money whose absence tormented him night and day, and how. His habit of keeping his head down wherever he happened to be simply meant he was on the lookout for anything of value, if not a lost treasure. Never mind that in fact he never did have money, at most the smallest of small change now and then, which wasn't good for anything, anything at all, or that at home he hardly ever laid eyes on money, and certainly not on banknotes. How could he get his hands on money? Yet he wasn't greedy to have money in his possession; were he to have some one day, he'd promptly go out and spend it, and he already knew, had known for a long time, where and for what.

As it happened, a "mushroom depot" was set up close to his village. It was the period after the Second World War when commercial activity and the economy in general were reviving in a form entirely different from that of the interwar years, and in particular commerce and dealings between the rural areas and the towns and cities, whose inhabitants were developing a taste for things they'd never eaten before (and not just imports from the tropics or elsewhere), and especially the market for woodland mushrooms, which, unlike "champignons," couldn't be raised in cellars or old mine tunnels but grew wild, there for the foraging, which could add to their exotic taste, at least off in the cities, giving them their reputation as a delicacy.

That mushroom depot, where the pickings from the entire, quite wooded, area could be exchanged for payment, and from which they were transported by the truckload to the city: that depot was what got the money-obsessed child started. Before that the future mushroom maniac had gone out in nature anyway at the drop of a hat. At the drop of a hat: usually what drew him was the trees' rustling, swooshing, or swishing, even just whispering, and to hear that he didn't venture into the woods themselves or wherever but crouched on the edge, and crouched and crouched and stayed and stayed, with his back to the trees and his eyes scanning the rather deserted countryside.

Not until the previously mentioned hankering for money came into play did he venture into the woods and then into the innermost reaches. The forests in the region where he grew up consisted mainly of conifers, and furthermore, with the exception of the sparser stands of larches up in the mountainous areas, almost exclusively of spruces, with their dense coats of needles, and these trees all grew close together, their limbs and branches intermeshed and interwoven, and as one plunged into the tangle of spruces it got dark and darker, to the point that after a while neither individual trees nor the forest as a whole could be made out, and it was darkest and most disorienting in the depths, which closed around one soon or even immediately after one ventured in from the perimeter: no sightlines between the trunks, with their mostly dead lower branches, into the open space that had surrounded him only moments before, none of the daylight that had shone on him only moments before, the only remaining light an unchanging deep dusk that didn't provide any usable illumination, and in the (invisible) treetops not merely "hardly a breath," to quote Goethe, but none whatsoever, not to mention the birdsong audible only a few steps back.

A kind of light did emanate instead from what could be found on the forest floor, sometimes half hidden in moss. The more often the child pressed on into those deep, dark woods, the more he was received by that light, even before he'd made any finds, yes, long before, and also time and again later on, even when no productive spots turned up; so he'd been thoroughly fooled by the light in the moss.

What kind of light had that been? A glow. Under the dull-gray tangle of dead trees and lichens glowed a treasure-trove light. How so? Those small clumps of chanterelles whose glow later beckoned to him, literally blinding him at first amid the gloom: a treasure? A treasure: something that netted you at most one or two little banknotes for even the best harvest when you turned it in for money at the mushroom depot, though more likely hardly a handful of halfway splendid coins? Aside from the fact that in those days the child was pleased just to have some change jingling in his pocket, and had a use for it and was proud, and how! to have "earned" it by his own efforts: this kind of finding, far from other people, the "madding crowd," deep in the woods, if the haul grew, even modestly, it did indeed count as treasure—that much was clear, clear as day!

At this point in the story of my mushroom maniac I've just realized, by the way, that my vanished friend saw himself from an early age as destined to be a treasure hunter, or, as he put it, called to be one. In his own eyes the child was thus already something like a chosen one, even if he wouldn't have described himself as such. Rather? More likely he'd have thought of himself as "not quite normal." In any case, every time he dashed away from his house and the village, crossing meadows, pastures, and cultivated fields, and headed uphill through the last of the orchards to the edge of the woods in order to "listen in" to all the sounds the leaves made—the edge of the woods consisted mostly of foliage trees—he did so and undertook that in the awareness of, or, you might say, the illusory belief in, a higher calling.

He experienced the spherical tossing of the trees' crowns in the wind, even when it produced no sound, as an order, or as an alternative law; that movement swung him into the sky, into the heavens. And at the same time it was a story all its own, a tale of swaying treetops, and nothing but, a tale of nothing, and of everything. Looking and listening became musing, in which he felt far more at home than in thinking of any kind. And oh, my! when the swishing and swooshing gradually became voiced, a voice! How that voice filled him with enthusiasm. For what? For nothing at all. Did he enter into or merge with the tossing of the treetops? It just felt right, as one feels when an arithmetic problem finally comes out right after many futile attempts. When he was older, even the wildest ocean surf couldn't compete with the fluttering of birches, the rustling of ash trees, the thrashing of oaks along the edge of the woods. The treasure existed, the one destined to be his from his earliest years. It wasn't the crushed aluminum cans and empty cigarette packs littering the local roadsides. So was it the spheres formed by the trees' crowns instead? Not exactly. What he expected from the trees' swishing and swooshing was no sense of self-sufficiency, he didn't yearn to be raptured or to find consummation in becoming no one and nothing. Listening in to it didn't mean becoming one with it. It functioned as a kind of summons, a push to act. But to act how? To do what? To be embraced by the rustling? Not completely, not wholly, not ever.

Whatever the case, when he set out for the edge of the woods, it was as a treasure hunter, a particular kind, though when he got there all he did—this is how I see him now, from my post at my writing table—was sit, pigheaded, and in the process becoming more and more pigheaded, all afternoon, mute and motionless except for sometimes scratching his head, blowing into a dandelion stem—which produces a drone that doesn't harmonize very well with the rustling of the leaves, more of a jarring note like a cow's fart—and finally shuddering repeatedly, not as a result of being overcome with emotion or even awe, but clearly because as time passes and dusk comes on he begins to shiver and shake in the cold, and finally he heads for home with his invisible treasure, where he snaps at his mother, who worried constantly even then that her son might disappear for good and now timidly utters a mild reproof, whereas every time he goes, it's to fulfill his special obligation to hunt for treasure—something his parents should realize without his having to explain it to them.

And in this connection it also occurs to me that as a child my maniac imagined, though for only moments at a time, or for only one, that he possessed magical powers. He thought he could feel the strength to work magic in his muscles, which at such a moment would fuse into a single magic muscle. And what act of magic or enchantment did he want to perform? He wanted to work magic on himself. –And how? In what form? –He wanted to whisk himself away, using the power concentrated in that muscle, in front of everybody. Out of everybody's sight, while remaining present at the same time. No, not in the same place, but still on hand, and more intensely so, to everyone's amazement. –And how do I see the child now after that moment of utmost concentration? –More pigheaded than ever. In general rather puffed up. And then I hear the child: clearing his throat. Giving a little cough. Giggling to himself, embarrassed but not defeated. And I catch a whiff, can positively smell it: my friend, the boy from next door, won't give up. He's positive that next time, and if not then, sometime after that, he'll manage to whisk himself away by magic, away from the rest of us.

The mushroom depot, where during two or three summers he exchanged his mushrooms for cold cash, was located in a house that stood all by itself at some distance from the village. This house, taller and wider than the others in the area, also differed from them in its construction and design: clunky and odd, neither a farmhouse nor a burgher's house, more like the "poorhouses" of the day, where behind each of the dusty windows, some of whose glass panes had been replaced with cardboard, one could sense rather than see a motionless human doll, its eyes wide but expressionless, the eyes and ears no longer registering anything, and certainly not the man or woman in the cramped room next door. And this building was in fact serving as a sort of emergency shelter or refugee residence, but for a single family that had fled after the war from a nearby Slavic country, or simply emigrated, and had temporary asylum here. The family lived–if one can call it that–only on the ground floor, occupying dark caverns without doors, while the two upper stories stood empty, probably uninhabitable in any case, having even from the outside the look of ruins, not from the war but from the pre-prewar period, as indeed the entire house, from top to bottom, including the ground floor, turned out, if one found oneself inside, keeping one's head down and not venturing more than a step beyond the entrance, to have none of the amenities of a house, and certainly none of a home, resembling, if anything, a tumbledown bunker: one more step, and it would come crashing down on top of one.

Yet the foreigners holed up on the ground floor were living there as if it were perfectly normal. Almost all the family members had a rather imperious air, even the children, including the younger ones. And that stemmed from the business into which the clan had literally thrown themselves soon after taking up residence there. They popped out like jackrabbits, one after the other, from their various nooks and crannies whenever my maniac turned up on their nonexistent doorstep to make his delivery, and one of them, who could also be a child, younger than he was, would already have set up the prewar scale with its two pans, one for his contribution and the other for the weights.

My friend was seldom the only one there to make a delivery. It did happen a couple of times, but only during the first summer, when the mushroom depot had just been established. Toward the end of that summer and much more so the following one, a crowd of local collectors would form outside the wreck of a house, and as time went on, the scale moved more and more from the house's interior, until finally it stood smack in the middle of the entrance to the cave, the emblem, as it were, of the market the family had cornered. And the others making deliveries always brought far more booty than the maniac, hauling it in bags, baskets, and rucksacks, their hands full, also pulling little carts, while he just strolled in with his finds. The older men and especially the old women knew where to look. Yet his rather meager offering was received by the lordly merchants with the same attentiveness from start to finish, weighed with the same care and converted into the bit of change. Lordly merchants, lordly merchandise: from summer to summer those terms became more appropriate for the immigrant clan. All the while the ruin that housed them remained unchanged. But their one delivery vehicle, a rusty tractor with a trailer, turned into several, then brand-new ones, and after three years one could see the majesties outside the same old ruin climbing into cars that bore no resemblance to the clunkers driven by most of the villagers, if they owned vehicles at all. To be sure, that kind of wealth—which it was, a particular kind of wealth, in that it was on display, unlike any other wealth in the area (the only other kind, that of the nobility, was kept out of sight)—ultimately flowed from more than the simple exchange that had been so lively precisely in that provisional shelter: with the passing years the clan, all its members included, had taken to the woods themselves to search, and by now knew better where to look than the one native or other who in return for a small pension or death-insurance policy had provided information about the best places.

By the third summer of his childish collecting mania he had to reckon with running into one, no, never just one but more and more members of the clan, even when he ventured almost to the tree line, hunting first among the spruces, then among the larches, and finally among the Arolla pines, and these competitors gave him to understand in no uncertain terms, with smiles at a distance, and then more unmistakable signals as they drew near, that there and then he had no right—not by hook or by crook, not by root or by branch, with no bells and no whistles—to be hunting for mushrooms.

What was strange about the whole thing: as he told me, the only member of that clan of collectors and dealers that stuck in his mind as an individual was the one who in all those years remained excluded from the business and even the family circle. Indeed, nothing else was conceivable for that person. It was someone who in those days was called "feeble-minded" or "retarded," a feeble-minded, mentally retarded girl. She hardly ever let herself be seen, or more and more she was kept hidden by the tribe that had blossomed into a clan. Basically he remembered only a single moment with the feeble-minded girl: having made his delivery and gloating in the weight of coins in his pocket, in a fit of high spirits, and of curiosity as well, he strolled around the back of the depot, still a semi-ruin, and came upon a tangle of poles that had probably been a rose arbor at one time—the one at his parents' house was still covered in blossoms—and there she was, a girl of about his own age. With round red splotches on her cheeks and bulging eyes that he remembered later as also red, the girl was perched on something that must have been a milking stool at one time, and she grinned, no, smiled at him with her thick lips. Could he slip back around the corner of the house and make himself scarce? No, she kept him there by addressing him, as matter-of-factly as if she'd been waiting forever for someone, someone like him, no, him personally. And what she said to him seemed to contradict those flaming cheeks and glowing eyes, and then, in retrospect, not so much after all. The light was too bright, she said, her head couldn't take it. God was trying to punish her, if only she knew why! His light kept ramming her forehead, but her brow bone was too thick, and God could pound and pound but not get through. Ouch, how He hurt her with that pain, and it never let up, but why? And suddenly she slid off her stool, pulled up her dress, a smock, actually, and relieved herself right in front of the other child, a stranger, while he fastened his eyes on the high shafts of her shoes, apparently meant to reinforce her weak legs, and the cuff of a woolen sock peeping out the top of one shoe—was the foot in the second shoe bare? no, the sock had bunched deep inside the shoe, had worked its way under her heel—a condition we described in those days as "starved to death"—the sock had starved to death in the depths of her shoe.

Not long after that the feeble-minded girl was sent to an institution far away, in a different region, since the mushroom-collecting clan could afford it now, and there she died a few years later. She was brought back to the ruin for burial, and he, by then no longer a child and also no longer a mushroom collector—he was earning the money he needed in other ways—watched the funeral procession, as his winter vacation was drawing to a close, from a window in his parents' house. It had snowed for days, but now the snow had turned to rain: dark gray light and a cold mist rising from the snow cover; the coffin was draped with a white cloth to indicate the girl's virginity, and the pouring rain made its whiteness stand out against the prevailing gloom and emphasized the coffin's geometry. It seemed to him later that this particular funeral procession had coincided not only with the end of his vacation but also with a final farewell—to the area, to the landscapes of his childhood, to his kith and kin.

My friend had had that obsession with money as a child because there was something he was bound and determined to buy. And under the conditions in which he grew up, the only possibility for obtaining the "medium of exchange" he so urgently needed was picking things that grew wild—raspberries and blackberries, and above all mushrooms, among which the previously mentioned yellow ones that went by such different names from country to country (more about those names later on in this story), constituted just about the only real items of value in those years right after the war, at least in the area where he lived.

And what did he want to buy with his mushroom money? You guessed it: books. But this boy next door wanted books entirely different from the ones I coveted. If the only ones that mattered to me were narratives, invented stories, products of the imagination—in short, literature—he was fixated on books, or anything printed—which he also called literature—that responded to his boundless desire for knowledge; slaked his searing thirst for knowledge (what I recall most vividly about him from our childhood: the way his mouth would go dry as he asked question after question). So he took his first mushroom money, and not only the first, and set out on foot down the main road, which in those days had little traffic, and walked half a day to get to town, returning with his rucksack, which still smelled (and stank) of mushrooms, full of brochures, which might have titles like ". . . : What you always wanted to know" or "The hundred and ninety-three definitive answers to . . ."

This early phase of his mushroom mania would probably have passed on its own in the fullness of time. But then, as he told me, it was of all things a nightmare that brought his relatively harmless obsession to a sudden end. One time he'd discovered a wooded spot way up on a mountainside that seemed never to have been found by a mushroom hunter—let alone plundered and pillaged by the local old-timers or the immigrant clan, who otherwise swarmed over the most remote forested areas. This spot turned out to be not just one spot but rather an entire territory, which in his imagination became a continent, spreading for hours and hours and inexhaustible. Wherever he looked, walked, ran, fell, turned off, swerved, leaped over brooks or fallen trees or gullies: yellow, yellow, and more yellow. No matter how much he collected, eventually using both hands, picking, harvesting, gathering: the yellow fungi in the mountain moss, "little foxes," as the clan members called them, translating the name from their Slavic language, the "fawnlets," the *finferli*, the *setas de San Juan* (names with which he would become familiar only later) simply refused to dwindle, the "yellowing"—"that word, like *bluing*, *greening*, and *graying*, would have been appropriate!" he told me much later—the "yellowing" would never cease. Was that perhaps the origin of the eye he developed for different colors—shades of red, shades of gray, shades of yellow?

But the same phenomenon that during the day, at least intermittently, had occasioned incredulous amazement, yes, delight, became transformed during the night that followed, which my mushroom maniac was forced to spend in a deserted Alpine hut, into something else. The sight of those mushrooms of St. John found its way into the young person's dreams. All night long he dreamed that he was crouching in the densest underbrush, then tumbling rather than hopping from one crouch to another, drawn from one scattering of yellow to the next, and on and on, all night long. Having everything go black before his eyes was nothing, was harmless, when compared with these unending swaths of yellow unfurling, no, convulsing before him, yellow, yellow, and more yellow before the dreamer's eyes. But no: the unceasing, unremitting yellow assailing the sleeper was not "before" his eyes—it kept leaping into his eyes, sneaking into them, flickering deep inside him as it did beneath his hands, forcing them to keep grubbing for it, until the incessant yellow curling, crinkling, and licking left him completely encircled: any minute now he'd be suffocated by this yellow times yellow times yellow; any minute now this yellow to a higher power, yellow to the third, fourth, fifth, etc. power, would cause his heart to explode in his chest—or the attack of toxic yellow would evaporate his heart's blood, turn it yellow.

Perhaps it wasn't only this nightmare that drove his early, youthful mushroom mania out of him. Yet the dream, of that much he was sure, did more than going away to study in far-off cities, more than his first loves, more than forming friendships different from those with childhood neighbors, to get him to leave the world of mushrooms behind, or at least beyond the horizons, beyond the seven mountains from which we both came, the more so since his mushroom money had enabled him to buy everything his heart, in those days still modest, desired.

That didn't mean, however, that thenceforth he avoided going into the woods, either in his native region or elsewhere. As a result of his collecting forays, the woods had become one of his elements, though his relationship to them differed from his earlier attachment to edges, rims, and clearings. He still picked mushrooms and brought them home with him, but without keeping an eye out or setting out to look for them on purpose—simply when he happened to come upon them. And it was still primarily those St. John's mushrooms, nightmare be damned. Even when he stumbled on so many that their sheer weight brought to mind the scale in the doorless entry to the depot, it never crossed his mind to sell his haul. Not that he no longer needed money—even after he'd left childhood behind, he still fell short year after year; but in the meantime something inside him resisted obtaining money through anything resembling a commercial transaction, at least of that sort; money should "come in" as a result of more noble activities—whatever those might be.

So he handed over to others what he found, by chance and in passing, in the woods, and that meant to his mother when he was home. She usually acted delighted—provided he didn't bring too many—as if he'd come bearing a treasure, though in her eyes, as in his, mushrooms had long ago ceased to be treasures, inasmuch as they had no commercial value, even for bartering. His mother also had to feign delight when she sautéed the yellow spawn on her kitchen woodstove, since neither she nor her boy liked the smell of them cooking, and didn't really enjoy eating them either. (In her son's case, that would change later.)

He experienced a different reaction at most in the fall, when before he headed back to the city to resume his university studies, he sometimes brought home from the edge of the woods, which he still cherished as in childhood as his "haul and windfall spot," those giant mushrooms, their caps often as big as a plate atop a tall, fragile stem, called "umbrella" or "parasol" mushrooms (what else?): when that happened, his mother didn't need to feign delight, just marveled at their form, because they looked so much more unusual, more unique, and perhaps for that reason also beautiful, and, after breading and sautéeing the caps like, or as, schnitzel, served them to her son and indeed the whole family, this time to their unalloyed pleasure. And woe betide anyone in the household who spoke ill of these peerlessly tender delicacies, which refused to allow any associations with ordinary mushrooms to come to mind or to the senses, delicacies that transcended any other special or exceptional thing, their taste infinitely far from that of any schnitzel, no matter how tenderized—woe betide anyone who allowed the concept left over from wartime (still in use to this day) of "meat substitute" to pass his lips instead of letting the parasol, pure and simple, melt in his mouth. And each time it did melt in the mouths of the family, all of them gathered around the table, harmoniously for a change, the delight spreading through the house, to the now cleared-out corner where the crucifix had hung, to the cluster of enlarged photos of family members lost in the war; it spread and spreads and will have spread, even to the son, at the time still excessively picky, who furthermore was reluctant, as decades later, when he was long since someone other than a son, and is still reluctant, to take some of what he himself gathered and brought home.

That, at least, is what he described to me, and in fact several times. Once, by the way, he'd served his own child a mushroom breaded according to his mother's recipe, presenting it as a schnitzel, *un escalope*. But the child's taste buds had refused to be fooled; at the very first bite he exclaimed, "You're lying!" which didn't mean the child stopped chewing; on the contrary.

Half a lifetime would pass after his first bout of mushroom mania, during which the world of mushrooms meant hardly anything to him. And if it did, more in a negative sense: after he'd acquired a house—which, strangely enough, stood in an isolated spot, separate from the other houses in his urban neighborhood, and was a partial ruin when he bought it—and soon after he'd settled in, together with his wife and child, and made the place livable, the fungal affliction known as dry rot began to spread through one of the foundation walls, eating its way through wood and mortar and even causing the blocks of granite to come loose and fall out, and there was nothing to be done; the whole wall had to be torn down (which by the way turned out not so badly for the house's interior).

Along with the half-dilapidated house he'd also become the owner of an overgrown yard in which, even after years of cutting down trees and brush, pulling up weeds, and digging up the ground, every year, in an entirely different spot from the one cleared the year before, so-called stinkhorn mushrooms sprang up, their stench wafting through the yard and the house, into the farthest corner, which until then might have been the enchanted refuge of love and sweet secrets, a stench that the mushroom's name didn't begin to convey. Yes, this growth that functioned as an enchantment-killer started out almost invisible among fallen leaves under a bush, rather like a snow-white layer of ice or grated horseradish, and actually sweet-smelling despite its mushiness, and then from one moment to the next, as if in a natural time lapse, shot up into a stinkhorn, the stem looking like Styrofoam, "which wasn't so bad," he commented, "but then the head–impossible not to associate with the head of a human penis, but one that upon being exposed to the air for the first time, above the ice, promptly rotted, melting gelatinously, and this dissolving, dripping mushroom cap, stinking to high heaven, a heaven that until then had held sway in my, in our, house–is attacked almost from the moment it emerges from the ground on all sides by a swarm of flies, seemingly from nowhere, which descend on the gelatinous mass so ferociously that the fragile Styrofoam stem snaps, and the head, together with its fuzzy covering of flies, crashes to the ground, which doesn't deter the flies for a moment–they just continue devouring it–nor does it moderate the carrion smell in the slightest; the sight of the blowflies even intensifying the charm-breaking stench? No, impossible for it to get any stronger."

During those decades of his life he had further unpleasant incidents involving mushrooms. But my old friend from the village didn't mention them, or left it to me to imagine various things on my own. Besides: even those he did tell me about, however much background he filled in and dramatized, more in jest than seriously, were incidents that carried hardly any significance, as did mushrooms altogether during that period. Disturbing incidents in general, with the exception of those described above, might unsettle him for a while, but they didn't mean anything; he viewed them as not really part of his life, not chapters, however brief, not even parenthetical remarks in the story of his life.

The story of his life, at least that half of his life, was shaped, after he moved away from our area, by the aesthetic principle Kant called "disinterested pleasure"; at least that's how he saw his life, had taken the idea into his head, and not only into his head, or had chosen to model his life on that notion, applying it to others as well, and that took him far, in more than one respect. Disinterested pleasure helped him achieve balance, not only to maintain distance but also to create distance, as a deed, an activity, and if it became necessary to engage in emphasizing, singling out, distinguishing, to do so in a measured way–which combined into a stable form of–no, not being just but rather doing justice. And pleasure in that context meant that in all undertakings, decisions, and interventions in which something, or everything, was at stake, he projected a cheerful acceptance that came across to some (a few), including me from time to time, as positively scornful, a harmony that–or so it seemed to me here–pictured itself as more and stronger than just his own personal harmony–a cosmic harmony, so to speak; whereupon he would reply to me, with that smiling equanimity that during his lord-of-the-world period could make my blood boil at certain moments, that this kind of acceptance was probably indigenous to the area from which we both came, where the tragic had never, ever been at home, through the centuries and to this day. "There's no such thing as the tragic for the likes of us. Tragic? Out of the question. (For God's sake, spare us your tragedies.)" During that phase of his life, my now-vanished friend considered himself far, infinitely far from mania of any kind, or he kept his distance from it, far, infinitely far from any false weights and measures.

He'd never expected to amount to anything. As a child, when asked what he wanted to be when he grew up, he'd been at a loss and had at most shrugged or, one of his seemingly innate talents, stared stupidly straight ahead, half seriously, half in jest. Hungry for knowledge though he otherwise was: he had no desire to know anything about his own future. As he saw it, there was nothing to know. And besides, from the time he was little he couldn't imagine that a person like him had anything like a future beckoning. The future didn't interest him particularly, just as, once his first obsession had dissipated, nothing else particularly, or in particular, interested him.

In this way my friend from the village, who didn't expect to amount to anything, actually did amount to something after all, albeit, as he gave me to understand more than once, only in the eyes of the world. "In my own mind I never got any farther than the edge of the woods, where I went to hear the wind in the treetops. Maybe outwardly, to all appearances, I amounted to something or other, but that's all. What am I saying: nothing else became of me!" Whatever the case: without intending or planning to, over the decades he did come to represent something to the outside world. He made a difference. He made a difference in all conceivable directions and parts of the world, and he made things happen. What did he make happen? According to what I heard in the meantime from out in that world, it certainly wasn't anything terrible, which confirmed me in my prejudice that those constantly working for the general welfare, if not for the benefit of all mankind, would do infinitely better to engage in insignificant tasks like sewing on buttons, collecting kindling, or even just lying around idle, because then at least they would be doing no harm.

For his making a difference and making things happen I have the following explanation—though I'm aware that this explanation stems entirely from fantasies I've been indulging in for quite a while about my dear vanished friend: his effectiveness resulted from a unique alternation between being intensely present and utterly absentminded, completely absent and completely present and vice versa, and vice versa again. From one moment to the next he could switch from being the personification of attentiveness to being missing in action, and the person with whom he'd just been interacting intensely would find himself in a flash facing a mere cutout or a hollow shell of a human being, on whose forehead he would be tempted to knock, sometimes even pound, shouting, "Hello, anybody home?" and seconds later the shell would not only be newly occupied but would represent the very spot where the authority superior to all other external authorities would do justice or at least promise justice—which for the moment was often exactly what one needed. That he could do his work with his left hand seemed right to him, and not only to him, for a long time, as did the fact that it didn't seem like real work.

And now my imagination further makes clear to me that this rhythm of his, the alternation between presence and absence, grew out of the alternation between his original passion for knowledge, actually more a craving, a lust for knowledge, and his tendency to flee head-over-heels from books and brochures, from "literature," to flee also from his house and the village, away from people, flee to the uninhabited, wordless, unspellable, indecipherable edge of the woods, which refused, absolutely refused to express anything, and whose rustling, swishing, and crackling bucked him up. But then back where he'd come from, without delay! His existence a constant game of switching between lust for knowledge!, sociability, and a secret—which involved no one else, by the way, and which he didn't divulge even to me, his only friend, until much later. Otherwise he wouldn't have been able to make such a difference in those later years, amounting to a good half of his life, before the outbreak of his maniacal obsession, of which he also became aware when it happened.

He made a difference, which meant that by alternating between presence and absence he built trust—except with those to whom trust didn't matter, who took trustworthiness for weakness. In this respect it was as if he were both my judge and my lawyer, though more my lawyer when the chips were down and he, the lawyer, was needed. He had in fact become a lawyer, a defense attorney, traveling to international courts of justice, and he helped many defendants—especially because the judge in him repeatedly manifested itself, as a sort of call to order. Many people also pictured him becoming a politician, on the world stage, as it were; fortunately that remained something they imagined, not shared by him; he still had no concept of what he might be when he grew up, couldn't picture himself as someone who'd "amounted to something," or as someone who'd become something, let alone someone who might yet become this or that.

Over the decades, my friend from the village didn't become a rich man, but he was, as the expression had it at one time, "comfortable." I never heard of his having enemies, but also, and this was strange for someone whom so many trusted, any friends. Instead I heard various things about him and women, or rather women and him, and that was also strange, since I'd never been able to picture him as a ladies' man—but I probably see it that way because I knew him as a child and then as a rather scrawny though athletic youth (in soccer and such there was that rhythm again of presence and absence, with which he faked out his opponents). And a "ladykiller"—a killer? And "lucky with women"—lucky? In my imagination I see us laughing, my vanished friend and me, in unison.

It was during this period of his—what's the term?—social ascent that I gradually lost track of him. Now and then he'd send me signs of life, though not mentioning any of what the newspapers reported about him. I could never fully believe the hearsay that reached my ears, but thought the newspapers were more reliable, God knows why; as someone occasionally mentioned or at least alluded to in the press, I should actually have remained skeptical: but when it came to people other than me, I tended to read anything in print fairly uncritically, at least in my earlier years, and even today, though now only when I first skim an article. According to the papers, I was supposed to know that my village friend and later man of the world "always wore Italian or French suits and English custom-made shoes, with silk ties for every season and even every time of day," was on his third or fourth marriage and had just separated from his most recent wife, an indigenous woman from Fort Yukon, Alaska—his wives, according to these accounts, had become more "exotic" each time—while other sources reported that it was the woman who had left him, and that from his first wife on it had always been the woman who walked out: Wasn't something odd going on there, and not necessarily something nice? And then what about children? In all those years, not a single one.

By contrast, one of his personal signs of life at around the same time: he mentioned that he'd just seen the first snowflakes blow through his yard. While he was raking leaves that morning, as usual the robin—"always the same one, or do I only imagine that?"—had fluttered out of the shrubbery, "landing without a sound on the freshly raked black soil, more silently than a leaf." He told me he was reading my story about life in the no-man's-bay and finding allusions in it to his own story. And besides—"this is just for you, don't tell anyone"—he'd met the woman thanks to whom he'd finally received the push he'd been lacking, which meant that in her company what he'd always dreamed of experiencing with a woman had finally "come true," in other words, he'd wanted to "save her" on the spot, "get her to safety," and himself as well, even if neither she nor he might actually need to be saved or gotten to safety—not at the moment—"not yet!" Whatever the case: they'd met each other halfway, and "not only figuratively." Furthermore, the woman came from "our part of the world, my friend," that, too, being what he'd always dreamed of. And to top it off: they'd both caught the bus at the same stop in the old days, though at fairly different times—but what were "all those different times in comparison to old times"?

He went on to tell me that from one day to the next—"or, if you will, overnight"—he and the woman had become an item, and they were expecting a child in the summer, whose name both of them secretly knew, without having to speak it out loud. "Yes, old friend: this woman has led me along secret paths, as your Wolfram von Eschenbach phrased it. Don't wish me luck; wish me goodness: that I may always be good. Pray for me. I need that. I feel that I'm too weak on my own, and of all times now, when things have finally turned serious. This woman trusts me, and how. But I don't trust myself. I'm afraid of myself. Yes, pray for me. Who prays for me? Weak though I feel on the one hand, on the other hand I feel chosen, and that's what makes me afraid of myself in this situation. Yes, ever since I ran head over heels to the edge of the woods to get away from the family, to be alone with the rustling of the leaves and the swishing of the branches, I've felt as if I'm chosen, also in this sense: People, what have I to do with you? And now I have this premonition again: Woman, what have I to do with thee?! I, who was always too weak for those closest to me, and at the same time? or for that very reason? chosen, or fooling myself into thinking I am: for something different, entirely different—a calling? Or, on the contrary, the chosen one from the beginning and therefore unfit for any kind of community. But taboo as the chosen one? Don't touch me, I'm taboo to you people?—Pray for me!"

Was that the time when the life of my friend, who would eventually disappear, began to develop into a story all its own? If that was the case, it occurred without suddenness or shock. What happened to him began very gently, and continued that way for a long time. At first, and that also remained true for a long time, the change involved only everyday things, to be specific, the kinds of ordinary things that to him had always represented an ideal, precisely because they helped shield him from his consciousness of being special, and were harmless besides, and were thus the kind of thing that did a person good: nothing more peaceable than that, but also—why not?—nothing more pleasurable than such everyday things, which he hoped to encounter in the future—nothing more childlike. Right?

The story, the actual, special one, began on a summer day, weeks before the birth of his child. He'd set out from his property for the nearby wooded hills, planning to take the shortcut to the city, a trail that ran gently uphill, and then had a much longer descent. He had nothing to do in the city but meet his wife, now late in her pregnancy, for dinner; he was temporarily on leave from the court where he was slated to defend yet another man accused of war crimes. Feeling impelled to walk rather than drive, and that over a considerable distance, as if for the sake of the unborn child, uphill, then down into the valley and uphill again, he left his car in the garage and also passed up the local rail line. Wearing a suit, tie, and hat (neither a Borsalino nor a Stetson), he made his way through the hilly wooded area that formed a barrier, but not that high a one, between his area and the metropolis.

The path led through a deciduous forest. What a difference between those trees and the spruce, fir, and pine forests we'd known as children. The woods in this country let light through from top to bottom, the trees—oak, Spanish chestnut, beech, and birch—spaced quite far apart, their various limbs and branches not intertwined, with hardly any underbrush, and when the sun came out it shone through the whole forest, even its farther reaches. The technical term "clear span" acquired a different meaning here. Initially this brightness had made him uncomfortable. In his former country there was a saying that white wine wasn't "real wine," and similarly he didn't consider these deciduous forests real forests. The gloom, the darkness, the crowding, the confinement, the sense of not finding one's way but having to fight one's way through: he missed all that. Besides, despite their clear span, these deciduous forests seemed unclean to him, no, actually dirty, or to put it differently, he missed the sense of cleanliness he'd experienced long ago in the evergreen forests, above all in their dark depths, despite the trepidation—cleanliness as part of that—he'd felt in their midst; even the maggot-ridden mushrooms, even the skeletons, strikingly white, of deer, foxes, hares in and on the moss, had radiated something pure there. An additional factor was that for a long time, perhaps up to that very summer day, he'd hardly registered these deciduous woods as places in their own right, as an environment, as a space or spaces, seeing them only as an in-between realm and a passage from his starting place A to his destination B—except for the one time when he and his future wife had been on their way to a different city and had passed through just such a forest, and suddenly she'd pulled him to one side—he didn't remember whether by his shirt or his belt, but at least not by his tie or his hair—had almost yanked him, with a facial expression that suggested that she was the one who had to rescue him.

When he'd crossed these deciduous forests on previous occasions, he'd never intentionally looked down at the ground. In general that was something he hadn't done anywhere in a long time, just as he usually didn't make a point of looking up at the sky—except for one time when he'd had to go on official business to a country involved in a civil war, and then only on clear, starry nights, when the bombs were sure to hit their targets. Official business or not: during his period as a man of the world his gaze was directed straight ahead, always at eye level.

That was the case as well on that summer afternoon as he hiked uphill, hat in hand, through the woods, with no one coming in the opposite direction. It must have been a steep section of the path, for how else would he have had at eye level what he later described to me as something "unexpectedly conspicuous" (his words) on the forest floor. It was a kind of eye level such as he'd never encountered before. Nothing of historic significance crept into the encounter, such as might have occurred between two statesmen or two artists; nothing fateful such as, though not recorded as part of human history, sometimes occurs between a man and a woman (and not just in the novels of Georges Simenon); nothing indescribable such as he, the defense attorney, had experienced more than once at eye level with the accused—and yet—and yet.

This eye level, however, was describable. "Well, would you look at that!" The object, the thing, was directly before his eyes and at the same time in his eye; it was describable. But there was no name for it, at least none that seemed to fit at that moment. Even "thing" or "object"—such terms didn't do it justice. "Don't laugh!" my friend said to me. "What suddenly, no, not suddenly, unexpectedly, met my eye: at that moment I took it in as something nameless, or, if I did have a name for it, I called it, in a silent exclamation to myself, 'a living being!'

preceded by an 'Oho!' such as Knut Hamsun often uses at the beginning of a sentence: 'Oho, a living being!' And lest I forget: even before that silent exclamation—only now, as I'm telling you this, does it come back to me—an even more silent one occurred, and that went as follows: 'This is it!'"

Oho! Would you look at that!: He felt as if, unbeknownst to him, he'd been waiting for this moment, for this sight, for this encounter, this coincidence. For how long? It was a stretch of time that didn't lend itself to measuring: "since time immemorial," and that could equally well mean from before his birth or just since yesterday. Wasn't he exaggerating, to himself first of all, as he suddenly stood there—can you believe it?—with his first-ever boletus right in front of him, not a particularly large one, but with a very straight stem, a gleaming reddish brown cap, untouched by any snail or other pest, and a pure white underside. Picture-perfect, or more like something from a magic kingdom? So this existed, was part, or a standard feature, of reality; revealed itself incarnate in this fabulous being as fully as anything could. "To encounter it at eye level," he wrote to me much later, "meant more to me than, or at any rate something different from, seeing a lion coming toward me through the trees—one of my frequent dreams in childhood—or, let's say, finding myself suddenly in the presence of a unicorn, conjured up from who knows where, and the experience was also entirely different from the legend of the hunter and future saint, Hubert, who in the depths of the forest came upon a stag with a crucifix in its antlers. My fabulous being, my first ever and, by the way, also my last up to now, had nothing in common with a mythical beast. It was both part of and an addition to the bright day and, instead of calling reality into question, casting a dubious light on it and, like the dream of the lion bearing down on me, pulling the ground out from under my feet, it solidified the ground and in equal measure the brightness of the day; my fabulous being heightened the day's reality for me, which I can't imagine happening with a unicorn popping out of the ground, besides which to this day I've never met an actual unicorn: to see it, like the lion, in the guise of a hunter, aiming its bow and arrow or whatever at the stag, would have made my heart beat faster, one way or the other. But believe me, at the sight of my first boletus, with more than half my life already past, it beat even faster—faster, believe it or not, than it ever had before!"

How could that be? He'd grown up in a densely wooded area, and starting in early childhood had "gone mushrooming," as we called it, looking for those he could sell, the yellow ones, had crept and crawled into the highest, most remote evergreen forests, and he'd never come upon that king of all fungi? Never. Not once. Or maybe one of them had stuck up like this one, in the grizzled moss there, gleaming amid the gray spruce litter and fallen needles, even more conspicuous than this one here, which was surrounded by reddish brown fallen leaves from the previous year, with the sun shining on them? And the child had overlooked it every time, precisely as something, or someone, so obvious, so apparent? Yes, possibly, or certainly. But how to explain that with all those other mushroom hunters in the woods the child had never seen a single boletus, not even in the hands of the forest-looting clan? Nothing but the eternal yellow had caught his eye in his competitors' baskets and other containers? Or did they keep the masters, the fabulous beings, hidden underneath so no one else would see them? But why did he also remember nothing but wave upon wave of yellow, crate upon crate, at the mushroom depot down in the valley? Hidden nooks into which no light penetrated where the uprooted kings frolicked? Intended for what market? Except that they'd never caught his eye at markets, or he'd hardly felt attracted to markets, even much later on in life, or then only for exotic fruits, those from overseas, the *ultramarinos*.

When I objected that my friend was making too much of this experience, at the age of almost fifty, with his "first boletus," he retorted in a letter, "And what about you and your 'Repetition' story, when you describe yourself setting out as a young man from our deep valley to cross the seven mountains, heading south, and there, on the slope of the seventh mountain, stumbling toward the sea, or also just the Karst, and, coming upon a palm frond there, or was it a fig sapling, or most likely just a fig leaf blown there by the wind, raising a paean to the 'event of the first fig tree'?! I have to say I prefer my 'first boletus,' the more so since it changed my life!" (At the time when my boyhood friend sent me that reply, he couldn't know or guess how or where he could go astray in his changed life.)

For the moment he crouched down on the side of the uphill trail next to the mushroom, which stood motionless in the summer wind, in contrast to all the other things and plants, including the tall trees, and then he sat down beside it in the dead leaves, without a thought for his suit, although usually even a bit of lint on his clothing bothered him. Time and again his gaze strayed from the object to the surrounding area, as if pulsing away from it, calmly, evenly, in ever-widening circles. In the stillness he quietly told himself what he was seeing, there, then over there. A blackberry bush was covered with reddish berries, not ripe yet, while deep inside the bush a couple of berries were already plump and black: strange that the berries the summer sun couldn't reach in their semidarkness should be ripe already. One of the miniature frogs that had metamorphosed in early summer from legless tadpoles into four-footed creatures and made their way by the thousands from the small lake down below up into the hilly woods, their intended living space, who knows how and for how long, came into view, a rarity, and hopped, no bigger than half of my friend's thumbnail, up the path, easy to mistake for one of the ground spiders skittering back and forth, and now and then one of its hops, weightless though the tiny creature was, caused a grain of sand to swirl into the air: the frog "a survivor from among countless thousands!" One of the oaks along the path had a tumorous swelling on its trunk, or was that a wooden sculpture of a pregnant giant? A group of mountain bikers pushed their bikes up the hillside, and as he sat there, instinctively blocking any view of the mushroom, which they, too, would have overlooked (though who knows?), he was greeted for the first time by such strangers, and not because he was in a suit and tie, and he returned the greeting—or didn't the mutual greetings take place simultaneously, as if it were the most natural thing in the world? Thanks to finding that small treasure, he'd had a sense of "I'm here! I'm here with you!" or simply "Here!" as never before.

Later he even stretched out beside the mushroom. As long ago on the edge of the woods, he was all ears now, though not listening for anything in particular. He simply began to listen, as one begins to walk, to reflect, to think, or also to hesitate. Hammering and the whine of power saws, not far off, not close by, from new houses, more and more of them, being built around the suburban lake. A constant quiet din in the blue sky—"quiet din"?—yes, from passenger planes, and in addition the periodic clatter of helicopters taking off and landing at the nearby military air base—"in addition"?—yes. Nothing bad could happen to the passengers up there, not now, not during this hour at any rate, not on this flight. And from the highways and beltways beyond the woods a roaring, droning, and humming, harmonious as never before, and in harmony with that the honking of horns, even ambulance and police sirens, and all that more or less distant racket in harmony with the swishing of the summery leaves above his head, heard this way for the first time, as well as the bumping and rubbing, the creaking, squeaking, even whistling and warbling, there, and over there, of one or several tree limbs being buffeted by wind gusts across or into each other. And the bad stuff happening or about to happen—now, now!—out there in the world, ears cocked for the sirens and the final crash? What do I care—let it happen—no big deal. To him, too, as he lay there, nothing bad could happen at that moment, or to his wife, along with the child she was carrying. The mushroom next to him would bring him, her, the three of them, luck.

Later on my friend couldn't remember how he'd finally picked his first boletus, the *hongo, jurček, vrganj, cèpe, Boletus edulis*. Had it been a picking? A digging-out? A yanking-out? A plucking? A twisting? What he could say for sure was this: he'd "claimed" it, without checking, by the way, to see whether any others might be nearby. And there's no doubt that for the rest of his hike to the top of the hill and down into the metropolis he neither squeezed it into one of his suit pockets nor hid it in his hat: he carried it openly, in the same hand that kept a firm grip on his hat, and strode along, without once altering that hold, through the remaining hours of the afternoon and into the evening, toward the place where he'd arranged the rendezvous with his wife, changing to the Métro from the bus he caught on the outskirts, and then on foot again. And not a soul noticed what he was balancing and maneuvering through the crowds, holding it next to his hat or in its brim, as if transporting a particularly delicate load.

Treasure? Transporting a treasure? Indeed, it seemed to him during those summer hours as if his daydreams from very early childhood, in which he sallied forth as a treasure hunter and found a treasure with whose help he could work magic, had been fulfilled, albeit with a treasure different from what he'd imagined as a child. Back then and there he'd pictured the treasure waiting, yes, waiting for him—"to whom am I saying this?"—as something metallic or mineral, or as a precious stone, at any rate as something hard and indestructible, something sturdy. And now: the treasure intended for him, the treasure that had been waiting for him all along—without his having any inkling of it—was something that at the first moment was certainly hard, sturdy in its own way, also elastic, but then soft and becoming softer, something unmistakably perishable, the initial elasticity gone, likewise the original pure fragrance—"nutlike," they called it?—the essence of fragrance, dissipated, not only as a result of exposure to the city air, and giving way to ambivalence; to experience something so transitory as his own special treasure: Wasn't that childish? The answer my friend gave as he hovered on the brink of complete mushroom mania, and also years and decades later: "No!"

When he got to the bar where they'd planned to meet and showed his wife the treasure he'd found—even she had failed to notice it—the pregnant woman opened her eyes wide, actually in alarm. She started, and the child in her womb with her. He had to persuade her to take the mushroom, still impressive, its cap shimmering with its last traces of moisture, the underside white as if it had just come into the light from belowground. She held the thing at arm's length and eyed it, less with admiration than with a certain horror. "How ugly!" she said, and it didn't help when he pointed out a lighter spot on the reddish brown cap in the form of an oak leaf that had fallen on it. Yet, as mentioned, she came from the country as he did, from the next village over.

She didn't change her mind until the bartender joined them. He, too, opened his eyes wide when he caught sight of the mushroom, but in his case it was astonishment, and the shock came from pleasure. He told them he'd used his day off to go to the woods, but it had been too windy, with the wind coming from the west, and in that kind of wind the mushrooms didn't poke out of the ground. How could that be, a bartender, and in a world-famous metropolis, as a mushroom hunter and even an expert? Did he perhaps come from the country, too, like his guests? Not at all; he was a city boy, he told them, through and through, and mushrooms simply happened to be his passion, especially the edible varieties, and that had been the case ever since his father had taken him along, when he was barely old enough to walk, leaving behind the urban plane trees and hiking up to the oaks, chestnuts, beeches, and birches.

And he picked up the rather heavy mushroom between his thumb and pinkie, a remarkable light touch that my friend committed to memory, and, using the small knife with which he usually cut lemon peel, orange slices, and other things, carved wafer-like pieces out of the mushroom, not out of the cap but from side to side across the bulging foot. And he did this on the counter, demonstrating it to the two of them: listen to the sound the flesh makes as it's being cut, what a sound, almost a tone, do you hear it? And look at those droplets oozing from the cut, no, welling up, and look, yes, see how they fizz, well up and fizz, colorless, clear: where have you ever seen drops of water that clear and brightsome?

And already the bartender had presented the plate with the almost transparent white disks, raw, with toothpicks stuck into them, to the couple, and my friend and his wife tasted the dish, without any other ingredients, tasted it without hesitation—the wife went first, by the way—and in the course of the hour consumed the entire mushroom prepared in that fashion, the eating remaining a tasting to the last.

Their sense of taste was awakened as never before. My friend savored the taste as never before. And that meant: with the help of this dish, thinking well and thinking good things, feeling good things.

And the evening meal after that? This kind of tasting had sharpened their appetite, and besides, the pregnant woman was always hungry, wanted in those days before giving birth to eat and eat, at every meal. And as it turned out or happened, on that same evening in late summer, the very bistro where the couple were sitting received a delivery of boletus for the kitchen. Why did he tell me this? Because they went on eating the same thing, though prepared differently, in a different form? Nonsense: the delivery struck him as a devaluation of his treasure. These mushrooms weren't larger, and certainly not more handsome than his, and they'd been collected in similar woods, just somewhat farther from the metropolis. But how many of them there were! They were dragged in, piled into crates meant for other kinds of produce—fruit and potatoes—so heavy that each crate needed two men to carry it, and the boxes and crates, filled to the brim, formed a seemingly endless procession from the front door and through the swinging door to the kitchen. From the kitchen, where the mushrooms were being weighed, an unending shouted litany of numbers could be heard, for a long time in kilos, then going into hundredweights, each of these amazing objects—wasn't a mushroom complete unto itself, and meant to stay that way?—translated into a unit of measure and eventually into a measure of quantity, and when the swinging door finally remained wide open—the entire truck empty at last, or was it two of them?—my friend, sitting at his table, while his wife ate and ate, swallowing almost without chewing, and seemingly oblivious to the entire scene, saw an enormous pile of boletus dumped onto the tiled kitchen floor, not by mistake but because one of the sous-chefs was using a hose to spray off the earth, sand, bits of fern and grass, just short bursts each time, not soaking the mushrooms. Quite a few of them had lost their caps or stems when they were emptied onto the tiles, and under the water pressure they broke up even more, and from a distance, in his eyes, which still had his single specimen before them, those thousands of boletus, the masses, the hundredweights, all the headless rumps, looked like rocks, a heap of rocks, blunt, heavy, and above all worthless, or at least cheap. And that was supposed to be a treasure? And only his own, the thing, the meager singleton, was supposed to have been a treasure?

The disenchantment didn't last. It affected him only that evening. By the next morning the magic had reasserted its power, in fact from the time he woke up, during the moments between sleeping and waking. The very absence of a magical object made it potent. "As desire?" I asked. "No," my friend replied, "as longing, or, if you prefer, as a hankering for adventure." He felt a surge of energy, in contrast to most mornings, urging him to get out and head for the woods, and not merely to the edge. He had time, after all, his work with the international tribunal on hiatus until further notice.

His wife's going into labor prevented him from setting out. It would not have taken much for him to resent her for that, if only for a fraction of a second. But then came the thought, "I'm the one who's going to save her," which in that case hardly made sense, by the way. Without haste or anxiety they made their way to the room reserved for her at the hospital, and when his wife and the child, through a series of unfortunate circumstances not relevant here, actually did have to be saved, he, the husband and father, wasn't the one who saved them. When it unexpectedly became necessary to operate, he was roaming the side streets, clueless, his ear cocked for the roar from the nearby soccer stadium, as he tried to guess from the shouting how the game was going. Upon returning to the hospital he was frightened, then relieved, then happy, and finally frightened again, the latter a reaction after the fact, which stayed with him for a long time.

That fright made him forgetful, and my childhood friend forgot about the mushroom, and mushrooms altogether. Or perhaps he didn't forget, but the thing became unimportant—no longer impinged on his imagination. His wife, his child, resuming his place in the legal profession, which, as he wrote to me, "thanks to the child" energized him anew: these things became "my one and all." To be sure, he didn't fail to take the newborn to the now-autumnal woods—his wife avoided them, being allergic to the air there, the flying particles of crumbling leaves and the spiderwebs brushing her face—where he eyed the sides of paths and the gaps between trees. But not once did he make a find, and that was all right by him, at least once he was out of the woods with nothing but the baby in his arms.

A year passed that way, and then another. The only minor aftereffect of the "treasure-find" (by now in quotation marks): he secretly dubbed the steep uphill path beside which he'd encountered that one boletus on that summer afternoon the "Prebirth Path," and it kept that name, by the bye, until my friend's disappearance.

As time went on, it happened more and more often that the lawyer took his files and made his way to the woods near his house. He imagined that, as he worked on his briefs, the quiet there, however incomplete, combined with the almost constant rustling of the foliage—the prevailing sound despite the proximity of the metropolis—would give him inspiration for possibly decisive additions, or pauses, moments of silence, tangents, that might also prove decisive. An illusion? A strange lawyer? Strange, maybe so. But what started out as an illusion eventually became a fact. His arguments had the desired effect and his clients, almost without exception, were exonerated.

The place where he sat in those days, on the ground, still in suit and tie, with his hat beside him, and leaned against a beech, the kind of tree known for its smooth bark, was an open space, almost a circle, not big enough to be an actual clearing, but too large, also too round, too geometric, to have formed by chance. It was an in-between space, true, but created by who knows whom many years earlier, maybe loggers for their camp, of which no trace survived? Man-made, at any rate. It wasn't deep in the woods but just a few steps from the perimeter, along which a broad, cleared strip ran, marking the location of a gas pipeline or the like. Yet the lawyer always sat there undisturbed, as if the round space, which he thought of as a medieval *thing* grove, were accessible to him alone and off-limits to any "unauthorized person." Furthermore, the approach to the spot seemed to have been blocked intentionally with brush piled as high as a palisade, and the one spot where a person could slip through seemed not only meant for him alone but also visible from the outset to him alone.

Another summer, but this time a forenoon, with sunshine (or maybe not). And after entering the *thing* spot, at the base of the beech that had become his study, as if waiting for him, a veritable collection of—yes, that's what they instantly became and were again—living beings, which had been not merely forgotten by him for a year and a day but also, as he now realized, betrayed. "So there you are again," he blurted out. "So here we are again." There they stood, amid the leaves from the previous autumn and among prickly empty beechnut husks: dozens of them, and all almost equally large and ramrod-straight, on identically slim, sleek legs, as—the mushroom maniac learned and preached this only later—only boletus mushrooms around beeches can stand in review—"if they grow there at all, which doesn't happen often, and if they succeed in thrusting their way up through the beeches' unusually choking and life-threatening layer of dead leaves and the spiky, sharp-cornered beechnuts!"

There were lots of them, and he soon stopped counting. But the main reason wasn't the number. Counting at all in view of such splendor struck him as improper. So many in one place was also rare. Never again would he encounter such a phenomenon, and whenever he heard others say that they'd found a mass of mushrooms so large "that they could've been mowed with a scythe," he knew that people who nattered on that way had no real insight into mushrooms, at least not as he'd come to know them.

Also strange, or perhaps not: when he did come upon a large number of mushrooms he knew to be tasty, he didn't perceive them as a "mass," just as he didn't view himself as a "mushroom lover"; that was a term he never uttered, and heard coming from the mouths of his fellow mycologists with growing disdain. "Mycologists"? No, the people who spoke of their finds in terms of "kilos" that they'd allegedly gathered in one minute flat and brought back from the woods "by the bucketful" were no experts, and certainly not scientists, just as he never became a mycologist, even though, as events unfolded, he sometimes used a microscope and also dissected mushrooms, likewise only from time to time; instead, as he occasionally admitted to himself, he simply became a mushroom maniac.

For a long time, at least for the decade that followed that morning at the base of the beech, his growing interest in and eventual passion for the world of mushrooms, far from narrowing his perspective, broadened his horizons; instead of darkening his mood, or so it seemed to me, they brightened it. This form of distraction did his head and his work good, and not only that. This he discovered within an hour of making his great find, after he'd twisted the dozens of mushrooms gently, gently out of the ground—each of them giving off a (barely audible) different tone (yes, this time indisputably a tone)—and had piled them one on top of the other: studying his files, taking notes, synthesizing, building his argument, then testing the argument, pulling everything together and reaching a final conclusion: all that proved easier than usual, came to him almost effortlessly. One glance at the reddish whitish brownish pyramid near his shoe-tips, and he was clear on what needed to be done next.

What happened with this newfound treasure at the end of that day—whether he brought it home to cook and serve, cut it in slices for drying, or gave it away—the mushroom maniac couldn't tell me. What mattered was that he'd always wished he could return home with something special, going back to when he still lived with his parents in the village, but nothing this special had ever turned up: he'd always returned empty-handed. Now he finally had something special, even if only he saw it that way, to carry over the threshold. (Oho, even his child would be wide-eyed.) And what counted even more: that first moment of catching sight and having caught sight of it. That moment stuck in his memory with great clarity when all the other moments in that day had long since faded.

And then, to his own surprise, he had something to add to his story: he'd been planning to go to the movies that evening to see a film he'd looked forward to for a long time. But after his fairy-tale experience of sighting the treasure, his desire to see the film had vanished, or he felt as though he'd already seen it, back in that in-between space. He did go to the movies after all, but by comparison with that moment in the morning, the experience felt meaningless. Time had dragged while he was at the theater, he said—which didn't mean the film bored him—dragged almost as much as life on earth had always dragged for him, since childhood, perhaps earliest childhood. Once, shortly after his student days, he'd dreamed of becoming a writer like me, and had actually written a novel, to which he'd given the title "My Life"; it consisted of only a few sentences, one brief paragraph, ending with the line, "Time on earth dragged for him." Only at the movies—even when the film bored him—had time seldom dragged. But from that morning on, it dragged when he was sitting in the darkened theater, which had previously always throbbed with energy, and from then on, as his mushroom mania brought increasingly intense sensations, time at the movies dragged just as much as all mushroomless being-on-earth.

Things didn't reach that point with my friend, however, until almost the end of his story, just before he disappeared, and I'm not there yet, not by a long shot. To begin with, his passion cured him of what he called "my time sickness," and not just apparently: for a good while his newly healthy relationship to time overflowed into his daily life, which had previously seemed so tedious, with hours upon hours that refused to end, and at moments seemed deadly. Now, as a result of his passion, he no longer saw life on earth as a drag, or if it did hang heavy now and then, it no longer felt interminable. His passion didn't make time pass more quickly or seem more entertaining; it made time fruitful, and that, too, for a good while. With the help of his passion, and precisely because of its unique character, time on Planet Earth actually became precious to him, his lifetime having taken on a material form. If earlier he'd gone to the movies to get through the day—oh, if only it were night already!—now the day couldn't be long enough for keeping watch and poking around in the woods. In the woods he gained a sense of proportion. There, apparently for the first time in his life, he felt "mindful," as if he'd been "out of his mind" up to then. On the threshold to the forest, he was gripped every time by boundless excitement, as if on the verge of a great deed, as if before a great day. And then finding, catching sight of them: better than any film for silencing the endless chatter in his head, silencing the repetitive, soulless messages, silencing the mindless melodies, silencing, and silencing, and silencing, let silence reign.

Time became especially material for him now as he turned into a learner again. In his childhood and youth he'd enjoyed learning, but then more and more the pleasure had faded. From a certain or rather an indefinite moment on, he'd almost decided he didn't want to know more than he already knew. And now, without any deliberate decision on his part, he was learning again; knowledge came flying to him without his lifting a finger.

What kind of knowledge was it? First of all, knowledge about mushrooms, about hunting for them, about promising locations, identifying and misidentifying the various kinds, being fooled, and also, why not, though in his case less worth knowing, culinary techniques. —What important lessons could one learn from mushroom hunting or mushrooming? What insights could one gain? What benefits could one derive (non-monetary)? —Wait and see! The relevant details won't be withheld. And besides, when it came to this new learning, he had one thing primarily in mind, something that went hand in hand with the specialized learning about mushrooms.

Despite having grown up in the country, he didn't know much about nature—in this respect he was no different from most country folk—and what he did know was largely confined to what could be useful or was to be feared. And now, so to speak as a by-product of his late-blooming passion for mushrooms, from one sortie to the next, from one "expedition" to the next—as he increasingly experienced his times in the woods—he became more knowledgeable about trees, especially their root systems, about the geological strata underfoot—limestone? marl? granite? slate?—about various kinds of wind—see the bartender in the heart of the city—and about cloud formations, planetary orbits, and phases of the moon. For instance, toward the end, when he was at the apex of his "expertise," he attended a mushroom researchers' conference where he, the star lawyer, was the keynote speaker and challenged the prevailing consensus that the light of the full moon had the greatest influence when it came to drawing mushrooms out of the ground. He argued instead for the new moon: on nights without moonlight, when only stars shone in the clear night sky, mushrooms, and especially the boletus, were veritably tugged out of the ground, and he documented that contention with various anecdotes that he had "experienced in person."

There was also something about him that equipped him especially well for finding or sighting anomalous phenomena, something one of his teachers had described as the "sick gaze": amid the prevailing homogeneity, which was probably just the result of normative routines, he'd had an eye, from a very young age, for anything contradictory, unusual, or unfamiliar, and now he immediately noticed striking, unusual colors, unexpected shades, contrasting geometry, any clearly pinnate or glowingly checkered forms amid the ordinary messiness, patterns in the midst of patternlessness.

He was also prepared for the objection that his newly acquired knowledge wasn't useful, in contrast to that of his early years. He recognized as well that with this additional, unintentionally amassed learning, a gift vouchsafed him without any effort on his part, he ran the risk of forgetting things essential to success in his profession. But as time became more and more material as a result of his mushroom hunting, he discovered that he wasn't forgetting any of the knowledge necessary for his legal work—in fact that knowledge, infused with fresh air, as it were, thanks to his involvement with nature, appeared before his mind's eye more distinctly and above all more clearly organized. He did forget some things, to be sure, but only the kind that constituted unnecessary padding, and that, too, contributed to the thorough airing-out of whatever legal conundrum he happened to be working on. And if his new forays into learning, if the entire subject of mushrooms and the insights it provided, did happen to be useless: in those years, in that decade, and later not only in summer and fall but also in winter and spring, he felt enriched by it, never mind that he couldn't buy anything with the proceeds, unlike with his early earnings from the depot—and had no desire to.

To tell the truth, he felt enriched less by his finds than far more by the accompanying phenomena, enriched, for example, by his newfound ability to distinguish the rustling of oak trees on summer days, at times almost a droning, from that of beeches, more like a swooshing, and that of birches, which even in a brisk wind was a swishing more than a rustling. It was an experience to learn about the different ways in which the leaves of all these trees fell in autumn: how the jagged maple leaves began with nose dives and then floated gently to the ground; how the boat-shaped chestnut leaves, the largest and at the same time thinnest in the forest, took the longest time to reach the ground, refusing to drop long after they'd begun to float free in the air, and again and again, just a moment before they touched the ground, becoming airborne again, and rocking and rolling upward once more; how all the fan-shaped acacia foliage let go of the branches and twigs almost at the same time and instantly hurtled to the ground en masse, followed by a couple of laggard leaf-fans, which, instead of plummeting together, sailed away singly; like—but go and see for yourselves!

He felt he'd gained something on a winter day when he spied a snakeskin quivering on a bare bough, and on a prevernal day a sunbeam, still at a very low angle, shining on a lizard cowering in a hollow in a bank of reddish yellow marl. From the flight patterns of various birds he read not the future, which during those serene years of mushroom hunting hardly ever "clouded his brow"—nothing but the present, the material current moment, the here-and-now—but instead compared the styles of flight, the altitudes, the times of day, and could identify from the sound made by different sets of wings what types of bird they belonged to. Likewise, as he plunged through the woods, he quite often came upon the ruins of bunkers, also several types of hidden bomb craters, filled with fallen branches and a half century's worth of dead leaves, along with tin mess kits and steel helmets, in other places pockets of currant and gooseberry bushes planted in an even more distant past—but even there, as he scrambled into and back out of the craters and collected the once-cultivated berries, now wild and shrunken, he felt no desire to know or intuit anything about the various pasts they represented, caring only to learn from the here-and-now.

At the time he was, or believed himself to be, nowhere near his later mushroom mania. With his passion, which, in his eyes, was entirely rational—in contrast to not a few other possible passions—and enriched him, he enriched others in turn, and not only his near and dear but also people he met by chance, who turned up unexpectedly. At any rate, this passion, instead of shutting him off from his fellow human beings, opened him up to them for the first time, contrary to his previous tendency to isolate himself on the edge of the woods.

How else would he have emerged from the woods with his finds as if with proofs of love?

The in-between space where he "settled in"—the expression he adopted—to prepare his appearances in court, "simultaneously"—his term again—became the post where he kept a lookout for his contemporaries. That in no way resembled those deer stands he and I knew from back home, often built high up in spruce trees along the forest perimeter, used by hunters and game wardens, and occasionally lovers. And nonetheless, settled on level ground in his in-between space, his personal realm, if not domain, he felt as if he were elevated above those who populated the forest during his working hours.

That impression came from the fact that he could see them without being seen. For their part, the fence or wall of thorny brush, piled up like a palisade and separating his in-between space from the outside world, looked impenetrable, although the path ran close by it, and while sitting inside, with his seat at a slight remove from the barrier, he could glimpse the figures of those coming from left and right, not recognizable in detail and in their specific features, but as outlines, each of them all the more distinctive—unique.

Just as he'd named the path where, before the birth of his child, he'd encountered his first boletus in the flesh the "Prebirth Path," he dubbed this path the "Migration of Peoples Path." He, the lawyer, had formed the habit of getting up from the spot in the in-between space where he worked and, for shorter or longer intervals—longer and longer as time passed—making his way to the trees behind him and beginning to search for you-know-what. And although he was never confident in advance, he found some every time. Every time? Yes, every time. And each find brought a surprise, a previously undreamed-of object/being, a new location, coloration, variation in form, scent. And almost every time he had a premonition about a new place to look, which signified that all his senses were on high alert. And on the rare occasion when he was mistaken, at the site of the mistake he would give his imagination free rein, and at the same time pay meticulous attention to what was missing, not present, absent. His lifelong boredom thus became a kind of vital tarrying. "Bored? Me? Not on your life!"

Once he'd retraced his steps to his spot in the in-between space, he not only managed to get back to work without missing a beat but also engaged with the figures passing by outside the brush palisade as he'd never come close to doing earlier in his life. Yes, those people out there, on the other side, were with him, and he admitted to himself that his previous intermittent displays of conviviality, the impressive figure he'd cut in society, had been nothing compared with the impulse that from the beginning had driven him away from others and isolated him: his chronic skittishness vis-à-vis other human beings.

But during the period in question, heartened by his work in that in-between space and also made permeable by his finder's luck, he not only participated; he became part of society. It happened time after time, no, it befell him, that he merged with one person or another passing outside his enclosure on the path, as long ago he'd merged on the edge of the forest with the swishing, swooshing, and roaring of the branches and limbs, merged entirely, from head to toe and to his very bones, with the swaying, crisscrossing, parting, and coming together of the trees' crowns.

Up to now his skittishness had never left him. Years ago, as a child he'd woken up once and seen his mother sitting at her sewing machine or whatever, and had felt completely and hopelessly cut off from her, and a silent wail had shaken him at the thought of that unbridgeable distance; so, too, much later with his own wife, even eye to eye, mouth to mouth, he'd experienced the distance between them as unbridgeable and had bewailed his inability to overcome it—whereas in reality, as he should have perceived it, every bit of that space between them was filled to overflowing; and secretly but all the more perceptibly his skittishness toward their offspring had increased, if possible: no matter how he longed for it, he would never become one with that other being, who needed it as much as he did, become one so that he/she/it would finally disappear in the act of merging, which would be tantamount to all-mercifulness.

But no: what he felt now, in the course of becoming permeable and merging with the figures behind the brush curtain, suddenly no longer total strangers, was infinitely far from mercy, because unlike with those close to him, it didn't involve love. What he felt was simply understanding, and as a result an ability to do justice to others more fully than he'd done "to date" in his professional capacity, and in a few cases he had the experience of becoming aware, in a sudden, but less alarming than calming manner, of others, above all of their previous lives, their origins, their having come from far, far away and being destined to go God knows where—which explained, as my friend admitted to me long afterward, the term "Migration of Peoples Path." That person on the other side of the barricade who just tripped, then swore in an incomprehensible language, fled years earlier from a country embroiled in a civil war, and that one who's pausing by a birch tree is remembering a relative who died long ago, and as he continues on he yawns loudly, but the way one yawns only after being startled, and the person who now crosses his path and sticks out a leg to trip him up, which he casually swerves to avoid, has long dreamed of becoming a saint, one for whom everyone he encounters, or at least in the area where he comes from, reverently steps aside to let him pass.

Sometimes this migration of peoples made him quiver with emotion, and this man who'd been so skittish or unnerved vis-à-vis others felt his head growing heavy from harboring all those continuing their journey inside him, a lovely heaviness. Whenever he left his in-between space after finishing his work—both sitting and formulating his oral arguments and searching for mushrooms, which gave the arguments their particular flavor, felt like work to him—and set out for home on the Migration of Peoples Path, usually in a dark suit and a light-colored silk tie, carrying his briefcase in one hand and in the other, in the early days wrapped in newspaper but later more and more openly, his two or three finds, as meager as they were striking, he saw himself becoming part or a member of the crowd on the world stage as never before in all the decades, as one of the actors, each of whom embodied a different role, which, however, precisely in its distinctiveness, contributed to the great play and helped extend its reach farther and farther.

Here, squatting in a circle or dashing along: schoolchildren on their all-day field trip into the woods. There, a group of hikers, a few youths among the many oldsters, standing and arguing where two paths crossed, obviously in disagreement as to which they should take. Over here now, one person doing pull-ups on the fitness equipment, while behind him another man waits his turn. Coming this way, a pair of horseback riders, spurring their horses in unison from a trot into a gallop. Now, single quiet runners over there, not the hordes from which the forest echoed earlier, during the noon hour. Over there, a young woman equipped for an entire day's hike, the forest here hardly more than a short stretch on her itinerary. Over yonder, an Asian family, a veritable tribe, from great-grandmother to great-grandchild—didn't that call to mind another tribe?—busy collecting edible chestnuts. And over there, the police patrol. And farther on, where the path widened out, retirees playing boules.

And he in harmony with all of them, a treasure hunter and at the same time an ordinary person, a fellow human, and indeed this kind of harmony, treasure aside, was something precious. Planet Earth had been merely playing along with him for half a lifetime. Now—here—it was playing with him, and he? Was playing his part. Was playing a part in this society. The society of the diverse, the fundamentally diverse—precisely of these—it existed! And one aspect of that was his perception, his certainty, that getting off the beaten path and being unfaithful did good for those entrusted to him, his near and dear, including "his" defendants, and did good in general.

And he, the one with mushrooms in his hands? For a while he'd still felt out of place, sticking out like a sore thumb in that setting. People like him, figures like him, who didn't keep to the paths or the running tracks but wove back and forth among the trees and bushes, also went in circles, taking one step at a time, unusually slowly, or just stood or squatted there, half hidden by the tree trunks and foliage, who emerged suddenly from a thicket and perhaps promptly disappeared into it again: to put it mildly, they couldn't become part of the play, above all not with those unfamiliar, off-putting objects that they held out in front of them or that bulged suspiciously in their shopping bags. In the best case, that is to say, the most harmless case, people like him were marginal figures, lacking any connection to the great drama; yes, they even disrupted the play, wandering into the middle of a scene in progress.

But then the moment came when he, strolling and spiraling along, in a rhythm so contrary to all the actors', and furthermore one of the few solitary figures—the runners mostly showed up in multiples, and even a singleton seemed like more than one—saw himself as a fellow actor. He belonged in the play. He supplemented it, spiced it up. Without his stopping, crossing, going off on tangents, stumbling out of the picture in the role of the mushroom gatherer, the world stage, at least during summer and fall, would lack something. Having someone like him on scene provided a breath of fresh air. And this fresh air enabled him to see every person who crossed his path as belonging there in his own unique way, and that included him, and taken together that yielded an image of society as never before, of human society, an ideal one.

Filled with this consciousness he left the woods and made his way through the crowded streets of the metropolis, freed once and for all of the skittishness toward others that he'd previously believed to be either a congenital quality or the churlishness imprinted by his village upbringing. Me, a marginal figure, maybe even an outlaw? Look here, people! And by that he also meant what he was carrying or holding in front of him. And not a few passersby played along, did as he asked, stopped in their tracks, swapping stories about how they, too, earlier . . . in the place they came from . . . except that they remembered their finds as much grander . . . And finally, at the end of the day, the collector's return home, a return very different from Brueghel's *Return of the Hunters*.

In that happy period, which he experienced at the same time as a sphere—a spherical phase—my friend the mushroom maniac hardly encountered a competitor. He seldom ran into other gatherers, and those he did come upon had their own places and areas where they searched; or the others went out at times different from his. It did happen now and then that his path crossed that of someone moving along like him, one step at a time, eyes on the ground, stopping and then proceeding with utmost caution, tracing his slow spirals through the woods. But unlike later on, the two of them didn't swerve to avoid each other and on occasion even showed each other their treasures, their treasure, and then one envied the other, which, according to one of the Middle Eastern religions, is "permitted," because such envy expresses the wish to receive the same thing or something similar, but without, as is the case with the naked, impermissible form of envy, wanting to deprive the envied person of what he has. And for a long while afterward he would remind himself of what a woman gatherer had said when she observed, as they inspected each other's finds, which were just about equal in number, size, and beauty: "There's enough for all of us, isn't there?" Yes, oho! So even the kind of envy permitted by God or the gods wasn't appropriate in that case. The gatherer was an old lady in a newsboy cap who was out in the rain, poking around in the fallen leaves with a thick stick. The only mushroom in her basket that differed from his was of a type said to have become highly radioactive as a result of the nuclear power plant disaster in you-know-where, and likely to remain that way for centuries, and when he felt obliged to point that out to her, she replied that she knew all about it, but at almost ninety she didn't want to worry about it.

His passion spread and deepened from one season to the next, his knowledge even from one day to the next, and it seemed to him that quite a bit of that knowledge could be extrapolated from his limited area to others. Rather minor insights increasingly filled him with the excitement of a discoverer, and he conceived the idea of using the break between court sessions for writing a mushroom book, one unlike any that had ever been written. That would make him not merely a discoverer but also a pioneer, and besides, or incidentally, my friend imagined that a mushroom book like that, fueled by his excitement and informed in its logical structure by his legal training, while also geared to a general audience, would be exciting to read and universal in its relevance. He pictured it as the great success of his life. As mentioned, he was already well-off, but his mushroom book, at once highly specialized and universal, would make him rich, and can you guess what he dreamed of doing? Buying himself a forest, a large one!

The mushroom book didn't get written. But in the course of time he shared with me a few things he meant to include in the book. I'm going to try here to flesh out some of his ideas, not exactly passionately, but on the other hand in no way "dispassionately"—a strange contemporary concept used to praise someone who suppresses all emotion when sharing something that he ought to share because the subject is urgent and he feels an urgent need to communicate it; I'm also presenting the story without much structure, because unlike my childhood friend from the village I never became a proper lawyer, despite having studied the same subject he did.

So here goes, as bits and pieces of his unwritten mushroom book come back to me in a somewhat disorganized fashion: my friend ascribed his talent, or gift, for discovering mushrooms that others failed to notice to that previously mentioned peculiarity that until his passion assumed an acute form had interfered most painfully with his living a full life. What he meant by that was his chronic tendency to get distracted, day in, day out, by one thing, no, the one form among the thousands and hundreds of thousands of forms in his field of vision that stood out, literally striking his eye, day after day, hour after hour, as the one entirely distinct from the rest. Up to that point, his sensitivity to the one completely different form, diametrically opposed to all other forms, exacerbated his awareness of his unnaturalness, and that was a source of suffering.

Getting sidetracked by an alien form had pulled him up short time and again, leaving him at a loss as to how to keep going, both in his work and also in what used to be called real life. In "no time" he'd find himself paralyzed, whether overwhelmed by the imprint of an insect run over on the road or stymied by a minuscule coffee or grease stain, by a hair, not even hair-thin, stuck to a page of the international penal code, or by the unusually curved collarbone, the irregularly shaped navel, the one milky spot in the eye, of the woman he'd just made love to for the first time, or was about to. What overcame him from time to time, in everyday life and in his profession, an apparent string of misfortunes, diverting his attention, against his will, from important matters to odd obsessions, throwing him off course, seemingly for good, and filling him with a sense of incompetence and everlasting guilt—that became an advantage, he thought, when it was a question of intuiting, tracking down, and uncovering mushrooms, no matter how hidden and camouflaged in the shade of the underbrush, and, as he was tempted to preach with mounting passion, initially only for his own benefit, almost a source of salvation. At least seeing the one distinctive form appear or shine forth among the innumerable nondescript forms (to vary what's already been described here—and to add some nuance) on the bed of fallen leaves in a forest didn't throw him off course, and neither did this one form paralyze him: it swept him away, and that meant that instead of distracting him it got him moving again. No, when it came to the world of mushrooms—this was the theme of the sermon on which my later vanished friend (whose proximity, physical as well, I've had the sense of feeling and smelling here for the last few days) planned to base his mushroom book—the imagined or actually unnatural character of his gaze would be set straight. That unnatural character was the sine qua non, he asserted, for seeking and finding, and not merely mushrooms but for seeking and finding in general; without that kind of unnatural character there could be no discoverer's eye in which, with which, and through which non-form could become form and form become treasure.

My friend also wanted to weave in the notion that each distinctive and significant form among all the nondescript ones to be found amid the leaves lying every which way on the ground—the tangled fern fronds, the countless lance-like blades of grass, the moss stems—also lastingly heightened his rather undeveloped sense of color, because each of those individual forms, no matter how small, "lit the way" for him, like the roses in Mörike's poem "Auf einer Wanderung," wine-red today, amethyst-purple tomorrow, mouse- or also tiger-gray the day after, and so forth.

His mushroom book wasn't meant to serve as a guide, or if it was, the kind of guide that he thought of as primarily for his own use. But more and more, in the jottings he sent me, he seemed to be addressing, at first surreptitiously, later openly, a wider audience. Initially his notes took the form of storytelling, the way one sometimes tells oneself a story to gain clarity on the subject, but as time went on he fell to theorizing and, at certain moments, almost proselytizing.

In particular he described how, with the passage of time, he'd adopted the practice—before he got to work searching for mushrooms in earnest—once he reached the woods in question, of traversing a stretch, a good-sized one, in which he could be sure that none of what he was looking for would be growing, or where there was nothing but trees and underbrush. As he walked through the area, keeping his eyes on the ground, where he knew he would see only sand and clay between the fallen leaves, he sharpened his vision, without having to do anything else, for what he hoped to see eventually, and as he got into the rhythm of walking, he began to see, precisely where there was nothing special to be seen; and when he reached the places that promised something more, his eyes were ready.

My mushroom maniac found it helpful, once on location, to adopt a manner of walking that he called his "search gait," and, with a sideways glance at me, also termed the "storytelling gait," a form of movement that time and again verged on coming to a standstill; yet, as he forged his way through trees and underbrush, he never faltered but rather maintained a steady rhythm; and when he finally did stop, the search gait had fulfilled its purpose; instead of stopping and starting, the idea had been to move in a particular way during the search, and that way proved fruitful as hardly anything else could.

He also described a variation on the search gait that involved walking backward, reflectively setting one foot behind the other. (Wasn't that a kind of progress: from the backward walking he'd done when he was at a loss to backward walking for the pleasure of it, and then to backward walking as a treasure hunter?) Or he admonished himself, whenever he'd walked back and forth for a good while with his eyes fixed on the ground, to pause now and then and look up from the ground at the treetops and the sky, not seeking anything in particular, his head thrown back and held in that position for at least a minute: after that, when he lowered his eyes again, infused with the light from the sky, how distinct the ground appeared, with the contours of objects that had previously appeared blurry now perceptible down to the smallest detail and the most inconspicuous form! veritably electrified by the captured glow. And more than once it happened that it was not until he'd looked up with such intensity that he spied at his feet what he'd been seeking for hours, sometimes days or weeks; or he discovered something entirely different, something he hadn't thought to look for, that he'd never laid eyes on in nature or seen depicted anywhere, something new to him; or after looking up he discovered on the forest floor neither the sought-after mushroom nor a different variety, nor an unknown third kind, in that way discovering nothing new other than, after the realm above his head, the realm at the tips of his shoes or boots: yes, that, too, he called a realm.

In his notes for the projected mushroom book my friend moved on from such admonitions directed at himself to actual commands. He ordered himself, for instance, whenever he'd failed for quite a while, in spite of employing his search gait, in spite of looking skyward, to catch so much as a glimpse of what he desired—he even described it in one place as "the object of my fervent longing"—to look instead for something else, and that meant not only different mushrooms, ones he deemed worthless, but also berries, including withered ones, or edible chestnuts, including dried-out, moldy, or charred ones: "Gather! Turn sideways! Bend down! Poke around! Turn! Dig!" This self-hectoring, also involving the collection of various other irrelevant objects, in the course of which one got so much closer to the ground and thereby found oneself back on the gathering track, was probably also meant to guide future readers of his mushroom book.

For a while he cloaked this concept in rather cautious recommendations. Thus he advised, "on the basis of many years' experience"—despite his having been at this not that long—searching either close to paths and roads or at a considerable distance from them: the large stretches between the roadside and the hard-to-reach interior of the forest weren't as a rule fertile ground for "our friends"—by which he meant the valuable mushrooms, which he'd initially called "my friends"; the majority, indeed almost all of his "treasures," he said, he'd found close to the road; once one got away from those edges, often nothing would turn up for a long, long time; and in the deepest parts of the woods, which first had to be discovered, in the tangle of underbrush there, in dirt, in ashes, at the dark foot of a half-dead, disintegrating tree, the ground littered with bullet casings, one treasure might be found, that, too, a rule: only that one, head and shoulders above everything else: "Hello, there, King!" One time he even burst out, "Salve, Imperator! Ave, Caesar!"

With something similar in mind he wrote how he'd imposed another rule on himself: to look as well in places where others had already searched, even when they, after obviously doing a thorough job, had turned everything upside down and inside out and had left the spot and the scene only moments earlier, and every time he'd found himself staring at—"no lie"—something his predecessors had overlooked, something "worthy of all honor."

He likewise recommended, when it came to certain varieties, not looking in places that had previously proved particularly productive: that, he said, was yet another rule: that in the course of the year, during the winter and spring, such populations would have moved on, traveling underground in search of water, dodging the wind, and often surfacing into the light and air at a remarkable distance; far off, to be sure, yet not too far, their whereabouts intuitable from their point of origin—the searcher had only to do what he himself had done, year in, year out: deploy his senses. So he also advised against looking in wooded spots where dogs had done their business, recommending, on the other hand, horses and their manure. And the mushroom maniac recommended even more insistently places in the woods where children had played, or were still playing now, before the gatherer's eyes, shouting rowdily and dashing back and forth. According to his notes, particularly promising and actually reliable spots were—"hard to believe but true"—those near children's swings, outside of the woods as well, in parks, meadows, people's yards.

In the projected mushroom book an entire chapter was supposed to be devoted to forests with bomb craters. The area where he lived, near the international court, had many such forests; the bomb craters went back to the end of the Second World War, and the bombers had been American, helping to drive the German occupying forces out of the country. The craters were long since empty, with no trace of the bombs that had exploded there, and the forests, all of them neighboring the military air base once used by the occupiers, had been given a sort of rhythm by the craters, so close to one another that some of them even overlapped. The craters varied in size, weren't all round, some of them having collapsed inward, and above all their depths differed, and their walls were more or less steep or shallow, often within the same crater. At the craters' bottoms, far below many years' worth of dead leaves, he'd come upon the richest sources, and sometimes he wouldn't even have to poke through and move aside the layers: the mushroom, the mushrooms would have come to light all by themselves, at least their caps, which, having grown up out of the craters, were larger than usual, and shaped almost like inverted funnels, with the peculiar feature that instead of being brown-red-yellow as usual, they appeared almost colorless, whitish or pure white like only the most deadly of the poisonous mushrooms, or "no, not white, actually pale," and under the caps the same pale stem, but again with the unusual feature that when it was dug out of the ground, it appeared long and longer, generally twice as long as that of fellow mushrooms growing outside of the crater ("the smell and taste, however, equally delicious").

But that wasn't the mushroom maniac's sole reason for wanting to devote an entire chapter to the bomb-crater forests.

He had an ulterior motive: simply to get his future readers to go walking in forests of that kind—to pass on to them the pleasure he derived from wandering back and forth, up and down though that bomb-crater landscape with its soft, thick padding of leaves. Whenever he'd spent hours crisscrossing those woods, he felt, even if he didn't score any finds, as though he'd been given a present, if only in that he breathed more freely or his sense for horizons had been roused. "As a result of going back and forth among the bomb craters?" —"Yes, that's right."

Toward the end, the mushroom book was supposed to shift its emphasis more and more away from mushroom hunting to walking. He still meant to tell the story of his mushrooming, to wrap things up, as it were, but also to show how with the passing years his passion had become not weaker but rather dual-tracked. For more and more often, when he had a choice among several paths on which to go mushrooming, he would choose the one that struck him as pretty or intriguing, even if it promised fewer or less-valuable finds. Over time, the path and walking had become at least as important as seeking and finding. In the area where we'd both grown up, people who lived higher in the mountains had rarely "gone mushrooming," let alone set out specifically to look for mushrooms. They lived so close to the woods, which were so summer-dense with them, at least with the yellow ones, the St. John's mushrooms, that they'd no sooner stepped outside than they had a basket or a bowl full; instead of the verb *search*, these folks used the word *pick*: "Up here we don't search, we just go out and pick!"

But that, as the mushroom maniac saw it, didn't count. Searching was indispensable. Walking was indispensable. The third element that had been added was choosing a pretty path, the prettier one, the prettiest one. And likewise: going out searching with several others, perhaps as part of a group:

that didn't count either. Only "going alone" counted—even searching as a twosome didn't count, the only exception being with a child. Especially frowned upon in his projected mushroom guide: searching with the help of a dog (only pigs found approval in his eyes). But then how to dig for those most desirable of all mushrooms, truffles? How to sniff them out? To address this topic, he sketched out the story of how one summer he, all alone, had found himself face-to-face with an actual truffle at the foot of a children's swing set: a black clump, aboveground, with the midday sun directly overhead: what odd dog poop there, but then a smell reaches his nose, almost two meters above the ground, the smell of a truffle—my goodness, it is one!—then grubbing it out with both hands and look: this roundish thing, how did it come to light? ah, the downpour the night before, washing the earth away and bringing the truffle to the surface without enlisting a dog or a pig—how heavy it feels in one's hand, the furrowed black ball fragrant, so fragrant, imparting that smell to the subsequent night of love and beyond—but that was no oak tree from among whose roots the knob was washed, also no other mighty tree familiar from mushroom guides, nothing but a spindly locust, hardly more than a shrub, one of the saplings planted along the nearby railway tracks, and no trace of a forest or forests; the truffle appeared between two rather bleak suburban developments, on the edge, no, in the middle of a playground.

After that, every summer, whenever it had poured overnight, my friend would make his way to that particular playground locust; but no second truffle ever turned up (and there was only that one night of love, which his mushroom book was of course not supposed to mention). On the other hand, looking for truffles was something that in his opinion didn't count when it came to mushrooming. In general, the last notes on his project have to do less with storytelling than with establishing rules, rules so strict that they seem like more than mere rules of a game, and what he may have had in mind degenerated into a catalogue of laws, instructions, declarations, and ideas.

Thus one day when he was in a forest again, he came upon children, and not for the first time, having a scavenger hunt, racing back and forth among the trees, uphill and down, and "the idea" occurred to him that their teachers or guardians would do better to send these youngsters out mushrooming. Whereas now, excitedly searching for a piece of paper hidden by grown-ups in a tree trunk, a bush, at the entrance to an abandoned foxhole, they were blind to anything else, not only mushrooms, and thoughtlessly broke, trampled, and crushed things, and with red faces, no longer childlike, and tongues hanging out, shouted through the woods at and over one another or, no longer with children's voices, bawled, out of breath, their eyes bulging out of their sockets, if they were looking for mushrooms, they would learn to move one step at a time, attentive not only to what they were seeking, breathless—which was not the same as out of breath—and their eyes, instead of bulging, would widen, and their occasional exclamations here and there would be genuinely childlike, even those of boys whose voices were changing.

With his own child, whom the mushroom maniac took along on his expeditions from the beginning, he'd seen how that kind of outdoor activity could prove effortlessly "educational," without a trained educator in the background and, educational or not, appealed to the child, "and not only mine," like hardly any other activity, with the additional factor that "my descendant" had a better eye for the things at his feet, "and not only because he was closer to them." Yes, indeed: this idea of his mattered, and was supposed to matter. "That experience would eventually provide," according to the notes for his mushroom book, "after even the last notions of society in this dear century of ours became bankrupt, a way to imagine, or, if you will, merely surmise—but why 'merely'?—that society, or society of some kind, still has a future. One day it will. It will again."

Altogether, to judge by the last notations, my friend's mushroom book was apparently meant to culminate in a portrayal of mushroom hunters not only as the model for a possible new society but also, paradoxical or not, as the last adventurers of the human race, if not the last human beings. The individual mushroom hunter: an adventurer, at once a last and a first human being.

Mushrooms as "the last adventure"? Clear as day to the mushroom maniac, who used the expression in analogy to "the last frontier," referring to the wilderness, the border beyond which at least a snippet of wilderness remained to be discovered. In Alaska and elsewhere, and certainly in the Himalayas, this frontier had ceased to exist long ago. But the last adventure still existed, who knew for how much longer, even if one could grasp only a snippet of a snippet of it.

Mushrooms as "the last wilderness"? According to my mushroom maniac, this, too, "as clear as day": in the sense that by now mushrooms were the only growing things on earth that categorically refused to allow themselves to be cultivated, civilized, let alone domesticated, which grew only wild, impervious to any human intervention.

But champignons, oyster mushrooms, woodtufts, all the Japanese *take*, and so forth: these could be planted and cultivated, couldn't they? Even truffles, though by roundabout methods, such as planting certain trees that served as hosts? Were those not mushrooms? "Clear as day for the third time": being able to cultivate them wasn't the adventure he was talking about; only those growing wild counted; the cultivated meadow champignons, oyster mushrooms, woodtufts, golden needle mushrooms, Chinese morels, honey fungi were a form of trompe l'oeil, cloned, and they were marketed under false names, not merely fundamentally different in color and odor, but also, in contrast to their namesakes, one and all lacking in character, "null and void both in one's hand and in one's mouth." And besides, the main mushroom folk, not only the hongos but also the brittlegills, delicious in a different way, the parasol mushrooms, the fairy-ring mushrooms (aka *senderuelas*, aka mountain nymphs), the *setas de los caballeros*, the St. George's mushrooms, the *setas de San Juan*, the monk's heads, the black trumpets or trumpets of the dead, the Jew's ears or jelly ears, the shingled hedgehogs, the sulfur tufts, the cauliflower fungi, the lumpy brackets: all of them remained impossible to cultivate, and as long as these last growing things on earth resisted cultivation, "my and our mushrooming will remain part of the resistance and the adventure of resistance."

The time for setting out, searching, finding, and continuing to search: "A song of eternity." And as for himself: inscribed into the Book of Life what he saw was not the many cases he'd won before the international tribunal but only his expeditions back and forth through the woods.

The mushroom-mania book was not supposed to include recipes. First of all, they weren't part of the project, and besides he was secretly counting on his readers: just as he would take them by surprise initially, they would reciprocate someday by surprising him with ideas and stories from their own kitchens and beyond.

With respect to the taste of mushrooms, which he had increasingly come to appreciate in the course of the years and the decades—in contrast to many other foods, in fact most others, for which he'd lost all appetite—his plan for the book provided some hints, they, too, entailing the notion of surprise. Each of the thousands and more edible mushrooms was "good for a surprise," he wrote, even those described in other mushroom books as tasting "mediocre" or, worse still, "worthless." Not one of them tasted "wild," according to him; whatever was wild in form, color, or smell could be counted on to transform itself in one's mouth into something gentle—the wilder the visual impression, the gentler the effect inside one, and not just in the oral cavity. Every other edible substance, including the tenderest meat, the freshest fish, even caviar—especially caviar—tasted vulgar and coarse by comparison with a little wild thing like that. Only a few rare plants could come anywhere near that taste, in which, however, an additional energy was at work, an energy beyond that of a mere plant; one had only to open oneself to it (taking care not to ruin one's taste buds beforehand with any other food). "Open yourself—and savoring slows eating to dining, and dining to tasting; and savoring, dining, and tasting endow our nourishing ourselves with heart and soul, as happens—all too rarely, alas—with eating, taking meals, and thanks to all that, peace settles over us, and at the same time, my God, rarer than rare, the throbbing of peace, coupled with, alas experienced only in a blue moon, the rising of what is next to godliness in you and me, dear reader: the starry heavens of the imagination! In what one-, two-, or three-star restaurant has that ever happened to you? And isn't it strange that a form of nourishment from the depths of the earth can raise your head toward the heavens?"

I wonder whether my mushroom maniac would really have become rich with that kind of mushroom book. Be that as it may: the project never came to fruition. In the initial years—and they lasted a good while, as he kept starting over, discovering new things—his passion contributed to his success in his profession. Every time he came upon something previously unknown to him, he felt strangely rich, but he didn't acquire riches that way. He did, however, have the means to fulfill a wish dream. So he bought himself a forest, far from the metropolis, where the countryside was still country: a small forest that formed a kind of island in a vast expanse of cultivated fields and pastures, with no ocean in sight. On one of his expeditions he'd fought his way into these woods through a dense natural hedge, and everywhere reddish yellow torches had flared toward him from the ground, the mushrooms we'd known in childhood that grew among the spruces next to the cow pasture and went by the graphic name of "bear's paws." And then? His new forest was invaded by a mushroom tribe as handsome as it was malevolent, the honey fungus, which devoured not only the bear's paws but also, in the space of a year, the entire stand of trees.

This loss aside, he'd gradually adopted the practice of addressing his mushroom finds, which increased in numbers as well as in varieties, as "business": "Hello there, business!"—"More business!"—"Look how well it's doing today, my business!" Nor was this spontaneous exclamation all. That finds in such quantities ipso facto sparked associations with selling, trade, and markets seemed as natural to him as anything, as his opening and closing arguments in court, and certainly more natural than my writing of books. Another reason was that my old friend from the village found it harder and harder to get his arms around all his treasures. There were so many that what he consumed hardly made a dent in the supply, and his wife and child, though they were willing to eat some for a while, were out of the question as regular recipients of his largesse, as were various neighbors, though he'd pictured them as his perfect customers—a barter relationship with them, he thought, would create a neighborhood such as he still saw as ideal from his youth in the village, but which no longer existed in reality, and certainly not in the towns that ringed the metropolis. And what about bringing his riches to market, the weekly or Sunday outdoor markets? That he planned in all seriousness to do; he felt veritably compelled to set out, in Italian, Balkan, or Afghan attire, each hand holding a heavy basket overflowing with mushrooms, to play the role of a vendor, a salesman, the more so since his wares looked infinitely fresher and more appetizing than all the limp, battered, fly-ridden stuff hauled in airless cargo containers or such from distant provinces and more distant countries, even continents.

The problem was that, whereas a century ago many or most of his delicacies had still been offered regularly at markets, as expected as they were in demand, that was no longer the case nowadays, and if it was, then only cultivated varieties: the reactions that could be expected to the originals, forgotten by almost the entire world, were the conventional snide comments about mushrooms. In this day and age, the so-called present, these finest fruits of the earth—those especially—weren't considered market-worthy: "Degenerate customers," he commented in his lawyer's jargon, "degenerate market!"

Furthermore, he realized that he wasn't cut out to be a businessman, not even a supplier or purveyor to markets, whether as a result of his ineradicable villager's ways or not. He had no ability to formulate a business plan or create a market for his product; he was not the marketing type.

A single time he plucked up his courage and brought a basket of porcini to a restaurant, an Italian one—of course—where he and his wife had dinner reservations; he secretly hoped that when the owner, from the Abruzzi region or Sardinia, caught sight of this magnificent collection, something would be set in motion that would assign him, the guest, the celebrity lawyer, the role of a simple merchant, a vendor, who could supply the very product, and perhaps even better varieties, for which a demand existed in this particular place. And that did in fact happen, though not in the form of buying and selling but, all the better, or more natural, in the form of barter, even if the two bottles of Abruzzi or Sardinian wine didn't really match the cornucopia of *funghi porcini*: he representing not only the mushroom maniac but also a figure in the natural-foods economy, someone from a bygone era, and when a taste of the bartered wine was poured for his wife, she favored him, her husband, with a look reminiscent of the girl from the neighboring village such as he'd never received so openly, from so far off, so lingering, and wouldn't enjoy again until this very day, as I write this, almost at the end of my mushroom-maniac story.

If in the early years his passion for the mushroom world had enriched not only his professional life and a whole slew of nice incidental matters but also his relationship with his wife and child ("Her, my wife's love, is a kind of humor," he told me at one point), that changed over time, which he failed to notice but which his wife noticed all the more clearly. In fact, unbeknownst to him, he began, in the grip of his "passion," to forget about her. The passion had become an addiction, a vice, and his wife's sense of humor abandoned her. From one day to the next she left the house, and took their child with her. She was running away, from the man and from the gifts he brought home daily, just for her, which he called "souvenirs"—he used the word as a term of endearment—and which were piling up in the cellar and the garage, and later not only there, soon succumbing to rot and mold.

Escapes like his wife's, with the most varied causes and auspices, have often been described over the centuries, so I needn't say more. Only one more detail: the mushroom maniac seemed not to notice that his beloved wife had fled or that the child he also loved, in a different way, was missing as well. The very next morning he had an hour to spare before flying to visit a prisoner in a distant country, and he used the time to hotfoot it to the woods. True enough, later, much later, actually, he named the path he took to get there the "Path of Absence."

But long before his dear ones' escape, his behavior, and his whole attitude toward the outside world–aside from the fact that those closest to him had gradually faded from his consciousness–had become fundamentally, obviously, emphatically different, had undergone a transformation. I heard that from his wife, who was forced to listen to his tirades every evening, and then every morning as well.

If he'd viewed himself at one time as a marginal figure but later, buoyed by the awakening of his passion, had come to think of himself as someone playing a crucial role in society, complementing others and on an equal footing with them in the universal drama of life, now he saw himself as someone who even as a child, a marginal figure listening to the rushing of the wind and letting himself be rained and snowed on at the edge of the woods, had secretly borne the scepter. –How so–as a mushroom hunter? –Yes, as a mushroom hunter, collector, expert.

This belief manifested itself in his growing tendency to belittle everything else, to dismiss it as "whatever," or ignore its existence altogether. Not only did he stop reading–with the exception of mushroom books, the subjects ranging from New Zealand over the High Atlas to the magnificent volume *The Mushrooms of Alaska*, books in which, by the way, the mushrooms were identical–but he no longer wanted to go to the movies, either with his wife or by himself, took no more trips, either alone or with the family; and to top it off, neglected his professional obligations as a lawyer, eventually not doing any work, even with his left hand.

He remained largely oblivious to these changes, and none of this was intentional. He had only to make some finds early in the morning—he set out for the woods earlier and earlier—to feel he'd done his day's work and reading files was no longer necessary; nor were the presentations to the World Court, for which he'd previously prepared so meticulously, weighing every word, every sentence, down to the pauses and the rhythm of the paragraphs. World Court? Researching mushrooms: that had become his entire world. The work in court, defending the accused, which had once engaged his heart: he hardly registered that anymore, giving no thought to those entrusted to him. Making finds in his woods—which had meanwhile become his "domain"—allowed him to imagine that anything he needed to do for his defendants had been accomplished, as others might fool themselves that they'd done their work by listening to music, and night owls might convince themselves that they'd done their work for the next day. With every treasure he found, he felt he'd managed to get his client exonerated, as if his brilliant closing argument had already been broadcast to the world.

Worse still: he'd begun, again unbeknownst to him and unintentionally, to despise the prisoners and defendants entrusted to him. Whereas previously he'd seen almost all of them as beautiful, now each time they appeared in court he found them more unattractive. Runts. Nonentities. Wrecks. Losers. Dead men walking, with no prospects, no future, no vision! He, on the contrary, had a vision! —Really? Thanks to the mushrooms, even though he specifically excluded from consideration those varieties alleged to produce visions? —"Thanks to his wood ears, his *ninfas*, his gray knights and Caesar's mushrooms," as his wife, the woman from the neighboring village, commented bitterly to me in a letter. If earlier, precisely as the "two-timer" in the woods, he'd empathized with his clients, the defendants from "all oppressed countries," he now looked down on them precisely for being the oppressed who, when they were incarcerated, were getting no more than they deserved.

Even worse, or maybe not, or maybe bad in a different way, was the fact that his disdain for the defendants entrusted to him gradually expanded to include the tribunal's personnel, making no distinctions among them and certainly not reserved for the judges ("It's not only that the judges are becoming more and more merciless; they're also dumb, dumb as posts, and the closer you get to them, the dumber they become") but extending to the interpreters, the prosecutors, and the defense teams as well. He admired only himself, and his admiration grew and grew, with no reference to his work, which meant hardly anything to him anymore; he saw himself as a Chosen One. Carefully slipped in among his files, botanical prints of more and more mushroom varieties, eventually adding up to a thousand and one, the images resembling foreign galaxies.

It wasn't due to malice on his part that one time, when the prosecutor was delivering his closing statement, demanding a life sentence for the miserable heap of a defendant, my friend reached into his robe and forgot himself and the world of the court as he contemplated and sniffed the object in the palm of his hand. Another story made the rounds for a long time: at a particularly solemn juncture in another trial, when, let's say, everyone rose to hear the verdict pronounced, the mushroom maniac, this time with the unmistakable intention of at least puncturing the seriousness of the proceedings, also rose from the defense table, but at the very moment when the triumvirate of international judges, yes, intercontinental judges, in what looked like a single movement, "to a man," donned their ceremonial bonnets, he, also using both hands, placed a ceremonial object on his own head: in reality an enormous umbrella mushroom, a *coulemelle*, a *culumella iganta*, a *Macrolepiota*.

People invited to his house—in the days when they still came, and in not insignificant numbers—had to be prepared, no matter what, to be served, from dusk till midnight, mushroom invocations, rhapsodies, symphonies, sonnets, fables, and cantatas, meaning less the various mushroom dishes than expressions of his intoxication, which increased from year to year. Eventually he had no other topic, even past the midnight hour. He refused to let any other subject come up. Mushrooms, as already mentioned, were the ultimate adventure, and he was their prophet. They occupied the most distant horizon, no, the only one. The world's axis turned on them, including the weather, which he categorized as either mushroom weather or non-mushroom weather. His first thought upon waking in the morning: "Off to the woods. Off to the woods. Off to the mushrooms!" His first thought? His only thought, in the course of time and the seasons, in summer and in winter? "Thought"? In any case, his only subject, all day and all evening, eventually with me as his sole audience, was a particular spot, as if it were a matter of immense importance, and he wasted not a word on the daily catastrophes in the world, of which more and more were occurring; he couldn't stop conjuring up and murmuring mysteriously about the one thing that preoccupied him.

His disdain spread to all those not of his kind, "excepting only us, his family, whom my dear husband has lovingly forgotten about . . ." As a mushroom hunter he also saw himself as a protector, and those two functions combined made him the lord of the woods, or, as he planned to call himself in his unwritten mushroom book, the "son of the path," a phrase translated from the Arabic that allegedly referred to a warrior, a warrior in the Holy War. Yes, he was waging war against everyone, at first surreptitiously, later openly, if only with words, against all those not on the same path as his kind, and not only in the forests, but there in particular. A curse even on the children playing there, shooting one another dead with toy guns, though at one time he'd seen them as future allies, if only they could have the right upbringing. "Little good-for-nothings! Leave the woods in peace!" (And in the end he didn't bother to keep that inaudible.) Shame on all the false treasure hunters, laying waste to the woods more drastically from year to year, not only with picks and shovels but with more and more sophisticated metal detectors, digging deeper and deeper trenches around the trees' roots. Shame on the cross-woods bikers, defiling even the most remote wood roads with artificial ramps, landing pads, and slalom obstacles excavated from the natural forest floor, as if even the wildest wilderness were just one more terrain they'd annexed. "You sons of bitches are going to pay for this, pay me, the son of the path, the one in charge!"

Yet his wife also told me how disarmed he'd felt on the rare occasions when a gun-toting child or one of the cross-woods speeders had unexpectedly greeted him (no seekers of metal treasures ever did so), and how one time he'd come home raving about the glowing skin and sparkling eyes of a sylvan athlete—contrasted with his own appearance, even when—precisely when?—he'd made the most amazing finds: his eyes dull and his cheeks inflamed from brushing against forest spiderwebs, his forehead scratched bloody by the broken tree limbs that he'd blundered into in his seeker's greed, which he called "yearning," and she added that if he hadn't been rendered one-eyed long since, like some of his ancestors, by the way, when a dead oak branch with a broken end as sharp as a thorn stabbed him in the corner of one eye, yesterday on the right and today on the left, he had his guardian angel to thank, who, in the area they both came from, was said to be an admonitory angel as well: "Watch out, friend: next time I won't be there to protect you!"

And finally she told me that he still set out wearing an elegant suit, with a smoothly knotted silk tie. —And came back all dirty? —Oh, no, never, not a spot on the fine worsted, or on anything. But instead, snags, especially in the lining, and that would happen to a newly purchased suit the first time he wore it to the woods, or at the latest the second time, and eventually it would be not just snagged but ripped, in more and more places, and, the last few times we got together, in tatters.

Not long after his wife and child—by now hardly a child—left the house, the mushroom maniac gave up his work as a lawyer and got ready to write his special mushroom book. But, "as mentioned," "as previously noted . . ." And with that, as he sent word to me shortly before he disappeared, began "the most gruesome period of my life." Since this experience, too, has often been narrated over the centuries, in conjunction with different causes and auspices, I can keep this account brief, despite the fact that it took years to come to a head, and besides, this account must content itself with remaining a summary, though that's not my style. Up to now I've drawn from the "Homeric spring" invoked by Antonio Machado for a sense of rhythm and an indication of tone. For what comes now, that spring is—how should I put it?—no longer bubbling; or this is no longer the place for it.

Gruesome? Yes. And at the same time, in the course of searching he enjoyed almost daily a moment of ecstasy; one depended on the other. The ecstasy came even when he didn't find anything for a change, which happened more and more infrequently: as he saw it, this ecstasy proved to him that he was a free person, "the freest of all, and the rest of you, you're our slaves, the slaves of my kind." His kind? Yes. Now, without a profession, he was free to go in search of his kind, the other special searchers, researchers, search-outers, who, he sensed, were just as much the last human beings as he was.

And that even seemed to prove true now and then, though no longer in the course of his actual searching, in the forest or other locales, as had sometimes been the case earlier—outside of the woods the number of such locales was increasing to an almost worrisome degree. And it proved true even less during the organized gatherings and annual conferences of mushroom experts or "friends," as they called themselves, from the entire world, which he had still attended in the beginning. He usually, or actually almost every time, felt himself to be in the presence of his kind when they revealed themselves by chance, for instance when he was among strangers at a bar. There didn't have to be a soccer game on the TV screen for a conversation to develop. A casual remark about mushrooms from one of the strangers, or about a specific mushroom, often overlooked, and a discussion among several of those at the bar would spring up, full of quiet enthusiasm, also for places, seasons, and especially nuances and shadings, such as no soccer game, no matter how exciting, and no other object on earth, could awaken.

But it never went beyond that. And when he learned more about the life circumstances of those he'd taken for his kind, it turned out that they embodied, the mushroom world aside, more the opposite of the free human beings he sought. In their daily lives they revealed themselves for the most part to be willing subordinates to their wives or whomever, underlings not worth talking with, subordinates of the most craven kind, as if their forays into the woods were just a hobby or pastime, one among thousands available—which couldn't be right, that much was obvious to his eyes and ears time after time in bars. And he met his kind even less, if possible, at conferences, and not at all at the mushroom researchers' world congress. Hardly a whisper of those free spirits with tongues of fire, their bodies set ablaze by the air of the world, whom his imagination had painted in anticipation. It certainly was odd that so many of these mushroom researchers seemed sickly, and imagined themselves to be ill. Not one of them stood there with head held high, which might seem natural, given their particular research area, but couldn't people walking around stooped over, their eyes on the ground, radiate a kind of sovereignty? Sovereignty over themselves. A person like that would need only to open his mouth, and, never mind the congress, let his voice ring out over the land, right? Allowing what Goethe called "the higher principle," meaning the spirit, to hold sway, right? Yet no voice rang out, let alone held sway. The only voices remained those suitable for the congress or council, a competition among experts presided over by a mushroom pope and with many antipopes, and that tone also dominated even the most agreeable socializing afterward, in the context of which he, the self-appointed free lord from the Kingdom of Mushrooms, wished he could go back to the nice spontaneity of those chance conversations in the bar. Not a few of the mycologists, most of them on the older side, appeared tired out after just a few steps in the park surrounding the conference center, and back in the auditorium, even if one of them was presenting a revolutionary theory on spores, there was a constant chorus of little coughs coming from the seats, where the participants kept their distance from one another, as if afraid of catching something—"all of which was unthinkable during my opening and closing statements in court." And yet: in the end—in his story there actually was an in-the-end now and then—these mushroom experts were probably all lost souls, as was perhaps the way it should be these days, and at the same time all of them, each in his own way, dedicated and kindhearted.

Yet they weren't his kind. He saw that now: there were no others like him, and he admitted that toward the end of his story—according to what I've heard to this point—without the arrogance, perhaps congenital, that for a while, when his mushroom mania was at its height, had become a veritable hauteur.

His arrogance and hauteur gone—and nonetheless he felt himself to be the one and only, the lone legitimate treasure seeker. He was and remained the sovereign, if now only in those moments of ecstasy, becoming shorter by the day, fading in a flash, and, worse still, seeming inauthentic. And *sovereign* meant: Where I am and trace my circles, spirals, and ellipses is my spot, and that spot is mine, and no one's permitted to disturb me there. Do me a favor and get out of my search field. Out of my sight. Away with you, slavish creature. And since, as a result of his solitary condition, he'd become newly conscious of prestige and presence, the figure he cut sent a message without his having to utter out loud the invective he had on the tip of his tongue (only his fingernails, contrasting with his otherwise elegant getup, couldn't be cleansed of woodsy soil, so far had it worked its way into the nail beds).

He insisted that no one disturb him, as if he were engaged in a particularly delicate and furthermore essential project that in the interest of society couldn't be postponed. If it were stymied, that would create an eternal source of misery for the general welfare, and besides, he personally would be done for. Yes, strange, or simply gruesome: in his moments of ecstasy he was simultaneously fearful. Fearful as the person who, as a special geometer, alone with his equally geometric and spherical movements through the forest, had and represented having all the time in the world, but could be ambushed into suddenly having no time—be snatched out of time—find that his time was up. "Curses upon you, Lucifer, false bringer of light!"

And that is what happened, and eventually daily. Each time the ecstasy he experienced as a searcher-out, researcher, and discoverer threatened to veer into panic. Initially he experienced that as a beautiful cosmic ritual that warmed his heart and brow, but then it imperceptibly turned into a gruesome and icy ritual beyond his control. The gruesome aspect became more and more inescapable the longer he kept on finding treasures (and every day he found and discovered more): as a result of all his scouting and tracking down, the space grew narrower and narrower, eventually shrinking to mere dots, one here, one there. If earlier his searching had created an entire environment, now his finding, especially in unprecedented quantities, made it shrink. How lovely and beneficial the single finds had been. What he now had could no longer be called space, and that meant: no more sense of spaciousness. During one interval he fooled himself into thinking he still had space by directing his gaze toward the treetops and crowns, and beyond that to the "firmament," by pretending to see the most distant possible horizons, and in the process he gambled away his space once and for all, because those glimpses, awfully brief in practice, never had a chance to become real gazing, and before they developed anything approaching consistency, he broke them off and went back to staring at the dots, yes, fixing his eyes on the ground. From being a southwest-northeast lord he'd become a dot slave. Yes, now he was the slave.

And with space thus gambled away—part of the cosmic rule?—the almost daily sense of time pressure, then time crunch, then complete untimeliness closed in. Remarkable: his kind of time pressure, his "time stranglehold," as he called it, came not from having too little time but from having too much—as his loss of space came from his losing all sense of proportion. And remarkable in a different way: what now and then saved him from panic was precisely the exterior world going into a panic, was panic-stricken nature. When, in a downpour or a storm, times and places became jumbled, not inside him but outside, in the outer world, he experienced that as a fundamentally different drama, as the salvation-bringing countermovement to his self-delusions and self-deceptions; as limbs came crashing down, as terrified birds whizzed through the air, as thunder crashed, he felt safe; though he continued to eye and spy sideways and rootward (only intermittently now, no longer incessantly), he felt part of the interplay of spaces and times in the panic-stricken world; he gained the gift of inner peace and opened his eyes wide, even when a falling limb grazed him or a lightning bolt startled him: in the second after the shock his sight was even sharper, and what he saw in those moments was, as had been the case long ago, surrounded by a glow; at least it wasn't just a dot. How his sense of place was restored amid the wilderness of the panicked world. How the man who had lost his way so grievously became a discoverer.

What also rescued him now and then from his increasing awareness of untimeliness was, paradoxically or not, those incidents, all too short, alas, in which he searched and searched and searched—he couldn't help it anymore—and found nothing. During hours of searching like that he did get more and more annoyed, but precisely that emotion helped him remain located in time, or, as he described it to himself, "in the here-and-now." And above all, after a futile day like that, stepping out of the depths of the woods into the open with hands and pockets empty, and finally, finally! reaching a place where there was nothing more to search for, indeed meant, "Ah, out into the open!" Except that not finding anything was the great exception, and became greater from one time to the next. "Seeking and not finding!": that notion hovered before him now as a kind of ideal. But how to put it into practice? It couldn't be made a reality, at least not by a mushroom maniac, and certainly not by one with no others of his kind.

What made him unique among the members of all the maniac subcultures? I wondered. Perhaps the fact that he, in addition to his mushroom mania, was, to borrow from Shakespeare, also a consciousness maniac, in the sense of "so consciousness doth make maniacs of us all." While he could embrace taking things as they came, laissez-faire, not interfering, as an ideal, at the same time he was constantly aware of what he was doing, at every moment, horrifyingly and ceaselessly aware—instead of letting things go, leaving well enough alone. His hyperconsciousness was the source of his dysfunctional relationship to time, an illness from which his mushroom mania seemed for a while to have cured him, only to have it erupt again in the end—ah, that he might be granted "a good end!"—and erupt all the more virulently. What was the worst symptom of his consciousness mania now? He pretended not to be searching, while surreptitiously making finds after all.

Curses upon him, and curses, whenever panic threatened, upon mushrooms! If he had eyes for anything, only for them. And more and more things tricked him into thinking they were mushrooms, even things that didn't have classic mushroom forms. He saw the small square chimneys on houses in his neighborhood as mushrooms, and at the sight of a thousands-of-years-old sculpture of the Three Kings from the Orient bringing their gifts to the newborn Son of God, what they held in their hands was not gold, frankincense, and myrrh but mushrooms. In the depths of night, constellations in the shape of mushrooms. In dreams fungi grew on his own body, not the usual chronic ones considered health problems but woodland mushrooms, the most sought-after, desirable, tasty ones. And even in the woods and pastures, the more plentifully the colonies grew, the more likely he was to mistake everything else lying around for mushrooms, which he bent down to gather: leaves, cow flops, even berries and flowers, rocks, dog poop, paper handkerchiefs, empty cigarette packs, feathers, condoms, rusty helmets, hundred-year-old mess kits, disarmed Teller mines.

So captivated was he by the mushroom shapes outside of and inside his head that he stopped seeing people's faces, that which he had once considered the most noble, "the visible third person." His wife, long since rid of him, told me he'd run into her once in the woods, but his eyes had gone straight to what she had in her hands. –And that was what? –A Caesar's mushroom, an *Amanita caesarea*, a yolk yellow that couldn't possibly be more glowing, in an egg-white wrapping, a true feast for the gods. –So had she become a maniac too? –Yes, for a change, playfully, in order to have a chance, possibly, to win the maniac-in-chief back. –And what happened then? –He actually looked up from the mushroom emperor and into her, his wife's, face. But he didn't recognize her, only admired her, as a stranger, more for her find than for her beauty.

On the verge of horror he began to hear the rustling and swishing of the trees, which as a child he'd loved and needed intensely, as hostile whispering behind his back, as hissing, sinister mumbling, an ill omen. The limbs rubbing against each other in the wind were talking about him. Even when he came upon the most lovable and beautiful mushrooms under the trees, now they were nothing more than "stuff" to him.

Stuff of the devil! Spawn of hell! And how cold, icy cold, this stuff felt in his hand, a mass even the hottest blood couldn't warm, on the contrary sending its coldness up his arm until slivers of ice worked their way into his innermost heart, which didn't stop him, however, as the local expert, from helping a group of hikers lost in the woods—there were more and more people lost these days—get back on track, or from being the first one to greet whomever he encountered, even if he didn't need a friendly face, and which didn't keep him from wondering why the great forest walkers of past centuries, as great as he was now, such as Walt Whitman or Henry David Thoreau, to mention only Americans, had never written poetically about mushrooms or so much as mentioned them. Why did you use trees only for gymnastics, to get your agility back after your stroke, Walt? And why didn't you, Henry, write about any plants other than those found in the woods of Massachusetts and Maine? And what kinds of peoples were those, like the Indians and Arabs, who thought mushrooms grew only in the vicinity of shithouses, or were *ḥarām*, proscribed, like pork, banished in days of yore from Paradise as unclean?

Was my mushroom-maniac friend trying to free himself from his love-hate when he spent several months crisscrossing the dunes and deserts of the earth? That I don't know. What I do know: that among the Tuaregs and in Yemen, in the sand of the desert and the dunes, whenever he found himself near oases he began to keep an eye out for mushrooms, and also dug out some that were adapted to the sand and the land, or "symbiotic," as the expression goes. And also in the middle regions of our Europe, to which he fled, allegedly to get away from mushrooms, he would stop at the base of cathedrals, in stadiums, even, I kid you not, on river-cruise boats, between subway tracks, in the cemeteries barest of vegetation, to at least catch a glimpse of them, or his head jerked in their direction, away from everything else, and sometimes he found them in the most impervious concrete, causing dismay after a fleeting moment of ecstasy. During the hour before he underwent nontrivial surgery he stood at a window in the hospital, casting a glance at the crown of the tree outside, after which he peered all the more intently and at the same time more with disgust at the roots—looking for what, do you think?

More and more often he burst out in litanies of invective aimed at the objects of his research: "Monsters. Monstrosities. Bastards. Stinkpots. Mothers of all pests." And the worst insults, in his eyes, were these: "Fairy-tale nerds. Maggot tales. Wolves in Red Riding Hood's clothing. Rumpelstiltskin with the thousand false names, 'Rumpelstiltskin' being the falsest of all! Out of my sight! Have mercy!"

Since there was no escaping from his former favorites anywhere on earth, from Tierra del Fuego to Siberia, he decided he might as well go home to his house and grounds, near the metropolis, close to the familiar woods. It's understandable, or understand it if you can, that by now he was drawn there no longer just involuntarily but against his will, no, driven, veritably chased there. His first thought, no, compulsion, upon waking long before daybreak: "To the mushrooms with you, get a move on!"

Thus another summer and fall passed, and winter arrived. Overnight the first snow fell, continuing into the next day, coming down thick and fast. That didn't prevent the maniac in the slightest from going out to search as he did every day; indeed it made him even greedier; although he was tormented by guilt and self-loathing, consideration of the almost knee-high snow spurred him on. By the way, there could be no talk of "consideration," and the snowflakes on his forehead, at one time tapping rather than engraving the great seal of life there: no such thing, not anymore.

Once in the forest, deep in snow, he began to dig, scrape, and scoop, using a bundle of search sticks, branches, then his bare hands, and finally his feet, left, right, like a soccer player: nothing but dead leaves from the previous autumn, in a variety of moisture-saturated colors, which he hardly noticed, glowing under the layer of pure white. Yet from years of experience he knew that in winter, from December until far into January, under the snow, which protected them from freezing, his dear ones—which they were even now, in spite of everything—still grew. And in particular, after the season of the so-called death trumpets—another of those misnomers, given the way these mushrooms flickered blackish gray, very much alive—he could count on finding their cousins, they, too, formed like mini-trumpets, but ranging from pale to dark yellow, which he, autocratic as he'd become, had renamed, changing their common name into "little earth butterflies," and, during the period when he still felt like using endearments, "earth mothlets." The Taxham apothecary, unlike many of our pharmacists today, had been extraordinarily knowledgeable about mushrooms, and had sent word to him that these trumpet chanterelles became even tastier after the first frost.

As it happened, that was the day before his disappearance; before he vanished from the earth. For hours he burrowed in the snow in vain, and an observer would have thought the parts of the forest through which my friend zigzagged had been desecrated by the others, the mechanized, automated treasure hunters, or rooted up by a horde of wild boars. Fortunately or unfortunately for him, it stopped snowing, and in the low-angled afternoon sun, from yet another hole he'd dug, the yellowish brown wings of a little earth butterfly twinkled at him, a single one, which at the moment of being discovered was greeted with its endearment. And the yellow of its little leg in the sun: where else in the entire world was a glow that could express a warmer welcome?

And from years of experience the mushroom maniac also knew that once one had finally, often after half a day of searching, caught sight of the first and seemingly only butterfly like this one "winging" its way out of the deep leaves while remaining motionless in place, one could be sure of uncovering, all around one, not singly but rather in bushels, clumped together in bunches and clusters, hundreds of the most delicious earth mothlets, uniquely tasty—like almost all mushrooms—in a trail that had been hidden in a sort of geometric pattern of furrows and fissures in the ground and extended far under the trees, so plentiful that as he was picking or plucking them (which he heard as music, "as if composed in unison by John Cage and Domenico Scarlatti"), he pictured a secret garden plot deep in the woods, part of a concealed secret plantation meant for him alone.

That is how it was that day, too, except that once discovered under the snow, the plots with the earth butterflies went on and on, all across the forest; the plantation stretched in all directions as if endless. The harvest became richer from one hour to the next, also heavier in all the containers he had with him, in his pockets, in his knapsack, and it demanded his infinitely repeated stooping and plucking. Now and then the yellow trail at his feet thinned out, seemed to break off for one or two paces—then flared up and fluttered anew with the next step. During the interval he'd hoped he would finally be able to stand up straight and head for home, his job finished. Anything to get out of the woods! But he couldn't do it. The trail of earth butterflies led ever onward. It wasn't only that he couldn't get away; those beasts, those no-goods, those sons of bitches wouldn't let him go. The mushroom sites, the mushroom beds, the mushroom meanders snaked along, twisted and turned, jerked their rattails, thumped their dragontails, tossed nooses out to catch him, ceaselessly, mercilessly.

Dusk came on, the December night descended without evening in between, and cursing, pleading, also whimpering and wailing, he continued to churn up the forest floor as a "forced harvest laborer" (a technical term from his time as a lawyer), first by the light of the snow, then with his headlamp, which, since his passion had become an addiction, he'd taken along every time he went to the woods. "Me, the hunter? Not on your life! I'm the mushrooms' victim!" (Another such technical expression.)

And then? The definitive outbreak of horror, and him running screaming or silently to bash his head against a tree trunk on the edge of the deepest of the many bomb craters? A different kind of "Great Fall"? Or, humming and singing as if everything were just fine, burrowing at the bottom of a crater through the snow, frozen by now, into the leaf litter? Nothing of the sort. As in the story of the Habakkuk, an alleged prophet in the Old Testament, he was seized by a lock of hair—you know what I mean?—and borne straight through the air to somewhere else entirely. —Borne by whom? —Not a clue. Come up with something yourselves. —Maybe by himself? —Maybe.

Who told me all that, about his last years before his disappearance, the last year, the last day? He told me himself, my old friend from the village, the later mushroom maniac, if not lunatic: he told me himself.

My intuition that he was making his way to me has been borne out. He's been keeping me company for the last few days, or we're keeping each other company, after the entire year of his absence. And as a result of his turning up, hale and hearty, I hope the smidgen of serenity has fluttered into his and my story without which my telling of it wouldn't get to where it wants to be and belongs, "into the open," as if someone other than me called for that.

It was the beginning of December again, though without snow, and one afternoon, while I was sitting, engrossed in his story, in my rather remote house, long ago a way station and overnight shelter for stagecoach or whatever horses in the fairly unpopulated landscape, then as now, between Paris and Beauvais, my old friend came walking down the lane, which saw a bit of traffic only in the morning and the evening. I recognized him by his footsteps, perhaps because I was expecting him "somehow," perhaps also because my hearing was sharpened by the concentration with which I'd been working. My old friend? His gait that of a youth, almost a child's, like a child's skipping, which no matter where I hear it is always the loveliest music.

I got up from my table here, where I'm writing the end of his story now, and before he had time to knock or call out, went outside and opened the door in the garden wall to which I'd attached the house number, fashioned from prehistoric shells gathered on the nearby steppe—in this area house numbers rarely have more than three or four digits—and without a trace of surprise at being welcomed this way, he entered what had always been, in what I think is the spirit of Virgil's *Eclogues*, my "poor" garden. —The only thing missing is that you'd put a candle in the window to light his way by night! —I'd done that the previous nights. —And that you received him with the salt of hospitality. —So I did.

Before crossing the threshold into the house, a stone structure that had stood the test of centuries, he hesitated, long past the interval that politeness required, and in that way I had a chance to study his appearance. I have an eye for details, too, though for ones different from his, and thus I observed that his fingernails were no longer encrusted with dirt, but instead were as manicured as one expects of people with a public persona like his. His forehead and cheeks were smooth, free of the bloody scratches he'd acquired daily during his period of forest mania, and unlike the last time I'd seen him, he held his back straight, supported by the elegance of his suit, obviously newly purchased, as he gazed, both ostentatiously and emphatically (the kind of multisyllabic words he liked to use in his opening and closing arguments in court), at eye level, though without specifically avoiding looking at the ground or sideways; at any rate, he seemed not to be afraid to look there. And at the same time, in the corners of his eyes there glimmered, as it always had, the Prodigal Son.

Only on that first evening did we speak of his period as a mushroom maniac. (He insisted on spending the night in the tiny addition to my house, at one time a toolshed, too small for a horse, even for shoeing, for which a horse would stand with its hindquarters outside, no?) Thinking to put his mind at rest, I told him that during the almost three years I'd lived here, I'd never seen a single mushroom in the bleak landscape all around, or at least not a single edible one or one worth searching for; the substrate was limestone and gypsum—not hospitable to vegetation of any value—and the soil in the sparse pockets of woodland dotting the infertile steppe consisted of nothing but rock fragments, sand, and silt—see the rare molehills, none of which contained even a grain of the dark loam usually found in forests—sterile crumbs, with at most blobs of mushy, oxygenless, pus-yellow clay. At best one might find a puffball here and there, but now, at the onset of winter—"this I needn't tell you"—they would contain nothing but brownish, blackish dust.

My friend seemed to have no need of reassurance; he ignored my comments. I also didn't reveal to him that I was sitting (and walking) with his story just then; besides, he realized that the subject of my work (and my game) had to go unspoken. "To me it's enough to know you're sitting at your table, and to see you there, near the window, from a distance, from the edge of the yard," he said: "that does a person"—he didn't say "me"—"good." He seemed to ascribe the questions I asked about him and mushrooms on the day he arrived to my wish to be distracted from my topic; besides, he commented, he, and the relationship between him and mushrooms, didn't amount to a story worth telling, let alone a book from my "quill"; and at one point I saw him turn over the only mushroom book in my house as he passed it so the cover illustration couldn't be seen. In my imagination I pictured him throwing the book in the fireplace. Or lighting the fire with pages he ripped out and crumpled up.

On another evening we were sitting by the fire, and he revealed that he was thinking of writing an anti-mushroom book, indeed an anti-forest book. Mushroom seeking, and seeking of any kind, caused one's field of vision to shrink, he asserted, to a mere dot. Blotted out one's vision altogether. And how one's eyes weighed down one's head when they remained fixed on the ground, and became dulled: one of the chronic disorders afflicting seekers was cataracts! Riffing on Goethe's poem "Selige Sehnsucht," he remarked that a seeker went from being a bright guest on this earth to a gloomy one. Forests and forest air were bad for one in the long run, dreadfully unhealthful, putting pressure on one's lungs, et cetera, emitting toxic fumes and ultimately bad stuff. And the jerky movements collectors made when they failed to maintain their "search gait" affected their hearts in the form of arrhythmia. And seekers in general, when they were out and about, more and more became grabbers, out of pure greed, and being greedy meant being looters. Oh, all those godless, self-centered collectors. All praise, on the other hand, to God-fearing hunters, who at least fell to their knees once in a blue moon (see their patron saint). Oh, those forests, those fucking forests, how they rustle, and rustle, and rustle.

During the day, while I was writing his story, he kept busy in the yard, where he made almost no noise, raking leaves or collecting fallen branches and twigs from the old apple trees for us to use in the fireplace come evening, and while working he never got dirt on himself, even on his shirt cuffs. I'd also pointed out to him where on the steppe, and especially in the fields, plowed and harrowed for the winter, he might find the snail shells and seashells deposited there millions of years ago by ocean tides, even the tiniest snail shell amazingly heavy in one's hand, and he returned every time with far more, and much more magnificent, finds than I'd come up with in all my years of collecting. He also brought pockets full of rose hips, which he transformed into a uniquely red—rose-hip red, of course—jam, and the following day he'd filled his pockets with hazelnuts, which he served roasted with the evening meal he prepared, with potatoes from the Atlantic island of Noirmoutier, hardly larger than the nuts, and a salad of sorrel and watercress from the Troësne (privet), a small river down on the plain at the foot of the plateau on whose edge, as previously mentioned, my former horse-changing station is located. All these things, as well as a few edible chestnuts, he veritably conjured out of his pockets, sleeves, and trouser cuffs upon returning from his forays. So apparently he hadn't been able to give up wanting to make magic and create enchantment. Instead of searching on the ground, he now made drawings, especially of things at eye level, primarily the silvery, translucent, intertwined poufs of the wintry copses, as if the need for twinings, whorls, curls, dappled and striped things, and anything spherical had stayed with him! No matter: every morning I found my shoes cleaned and polished, my rubber boots washed, and every third day my friend rubbed the flint flagstones in the house with olive oil—which imparted a different kind of shine.

Every day when I'd finished my work, the two of us would set out for a walk before December's early dusk, each time in a different direction, and usually not coming home until long after dark. I had the impression Orion was moving across the winter sky from east to south and then toward the west faster than in all previous years; was that an effect of advancing age? In the canalized Troësne I saw the black humps of giant rats, in reality a particular kind of beaver, known hereabouts as "Chilean" beavers, God knows why; the hunter waiting next to us on the bridge over the canal informed us that they made an excellent ragout. Upon seeing the silhouettes of two stocky, short-legged horses in a nocturnal pasture we imagined ourselves riding them bareback, with no particular destination, as we'd done in our youth in the village on two broad-backed, short-legged plow horses, from one end of the village to the other. In another pasture stood a mighty bull, one big bulging muscle, as it were, from his hooves almost to his horns, his coat a white that didn't fade even in the dark, the testicles beneath his haunches looking like two oversized calabashes. One time a falling star flashed straight across the firmament, like a match being struck on a stone wall or somewhere by a hero in a Western or someone, and the clouds stacked up clearly from horizon to horizon looked like a tractor's tire tracks. Wild hares kept leaping across the steppe in the prewinter grass from one hiding place to the next.

One evening we also hiked to the distant village and stood there at the bar with two or three habitués who'd been coming for years, and my friend, with his eye for clothing, commented that often "lonely people have markedly sharp creases in their trousers." I refrained from commenting that at certain moments during these days he himself had seemed like one of the lonely. How did that manifest itself? For instance, when he, who'd just seemed the more balanced of the two of us, suddenly became clumsy, was literally overcome with clumsiness, bungling everything he touched, dropping everything he picked up. And in what other ways? Without a clock he always knew exactly what time it was, even when he'd been sleeping, and to the minute; and whenever numbers appeared, on a thermostat, on my car's tachometer, he read these numbers as the time, as current, real time. Once, long ago, he'd sent word to me that the one thing he was proud of was having time—precisely because he'd learned what it meant to have no time, which meant: the dragon in one's heart, one's heart as a dragon. So to this day he hadn't been cured completely of his original time problem, his malignant boredom.

His birthday rolled around, and to celebrate it with my friend, I put my work aside, and we headed out along roads, past villages, across fields, through thickets—"There's no way to get through here" (me) —"But of course we can get through" (him)—and past more villages and along more roads to the inn on the other side of the plateau's hill, called, no joke, Auberge du Saint Graal, "At the Sign of the Holy Grail." (At one point the name was changed, then changed back to its original form.)

We set out long before sunrise, which, as he knew, would take place on his birthday at eight thirty-three. The clouds on the eastern edge of the plateau, almost the southern edge, were rimmed in gold, and the old birthday boy burst out, "Gloria!" The wind in our faces as we cut across fields felt almost warm, whereupon my friend remarked that it was blowing from Yemen, from Paradise. At the end of a tree-lined avenue, a blue covered wagon: sky blue. More than ever my companion for the day resembled Richard Widmark, the ageless, reticent, then unexpectedly high-spirited actor. And I was his partner in *Two Rode Together*? That would be nice, would have been nice. But at any rate I took my partner seriously, seriously as only James Stewart took a partner and/or opponent seriously. The partner? The subject? His. Ours. Our shared adventure. And what did I hear at the same time from the man at my side? "Strange: that light in the sky's like the light during the funeral of the virginal idiot girl."

We didn't hike, let alone march; we trudged. "Finally I'm trudging again," he said. And the even beat of our trudging, especially through leaves, sounded to me like a train chugging along, a very slow one, incapable of getting up to full speed—and that was fine!—and I recalled the way someone had described my *Essays*: "like a slow milk train at daybreak." And so we trudged along. Trudged, trudged, trudged. The music of trudging, a different kind of caravan music.

When the path, provided we were on one, became too narrow for us to walk abreast, my friend took the lead, and I saw his back covered with burrs, which also clung to me in bunches and clusters. Now and then he turned his head and told me fragments of his story that were new to me, as if they were things he'd survived long ago: just as in the Second World War partisans had disguised themselves as mushroom seekers, he'd disguised himself for the woods one time as a partisan, in order to find what he'd set his heart on, and another time he'd drawn a map of the entire area with all the "treasure locations" marked, intended as a legacy or bequest for his child. And once, looking over his shoulder, not so much at me as into thin air, he exclaimed, "How lucky I've been, all my life! And how deluded I was, time and again, sometimes bitterly, sometimes beautifully. Beautifully deluded!" And as he said that, he stepped on an old puffball, full of holes, on the edge of a meadow, whereupon the blackish brownish smoke puffed out of the mushroom, a movable threshold at the entrance to winter.

Toward noon the sky closed down, it turned colder, and the wind changed direction, coming from the north. After we'd passed the woodland grave of Arthur Têtu and were climbing to the ridge, the highest in this direction between Paris and the ocean at Dieppe, it began to rain, and soon we felt showers of hail striking our faces, which didn't really bother us, "us"—as my friend from village days turned to shout—"sons of the mountains!" Before that we'd passed through the village of Chavençon on the far-flung plain and had both stepped onto the cattle scale, long since out of use—no livestock markets anymore—and swung and swung and rocked and rocked, reluctant for a while to continue our hike.

Later, in the afternoon, the sun came out again, the wind died down, and the blue became a bluing, the motionlessness of the clouds became a piling up, the last green became a fresh greening; and when we, halfway up to the ridge, not yet in the large forest, the only one in the whole area, crossed a cow pasture, I was the one involuntarily looking out for *senderuelas*, aka *carrerillas*, aka mountain nymphs, aka Scotch bonnets, which I knew grew here in fairy rings every year until late December: yes, hm, my friend had infected me for a while with his mushroom mania—and I actually saw the nymphs from a distance forming lasso loops, so I quickly pulled my friend aside and pretended I'd taken a wrong turn. And he asked in response, "Are we still in that time?" And I: "We're in that time, finally!" And there in the pasture stood the two old plow horses, and we swung ourselves onto their backs as we had in our village childhood, for only a short stretch, but it was enough for the horses to turn into riding horses, swaying, whinnying, sniffing the air—for what? And for a moment one of the animals turned into a donkey, sighing and braying across the countryside, while its partner snorted in response.

After that through the big forest, with oaks, Spanish chestnuts, and beeches bright in the distance instead of the tangles of bushes more common in that area: Yes, was that the idea? —Yes, that was the idea. —Whose? —Mine. My daydream. My plan. A divine plan like that: it existed.

Before we reached the edge of the forest, the sky closed in again, and it began to snow, for the first time this year, and as quietly and heavily as it always did the first time. "Or for the last time?" (That was him again.) In the twinkling of an eye, the old, new white world, and the birthday child now walked behind me—though from here to our destination, the inn at the foot of the hill on the other side, we had a broad path all the way—literally walking in my footsteps, our trudging no longer the chugging of a locomotive but rather a creaking, not unlike the call-and-response of two ravens, which turned, on the edge of the woods, into the creaking call of a single raven: the other one, following behind, had paused before the trees along the edge, which were being buffeted by the snowy wind, and I heard him saying to himself, "Being in the rustling, in the midst of the action. And up in the crowns the great weaving, the act of weaving and the woven material in one. Oh, why didn't I stick to the edges of the woods?" A great roaring there along the edge, and clattering of the leafless limbs like that of a festival canopy. At our feet a dead carrier pigeon, as if it had hurtled out of the sky that very moment and into the fresh snow, digging a crater, a message tied to one leg. But we didn't want to know what was in it.

Onward, uphill and into the woods, where what was meant to happen happened, and as was also planned, if you don't mind. And by whom? See above. Precisely in the thick snow, smooth everywhere else to the right and left of the path—the weather forecast was proving to be accurate—in one spot a form emerged all the more distinctly, something that might have been a Teller mine if it had been lying flat on the ground. But the thing in this form wasn't lying; it was standing upright, sticking up. And did the mushroom maniac pounce on it—"Hey, you!"—as planned (as a sometime fellow maniac I knew the spot and knew that even in early winter one more boletus grew there)? No, contrary to plan, he first took a few steps back. But then, after exclaiming, "Hey there, you're the right one for me!" he went toward that round shape, or rather strode toward it, slowly, in circles, spirals, ellipses.

In the end, however, what had to happen didn't happen, or what was planned, dreamed up, providentially provided for; as inspiration willed: at the last minute, before the maniac bent down or, heaven help us! even went down on his knees, someone appeared on the scene and got there first. Someone? A tall figure. A woman. The woman. The one. Summoned by me, or whomever, to his birthday. There she stood before him, as if on a far, far horizon, and this time he didn't look at the thing she was holding but at her face, and he recognized her. Long ago he'd seen himself as her savior. Or as the one who completed her. And now? Now it was the exact opposite. Did he walk toward her? No. Although she was only two, three, at most four steps away, he ran, from where he stood, ran to her. It's only children I've ever seen run that way from a standing position, to their father, to their mother, or to another person. In summer the ridge would have been rimmed with blueberry bushes. And now? *Time stood still / on Blueberry Hill.*

And our trio dined happily and contentedly at the Auberge du Saint Graal in the village of Grisy-les-Plâtres on the other side of the chain of hills; *plâtre* means gypsum. The inn's address: Place du Soleil Levant, the Place of the Rising Sun. The appetizer: I'll let you guess this time. And in the middle of the meal we three were joined by a fourth person, more or less unexpectedly. O youth. O rejuvenated world.

But is this too much of a fairy tale in the end? Maybe so: in the fairy tale he was cured. But in reality . . . Here's what inspiration, or whatever or whoever, has to say about that, however: in the worst-case scenario, the fairy-tale element is the realest thing there is, the essential thing. Air, water, earth, and fire as the four elements, and the fairy-tale moment as the fifth, the additional element. In a story, this one at least, from the mushroom world, the fairy-tale element has its place, as an answer to the daily toxic chatter, to the days of toxic rain in summer and fall, to the toxic phone calls year after year from international call centers, to the never-ending toxic happenings being cooked up in the devil's workshop.

At a late hour in the Auberge du Saint Graal we tried to guess what time it was. All four of us guessed wrong. But the one who guessed most wrong and miscalculated most egregiously, that was him.

—MARQUEMONT/VEXIN–
CHAVILLE–MARQUEMONT,
NOVEMBER–DECEMBER
2012

ESSAY ON TIREDNESS

Translated by Ralph Manheim

IN THE PAST I KNEW TIREDNESS ONLY AS SOMETHING TO BE feared.

When in the past?

In my childhood, in my so-called student days, in the years of my first loves, then more than ever. Once during midnight Mass, sitting with his family in the densely crowded, dazzlingly bright village church, the child breathed in the smell of wax and woolen cloth and was overcome by a tiredness that struck with the force of a sickness.

What kind of sickness?

The kind that is said to be "nasty" or "insidious"—for this was a nasty, insidious tiredness. It denatured the world around me, transforming my fellow churchgoers into felt-and-loden dolls that were hemming me in, transforming the resplendently decorated altar in the hazy distance into a torture chamber enhanced by the confused rituals and formulas of the servers, and the sick, tired child himself into a grotesque elephant-headed figure, as heavy and dry-eyed and thick-skinned as that animal. My tiredness removed me from the substance of the world, in the event the winter world of snowy air and solitary sled rides under the stars at night, after the other children had gradually disappeared into their houses, far beyond the fringes of the village, alone, winged with enthusiasm: utterly present, in the stillness, in the whirring of the air, in the blueness of the ice that was forming on the road—"it tingles" is what we used to say of that pleasant cold. But there in the church the child, held fast by tiredness as in the grip of an Iron Maiden, experienced a very different kind of cold, so much so that in the very midst of the Mass he begged to go home, which just then meant no more than "out." Once again I had spoiled one of my parents' rare opportunities, becoming rarer as the old customs died out, for social contact with the neighbors.

Why must you always accuse yourself?

Because even in those days my tiredness was associated with a feeling of guilt, which intensified it and made it acutely painful. Once again I had failed my family: one more steel band tightened around my temples, a little more blood drained from my heart. Decades later, a feeling of shame comes back to me at the thought of that tiredness; but strangely enough, though my parents later reproached me with one thing and another, they never mentioned my attacks of tiredness.

Was the tiredness of your student days similar?

No. The guilt feelings were gone. In lecture halls, on the contrary, my tiredness made me angry and rebellious. Ordinarily, it was not so much the foul air, or being cooped up with hundreds of other students, as the lecturers' lack of interest in what was supposed to be their subject. Never since then have I encountered a group of people so uninspired by what they were doing as those university professors and instructors; any bank teller counting out notes that don't even belong to him, any road repairer working in the overheated air between the sun overhead and the tar boiler down below seemed more inspired. Stuffed shirts, whose voices never vibrated with the astonishment (that a good teacher's subject arouses in him), with enthusiasm, with tenderness, with self-doubt, anger, indignation, or awareness of their own ignorance, but droned incessantly on, intoned—needless to say not in the deep chest tones of Homer, but in tones of examination-oriented pedantry, interspersed now and then with a facetious undercurrent or a malicious allusion addressed to those in the know, while outside the windows green went blue and finally darkened, until the student's tiredness turned to irritation and his irritation to rage. And again as in childhood that feeling of "Let me out! Away from the lot of you in here!" But where to? Home, as in childhood? But there in my rented room, a new tiredness unknown in my childhood was to be dreaded: the tiredness of being alone in a rented room on the outskirts; solitary tiredness.

But what was to be dreaded about that? Wasn't there a bed right there in your room, along with the chair and the table?

An escape into sleep was out of the question. For one thing, that sort of tiredness brought on a paralysis in which it became virtually impossible to bend my little finger or even to bat an eyelid; my breathing seemed to stop and I froze inside and out into a pillar of tiredness. In the end, I dragged myself into bed, but after a quick fainting away from wakefulness—with no sensation of sleep—my first attempt to turn over shook me into a sleeplessness that usually went on all night. For, in my room alone, tiredness always set in late in the day, at dusk. Many others have spoken of insomnia, how it comes to dominate the insomniac's view of the world until, try as he may, he cannot help regarding existence as a calamity, all activity as pointless, and all love as absurd. The insomniac lies there waiting for the gray of dawn, which to him signifies the damnation not only of him alone in his insomniac hell but of all misbegotten humanity relegated to the wrong planet . . . I, too, have been in the world of the sleepless (and even today I still am). In early spring the first birds are heard before dawn—often enough bearing a message of Easter—but today they screech derisively at me in my cell-bed: "One-more-sleepless-night." The striking of the church clocks every quarter of an hour—even the most distant ones are quite audible—gives notice of another bad day. The bestiality at the heart of our world is manifested by the hissing and yowling of two battling tomcats. A woman's sighs or screams of so-called passion start up suddenly in the stagnant air, as though a button had been pressed, setting some mass-produced machine in motion directly above the insomniac's head, as though all our masks of affection had fallen, giving way to panic egoism (that's no loving couple, only two individuals, each bellowing his self-love) and vileness. To those frequently afflicted by episodic states of sleeplessness, if I understand their stories right, such states may form a chain of continuity and come to be regarded as permanent.

But you, who are not a sufferer from chronic insomnia: Are you planning to tell us about the insomniac view of the world or that engendered by tiredness?

As might have been expected, I've started with insomnia and shall go on to the view resulting from tiredness, or rather, in the plural, I shall talk about the divergent views of the world engendered by different kinds of tiredness. How terrifying, for example, at one time, was the kind of tiredness that could crop up in the company of a woman. No, this tiredness did not crop up, it erupted like a physical cataclysm, a phenomenon of fission. And, as a matter of fact, it never confined itself to me alone, but invariably struck the woman at the same time, as though coming, like a change in the weather, from outside, from the atmosphere or from space. There we lay, stood, or sat, as though our being together were the most natural thing in the world, and then before we knew it, we were irrevocably sundered. Such a moment was always one of fright, even of horror, as in falling: "Stop! No! Don't let it happen!" But there was no help; already the two of us were irresistibly recoiling, each into his own private tiredness, not ours, but mine over here and yours over there. In this case, tiredness may have been only another name for insensibility or estrangement—but for the pressure it exerted, its effect on the environment, *tiredness* was the appropriate word. Even if the phenomenon occurred in a large, air-conditioned cinema. The cinema became hot and cramped. The rows of seats became crooked. The colors and the screen itself took on a sulfurous hue, then paled. When we chanced to touch each other, both our hands recoiled as from an electric shock. "In the late afternoon of the ——, a catastrophic tiredness descended out of a clear sky on the Apollo Cinema. The victims were a young couple sitting shoulder to shoulder, who were catapulted apart by a blast of tiredness. At the end of the film, which, incidentally, was entitled *About Love*, they went their separate ways without so much as a word or a glance for each other." Yes, divisive tiredness of this kind struck one mute and blind. Never in all the world could I have said to her: "I'm tired of you"—I could never have uttered the simple word *tired* (which, if we had both shouted it at once, might have set us free from our individual hells). Such tiredness destroyed our power to speak, our souls. If at least we had been able to go our separate ways. No, the effect of such tiredness was that having separated in spirit we were constrained to stay together in body. And it is quite possible that those two, possessed by the devil of tiredness, came to inspire fear.

In whom?

In each other, for one thing. Doomed to remain speechless, that sort of tiredness drove us to violence. A violence that may have expressed itself only in our manner of seeing, which distorted the other, not only as an individual, but also as a member of the other *sex*. Those ugly, ridiculous females (or males), with that innate female waddle or those incorrigible male poses. Or the violence was covert, indirect, the routine swatting of a fly, the half-absentminded rending of a flower. Or we might do something to hurt ourselves; one might chew her fingertips, the other thrust his finger into a lighted flame or punch himself in the face, while she threw herself on the ground like a baby, but without the baby's layers of protective fat. Occasionally, one of these tired individuals would indulge in physical aggression, try to shove his/her enemy or fellow prisoner out of the way, or deliver himself from her with sputtered insults. This violence seemed to be the only escape from the tiredness-couple, for once it was over, they usually managed to separate for the time being. Or tiredness gave way to exhaustion, and then at last they were able to catch their breaths and think things over. Sometimes one would come back to the other and they would stare at each other in amazement, still shaken by what had just happened, yet unable to understand it. At that point they might be able to look at each other, but with new eyes: "What could have come over us in the cinema, on the street, on the bridge?" (Once again we found a voice with which to say that, the two of us together in spite of ourselves, or the young man might speak for the young woman, or the other way around.) To that extent, a tiredness imposed on two young people might even augur a transformation—from the carefree love of the beginnings to something serious. Neither of us would have dreamed of reproaching the other with what he had just done; instead, we simultaneously opened our eyes to one of the drawbacks (irrespective of personalities) of life *à deux*, of a man's and woman's "growing" together, a drawback formerly diagnosed as "a consequence of original sin" and today as God knows what. If both succeed in escaping from this tiredness, it is to be hoped that this realization, accessible to couples who have survived a catastrophe, will enable them to stay together for the rest of their lives, and that such a tiredness will never happen to them again. And they lived together happy and contented until something else, something much less puzzling, much less to be feared, much less astonishing than that tiredness, came between them: habits, the humdrum, day-to-day business of living. But is this divisive tiredness confined to relationships between a man and a woman? Doesn't it also intervene between friends?

No. When I felt tiredness coming on in a relationship with a friend, there was nothing catastrophic about it.

After all, we were together for only a limited time, and when that time was up, we went our separate ways, confident of remaining friends in spite of that one slack hour. Tiredness between friends was not a danger, while to young couples it was, especially if they hadn't been together for long. In love—or whatever we choose to call that feeling of fullness and wholeness—as opposed to friendship, tiredness suddenly threw everything off balance. Disenchantment: all at once the features vanished from his/her image of the other; at the end of a second of horror, he/she ceased to yield any image; the image that was there a second ago had been a mere mirage. Before you knew it, all might be over between two human beings. And the most terrifying part of it was that when this happened all seemed to be over with myself: as I saw it, I was as ugly, as insignificant as the woman with whom only a short while before I had visibly embodied a way of life ("one body and one soul"); each of us wanted him/herself as well as the accursed opposite to be demolished and wiped out on the spot. Even the things around us disintegrated into futilities: "How tired and unlived-in the express train blows by" (recollection of a line in a poem by a friend); and there was reason to fear that couple-tiredness would expand into the world-weariness, not of any particular individual, but of the universe, of the flabby leaves on the trees, of the river's suddenly sluggish flow, of the paling sky. But since such things happened only when a woman and a man were alone together, I became more and more careful as the years went by to avoid prolonged tête-à-tête situations (which was no solution, or at best a cowardly one).

But now it's time for a very different question. Isn't it just your sense of duty—because they are part of your subject—that makes you speak of the insidious, frightening varieties of tiredness—and isn't that why you seem to speak of them so clumsily, long-windedly, and, for all the exaggeration—because I can't help thinking that your story about "violent tiredness" was exaggerated if not invented—halfheartedly.

My way of speaking about malignant tiredness was worse than halfhearted; it was heartless (no, this is not a mere pun, of the kind that for its own amusement betrays an idea). But in this case I don't regard the heartlessness of my discourse as a fault. (And what's more, tiredness isn't my subject; it's my problem, a reproach that I am prepared to incur.) And in dealing with the remaining varieties of tiredness, the non-malignant, the pleasant, the delightful, which have prompted me to write this essay, I shall try to remain equally heartless, to content myself with investigating the pictures, or images, that my problem engenders in me, with making myself at home in each picture and translating it as heartlessly as possible into language with all its twists and turns and overtones. To be "in the picture" is enough for my feeling. If I dare wish for something more to help me carry on with my essay on tiredness, it will probably be a sensation: the sensation of the sun and the spring wind on Andalusian mornings in the open country outside Linares. I should like to hold it between my fingers before sitting down in my room, in the hope that this marvelous sensation between my fingers, enhanced by gusts of wind scented with wild chamomile, may carry over to the coming sentences about *good* tiredness, do them justice, and, above all, make them easier and lighter than the preceding ones. But even now I am pretty sure that tiredness is difficult. Morning after morning, the gusts of wild chamomile are more denatured by the pervasive stench of carrion; still, I shall continue, as always, to cede my right to complain about the smell to the vultures, who feed so well on the carrion. —Very well, then, on this new morning, let us rise and proceed, with more light and air between the lines, as there should be, but always close to the ground, close to the rubble between the yellowish white chamomile flowers, with the help of the symmetry of the pictures I have known. —It is not entirely true that the only tiredness I experienced in the past was of the frightening variety. During my childhood in the late forties and fifties, the arrival of the threshing machine was still an event. The grain was not harvested automatically in the fields—by a combine that takes in the sheaves on one side, while sacks of grain all ready for the miller tumble out on the other side. No, the threshing was done in our home barn by a rented machine that went from farm to farm at harvest time. Its use required a whole chain of helpers. One of these would lift a sheaf of grain out of the farm wagon, which remained in the open because it was much too wide and piled much too high to get into the barn; he would toss it down to the next, who would pass it on, avoiding as far as possible leading with the "wrong," "hard-to-handle," or "ear" end, to the "big man" in the great rumbling machine, which, making the entire barn tremble with its vibrations, would swing the sheaf around and push it gently between the threshing cylinders. Straw came pouring out at the back of the machine, where it formed a pile which the next helper, with a long wooden pitchfork, would pass on to the last links in the chain, the village children, as a rule all present and accounted for, who, having taken their positions in the hayloft, moved the straw into the farthermost corners, thrusting and kicking it into the last open spaces they could find, working more and more in the dark as the straw piled up around them. All this—it grew lighter in the barn as the unloading and threshing proceeded—went on without a break in a smoothly coordinated process (which, however, the slightest false move could halt or disrupt) until the wagon was empty. Even the very last link in the chain, often on the verge of suffocation toward the end of the threshing operation, wedged between two mountains of straw and unable to find room in the dark for the last handfuls thrust at him, could disrupt the whole chain by slipping away from his post. But once the threshing was happily over and the deafening machine—impossible to make yourself understood, even by shouting directly into someone's ear—switched off: What silence, not only in the barn, but throughout the countryside; and what light, enfolding rather than blinding you. While the clouds of dust settled, we gathered in the farmyard on shaking knees, reeling and staggering, partly in fun. Our legs and arms were covered with scratches; we had straw in our hair, between our fingers and toes. And perhaps the most lasting effect of the day's work: the nostrils of men, women, and children alike were black, not just gray, with dust. Thus we sat—in my recollection always out of doors in the afternoon sun—savoring our common tiredness whether or not we were talking, some sitting on a bench, some on a wagon shaft, still others off on the grass of the bleaching field—the inhabitants of the whole neighborhood, regardless of generation, gathered in episodic harmony by our tiredness. A cloud of tiredness, an ethereal tiredness, held us together (while awaiting the next wagonload of sheaves). And my village childhood provided me with still other pictures of "we-tiredness."

But isn't it the past that transfigures?

If the past was of the kind that transfigures, it's all right with me. I believe in that sort of transfiguration. I know that those years were holy.

But isn't the contrast you suggest between manual work in common and solitary work on a harvest combine mere opinion and therefore suspect?

When I told you all that, it wasn't for the sake of the contrast, but of the pure picture; if such a contrast nevertheless forces itself on the reader's attention, it must mean that I haven't succeeded in communicating a pure picture. In the following, I shall have to take greater care than ever to avoid playing one thing off, even tacitly, against another or magnifying one thing at the expense of something else, in line with the Manichaean all-good or all-bad system, which is dominant nowadays even in what used to be the most open-minded, opinion-free mode of discourse, namely storytelling: Now I'm going to tell you about the good gardeners, but only to prepare you for what I shall have to say about the wicked hunters later on. The fact is, however, that I have affecting, communicable pictures of manual workers' tiredness, but none (thus far) of a combine operator's. Then, in our shared tiredness after threshing, I saw myself for once sitting in the midst of something resembling a "people," such as I later looked for time and time again in my native Austria, and time and again failed to find. I am referring not to the "tiredness of whole peoples," not to the tiredness that weighs on the eyelids of one late-born individual, but to the ideal tiredness that I would like to see descending on one particular small segment of the second postwar Austrian Republic, in the hope that all its groups, classes, associations, corps, and cathedral chapters may at last sit there as honestly tired as we villagers were then, all equals in our shared tiredness, united and above all purified by it. A French friend, a Jew, who was obliged to live in hiding during the German occupation, once told me, all the more movingly because his memories were transfigured by distance, that for weeks after the Liberation the whole country had been bathed in radiance, and that is how I should imagine an Austrian work-tiredness, shared by all. A criminal who has escaped scot-free may often manage to doze off, whether in a sitting or a standing position. His sleep, like that of many a fugitive, may be prolonged, deep, and stertorous, but tiredness, not to mention the tiredness that knits people together, is unknown to him; until the day when he snores his last, nothing in all the world will succeed in making him tired, unless perhaps his final punishment, for which he himself may secretly yearn. My entire country is alive with bouncy indefatigables of this breed, among them its so-called leaders; instead of joining the army of tiredness for so much as one moment, a swarming mob of habitual criminals and their accomplices, very different from those described above, of elderly but untiring mass murderers of both sexes, who throughout the country have secreted a new generation of equally tireless young fellows, who even now are training the grandchildren of the senior murderers to be secret-police agents, with the result that in this contemptible majority-country the many minorities will never be able to join forces in a community of tiredness; in this country, everyone will remain alone with his tiredness until the end of our political history. There was a time when I actually believed in the International Court of Justice, when I thought it could do something about my country (I'm not obliged to tell you how long ago that was). But that International Court seems to have gone out of existence; or, to say it in a different way: its decisions have not been put into effect within the borders of Austria and—as I have been forced to recognize since my brief moment of hope—never will be. There is no International Court of Justice, and the

Austrians, I am obliged to go on believing, are the first hopelessly corrupt, totally incorrigible people in history, forever incapable of repentance or conversion.

Isn't that last assertion a mere opinion?

It is not an opinion but a picture. For what I thought I also saw. What may be opinion and therefore untrue is the word *people*, for what I saw in my picture was not a "people" but the unrepentant "gang of the untired." True, this picture is contradicted by other pictures, which in the interest of fairness demand attention; but they do not penetrate as deep as the others; at the most, they offer a counterweight. My ancestors, as far back as I can trace them, were *Keuschler*, small, landless peasants; if any of them were skilled in a craft, it was carpentry. Time and again, I saw the carpenters of the region grouped together as a people of tiredness. That was in the days of the first rebuilding after the war. As the oldest of the children, I was often sent by the women of the family, my mother, my grandmother, and my sister-in-law, to deliver warm lunch pails to the construction workers in the area. All the men in the family who had not been killed in the war, even for a time my sixty-year-old grandfather, worked there with other carpenters putting up roofs. In my picture they sit eating their lunch not far from the frame of a house—once again that special way of sitting!—on rough-hewn beams or on peeled but not yet planed tree trunks. They have taken their hats off, and their foreheads with the hair plastered to them look milky white in contrast to their dark faces. All seem sinewy, fine-boned, and sparely built, I can't recall a single potbellied carpenter. They eat slowly and in silence; even my German stepfather, the "carpenter's helper," who could hold his own in the strange country and the unfamiliar village environment only with the help of his big-city bluster (may he rest in peace). After the meal they sat awhile, gently tired, talking, without jokes, without complaining, without raising their voices, mostly about their families, sometimes quietly about the weather, until in the end their work arrangements for the afternoon crowded out all other topics. Though there actually was a foreman, I had the impression that none of these workers dominated or commanded; this in a way was part of their tiredness. And yet, despite their heavy, inflamed eyelids—typical of that kind of tiredness—all were wide-awake, each one of them was presence of mind personified ("Here it comes!" An apple is tossed. "Got it!") and lively (time and again, several at once would spontaneously burst into a telling of stories: "Before the war, when Mother was still alive, we'd go and see her at the hospital in Sankt Veit, and that night we'd hike back home, a good fifty kilometers, by way of the Trixen Valley . . ."). The colors and shapes of my pictures of the fragmentary community of tiredness are the blue of work denims, the straight red marks that the guideline slaps on the beams, the red-and-violet of oval-shaped carpenter's pencils, the yellow of yardsticks, the oval of the air bubble in the spirit level. By now the sweaty hair on our temples had dried and fluffed up; the hats, which have been put back on, are free from badges, and pencils rather than chamois beards have been stuck in the bands. If transistor radios had existed in those days, I'm pretty certain they'd have stayed away from those building sites. Yet a kind of music seems to reach me from there—the music of clairaudient tiredness. Not to forget the way those places looked; again I say: it was a holy time—episodes of holiness. I myself, of course, was not one of those tired people (as I had been one among the servants of the threshing machine), and I envy them. But when later, in my adolescence, I might have been one of them, it became a very different matter from what it had been in the imagination of the lunch-pail carrier. When my grandmother died and my grandfather was pensioned and gave up farming, the great household community of the generations—others in the village as well as ours—went out of existence. My parents built a house of their own, and everyone in the family, down to the smallest child, had to help with the building. For me, too, a job was found, and I learned an entirely new kind of tiredness. My work in the early stages consisted largely of pushing a wheelbarrow loaded with stone blocks uphill to the building site, which was inaccessible to trucks, over a plank walk that had been laid over mud. I no longer saw it as work done by us all in common, but as sheer drudgery. The effort of pushing those loads uphill from morning till night took so much out of me that I no longer had eyes for the things around me, and could only stare straight ahead at the jagged gray stones I was hauling, at the gray streams of cement that came rolling down the path, and above all at the joints between planks, which regularly forced me to lift or tilt the barrow slightly on the corners and curves. Often enough, when we came to these gaps, my wheelbarrow capsized, and I with it. Those weeks taught me what forced labor or slavery might be. At the end of the day, I was "wrecked," as the peasants put it; my hands were bruised and my toes burned by the concrete that had oozed between them. Destroyed by tiredness, I would flop (rather than sit) down. Unable to swallow, I could neither eat nor speak. This particular tiredness—and that may have been its special characteristic—seemed to be terminal; one would never get over it. I fell asleep the moment I lay down, and awoke in the gray of dawn, when it was almost time for work, more exhausted than ever, as though the cruel drudgery had cleaned me out of everything that might have contributed to the most elementary sense of being alive—the feel of the early light, the wind on my temples—as though there would never be an end to this living death. Until then, when confronted by unpleasant chores, I had always been quick to think up dodges and evasions. Now I was even too worn out to shirk in my old familiar ways: "I have to study; there's an exam coming up"; "I'm going to the woods to gather mushrooms for all of you." In any case, nothing I could say would do a particle of good. Though, come to think of it, I was working for my own benefit—our house—my tiredness was invariably that of a hired hand, an isolating tiredness. Of course there were other jobs that were equally dreaded by just about everyone, such as digging ditches for water pipes: "This job is a bitch, a devil!" But oddly enough, my dead-tiredness lifted in time, giving way, to "carpenter-tiredness"? No, to a feeling of sportsmanship, to a Stakhanovite ambition, combined with a kind of gallows humor. I experienced still another kind of tiredness in my student days while working the morning shift—from early morning to early afternoon—in the shipping room of a department store during the Christmas and Easter rush, to make a little money. I'd get up at four to catch the first streetcar, urinate into an empty jam jar in my room so as not to disturb the landlady, and leave the house unwashed. The work was done by artificial light on the top floor of the building; it consisted of dismembering old cartons and with a gigantic guillotine cutting out enormous rectangles that would be used to reinforce the new cartons being packed in the adjoining room. In the long run, this activity, like chopping or sawing wood at home, did me good by leaving my thoughts free but, thanks to the steady rhythm, not too free. The new tiredness made itself felt when we stepped out into the street and separated after the shift. Alone in my tiredness, blinking, my glasses coated with dust, my open shirt collar soiled and rumpled, I suddenly had new eyes for the familiar street scene. I no longer saw myself as one with all these people who were going somewhere—to the stores, the railroad station, the movies, the university. Though wakefully tired, neither sleepy nor self-absorbed, I felt excluded from society—an eerie feeling. Moving in the opposite direction from all these other people, I was headed nowhere. I entered a lecture hall with the feeling that this was a forbidden room, and I found it even harder than usual to listen to that droning voice; what was being said wasn't meant for me, I hadn't even the status of a "special student." Every day I longed more and more to be back with the tired little group of morning-shift workers up in the loft, and today, when I try to recapture the picture, I realize that even then, when I was very young, only nineteen or twenty, long before I seriously took up writing, I ceased to feel like a student among students—an unpleasant, rather frightening feeling.

But isn't there something vaguely romantic about the way you derive all your pictures of tiredness from farmhands and manual laborers, and never from the upper or lower middle class?

I've never come in contact with a picturable tiredness among the middle class.

Can't you at least imagine one?

No. It seems to me that tiredness just isn't right for them; they regard it as a kind of misbehavior, like going barefoot. What's more, they can't supply an image of tiredness, because their activities don't lend themselves to that kind of thing. The most they can do is look "weary unto death" at the end, but we can all manage that, I hope. Nor am I able to visualize the tiredness of the rich and powerful, with the possible exception of deposed kings, such as Oedipus and Lear. On the other hand, I can't conceive of fully automated factories disgorging tired workers at closing time. I see only big, imperious-looking louts with smug faces and great flabby hands, who will hurry off to the nearest slot-machine establishment and carry on with their blissfully mindless manipulations. (I know what you're going to say now: "Before talking like that, you yourself should get good and tired, just for the sake of fairness." But there are times when I have to be unfair, when I want to be unfair. Anyway, I'm good and tired already from chasing after images, as you accuse me of doing.) Later on, I came to know still another kind of tiredness, comparable to what I experienced in the shipping room; that was when I finally started writing in earnest, day after day for months at a time—there was no other way out. Once again, when I went out into the city streets after the day's work, it seemed to me that I had lost my connection with all the people around me. But the way I felt about this loss of connection wasn't the same anymore. It no longer mattered to me that I had ceased to be a participant in normal everyday life; on the contrary, in my tiredness verging on exhaustion, my nonparticipation gave me an altogether pleasant feeling. No longer was society inaccessible to me; I, on the contrary, was now inaccessible to society and everyone in it. What are your entertainments, your festivities, your hugging and kissing to me? I had the trees, the grass, the movie screen on which Robert Mitchum displayed his inscrutable pantomime for me alone, and I had the jukebox on which, for me alone, Bob Dylan sang his "Sad Eyed Lady of the Lowlands," or Ray Davies his and my "I'm Not Like Everybody Else."

Wasn't that sort of tiredness likely to degenerate into arrogance?

Yes, I'd often, in looking myself over, surprise a cold, misanthropic arrogance or, worse, a condescending pity for all the commonplace occupations that could never in all the world lead to a royal tiredness such as mine. In the hours after writing, I was an "untouchable," enthroned, so to speak, regardless of where I happened to be: "Don't touch me!" And if in the pride of my tiredness I nevertheless let myself be touched, it might just as well have never happened. It wasn't until much later that I came to know tiredness as a becoming-accessible, as the possibility of being touched and of being able to touch in turn. This happened very rarely—only great events can happen so rarely—and hasn't recurred for a long while, as though such miracles were confined to a certain segment of human existence and could be repeated only in exceptional situations, a war, a natural catastrophe, or some other time of trouble. On the few occasions when I have been—but what verb goes with it?—*favored*? *struck*? with such tiredness, I was indeed going through a period of personal distress, during which, fortunately for me, I met someone who was in a similar state. This other person always proved to be a woman. Our distress was not enough to bind us; it also took an erotic tiredness after a hardship suffered together. There seems to be a rule that before a man and a woman can become a dream couple for some hours at a time they must have a long, arduous journey behind them, must have met in a place foreign to them both and as far as possible from any sort of home or hominess, and must have confronted a danger, or perhaps only a long period of bewilderment in the midst of the enemy country, which can also be one's own. This tiredness, in a place of refuge that has suddenly become quiet, may suddenly give these two, a man and a woman, to each other with a naturalness and fervor unknown in other unions, however loving; what happens then is "like an exchange of bread and wine," as another friend put it. Sometimes when I try to communicate the feeling of such a union in tiredness, a line from a poem comes to mind: "Words of love—each one of them laughing . . ." which isn't far from the "one body and one soul" cited above, though in that case both bodies were steeped in silence; or I would simply vary the words spoken in a Hitchcock film by a tipsy Ingrid Bergman while fondling the tired and (still) rather remote Cary Grant:

"Forget it—a tired man and a drunken woman—that won't add up to much of a couple." My variation: "A tired man and a tired woman—what a glorious couple that will be." Or "with you" appears as a single word, like the Spanish *contigo* . . . or in German (or English), perhaps instead of saying: "I'm tired of you," one might say: "I'm tired with you." In the light of these extraordinary findings, I see Don Juan not as a seducer but as a perpetually tired hero who can be counted on to be overcome by tiredness at the right time in the company of a tired woman, the consequence being that all women fall into his arms, but never waste a tear on him once the mysteries of erotic tiredness have been enacted; for what has happened between those two will have been for all time: two such people know of nothing more enduring than this one entwinement, neither feels the need of a repetition; in fact, both dread the thought. That's all very well, but how does this Don Juan bring on his forever new tiredness, which makes him and his mistress so wonderfully ready to succumb? Not only one or two but a thousand and three such simultaneities which, down to the tiniest patch of skin, engrave themselves forever on this pair of bodies, each and every impulse being genuine, unmistakable, congruent, and of course spontaneous. In any case, you and I, after such ecstasies of tiredness, would be lost to the usual bodily fuss and bother.

What did you have left when it was over?

Even greater tirednesses.

Are there, in your opinion, even greater tirednesses than those already referred to?

More than ten years ago, I took a night flight from Anchorage, Alaska, to New York. It was a long haul from Cook Inlet, great ice floes rushing in at high tide and galloping back into the ocean at low tide, a stopover amid snow flurries in the gray of dawn in Edmonton, Canada, another in Chicago after much circling around the airfield and waiting in line on the runway under the harsh morning sun, to the final landing in the sultry afternoon, miles out of New York. Arriving at the hotel, I felt ill, cut off from the world after a night without sleep, air, or exercise, and wanted to go straight to bed. But then I saw the streets along Central Park in the early-autumn sunlight. People seemed to be strolling about, as though on a holiday. I wanted to be with them and felt I'd be missing something if I stayed in my room. Still dazed and alarmingly wobbly from loss of sleep, I found a place on a sunlit café terrace, with clamor and gasoline fumes all around me. But then, I don't remember how, whether little by little or all at once, came transformation. I once read that depressives can be cured by being kept awake night after night; this "treatment" seemed to stabilize the fearsomely swaying "suspension bridge of the ego." I had that image before me when the torment of my tiredness began to lift. This tiredness had something of a recovery about it. Hadn't I heard people talk about "fighting off tiredness"? For me the fight was over. Now tiredness was my friend. I was back in the world again and even—though not because this was Manhattan—in its center. But there were other things, many, in fact, one more enchanting than the last. Until late that night I did nothing but sit and look; it was almost as if I had no need to draw breath. No spectacular breathing exercises or yoga contortions. You just sit and breathe more or less correctly in the light of your tiredness. Lots of beautiful women passed, sometimes an incredible number, from time to time their beauty brought tears to my eyes—and all, as they passed, took notice of me. I existed. (Strange that my look of tiredness was especially acknowledged by the beautiful women, but also by children and a few old men.) Neither they nor I thought of going any further and trying to strike up an acquaintance. I wanted nothing from them; just being able to look at them was enough for me. My gaze was indeed that of a good spectator at a game that cannot be successful without at least one such onlooker. This tired man's looking-on was an activity, it did something, it played a part; because of it, the actors in the play became better, more beautiful than ever—for one thing because while being looked at by eyes such as mine they took their time. As by a miracle, the tiredness of such an onlooker nullified his ego, that eternal creator of unrest, and with it all other distortions, quirks, and frowns; nothing remained but his candid eyes, at least as inscrutable as Robert Mitchum's. The action of this selfless onlooker encompassed far more than the beautiful female passersby and drew everything that lived and moved into its world-center. My tiredness articulated the muddle of crude perception, not by breaking it up, but by making its components recognizable, and with the help of rhythms endowed it with form—form as far as the eye could see—a vast horizon of tiredness.

But the scenes of violence, the clashes, the screams—did they become friendly forms on the vast horizon?

I have been speaking here of tiredness in peacetime, in the present interim period. In those hours there was peace, in the Central Park area as elsewhere. And the astonishing part of it was that my tiredness seemed to participate in this momentary peace, for my gaze disarmed every intimation of a violent gesture, a conflict, or even of an unfriendly attitude, before it could get started—this by virtue of a compassion very different from the occasional contemptuous pity that comes of creative tiredness: call it sympathy as understanding.

But what was so unusual about that gaze? Its special character?

I saw—and the other saw that I saw—his object at the same

time as he did: the trees under which he was walking, the book he held in his hand, the light in which he was standing, even if it was the artificial light of a store; the old fop *along with* this light-colored suit and the carnation he was holding; the salesman *along with* his heavy suitcase; the giant *along with* the invisible child on his shoulders; myself *along with* the leaves blowing out of the park; and every one of us *along with* the sky overhead.

Suppose there was no such object?

Then my tiredness created it, and in a twinkling the other, who a moment ago had still been wandering about in the void, felt surrounded by the aura of his object . . . And that's not all. Because of my tiredness, the thousands of unconnected happenings all about me arranged themselves into an order that was more than form; each one entered into me as the precisely fitting part of a finely attuned, light-textured story; and its events told themselves without the mediation of words. Thanks to my tiredness, the world cast off its names and became great. I have a rough picture of four possible attitudes of my linguistic self to the world: in the first, I am mute, cruelly excluded from events; in the second, the confusion of voices, of talk, passes from outside into my inner self, though I am still as mute as before, capable at the most of screaming; in the third, finally, life enters into me by beginning spontaneously, sentence for sentence, to tell stories, usually to a definite person, a child, a friend; and finally, in the fourth, which I experienced most lastingly in that day's clear-sighted tiredness, the world tells its own story without words, in utter silence, to me as well as to that gray-haired onlooker over there and to that magnificent woman who is striding by; all peaceable happening was itself a story, and unlike wars and battles, which need a poet or a chronicler before they can take shape, these stories shaped themselves in my tired eyes into an epic and, moreover, as then became apparent to me, an ideal epic. The images of the fugitive world meshed one with another, and took form.

Ideal?

Yes, ideal: because in this epic everything that happened was right; things kept happening, yet there was not too much or too little of anything. All that's needed for an epic is a world, a history of mankind, that tells itself as it should be. Utopian? The other day I read here on a poster: "La utopia no existe," which might be translated as "The no-place does not exist." Just give that a thought and history will start moving. In any case, my utopian tiredness of that day was connected with at least one place. That day I felt much more sense of place than usual. It was as though, no sooner arrived, I in my tiredness had taken on the smell of the place; I was an old inhabitant. And in similar spells of tiredness during the years that followed, still more associations attached themselves to that place. Total strangers spoke to me, perhaps because I looked familiar to them, or perhaps for no particular reason. In Edinburgh, where after looking for hours at Poussin's *Seven Sacraments*, which at last showed the Baptism, the Lord's Supper, and the rest in the proper perspective, I sat radiant with tiredness in an Italian restaurant, feeling self-conscious about being waited on—an exceptional state related to my tiredness; all the waiters agreed that they had seen me before, though each in a different place, one in Santorini (where I have never been), another last summer with a sleeping bag on Lake Garda—neither the sleeping bag nor the lake was right. In the train from Zurich to Biel after staying up all night celebrating the end of the children's school year, I was sitting opposite a young woman who had spent an equally sleepless night at a party celebrating the end of the Tour de Suisse bicycle race. On the instructions of the bank she worked for, which had co-sponsored the Tour, she had performed the duties of a hostess, distributing flowers and kisses to each prizewinner as he stepped forward . . . Her story came tumbling out of the tired woman as spontaneously as if we had known everything else about each other. One racer, who had won twice in a row and was rewarded with a second kiss, was so engrossed in his sporting prowess that he no longer recognized her, as she told me cheerfully, admiringly, and without a trace of disappointment. In addition to being tired, she was hungry, and she wasn't going to bed, she was going to eat lunch with her girlfriend in Biel. There, I realized, was another explanation for her unsuspecting trustfulness: in addition to *her* tiredness, her hunger. The tiredness of the well fed can't manage that. "We were hungry and tired," says the young woman in Dashiell Hammett's *The Glass Key* in telling Sam Spade her dream about the two of them: what brought them together, then and later, was hunger and tiredness. It seems to me that apart from children—the way they turn around and stare expectantly at the man sitting there—and other tired people, idiots and animals are most receptive to such tiredness. A few days ago an idiot here in Linares, hopping along absently hand in hand with a member of his family, seemed as startled at the sight of me, sitting on a bench exhausted by my literary efforts of the morning and afternoon, as if he had taken me for a fellow idiot or something even more amazing. Not only his Mongoloid eyes but his whole face beamed at me; he stopped still and had to be literally dragged away—his features expressing pure pleasure, simply because someone had seen him and acknowledged his existence. And this was not a unique occurrence. In many a time and place the idiots of the world, European, Arab, Japanese, presenting the drama of themselves with childlike pleasure, have been drawn into this tired idiot's field of vision. Once in Friuli, not far from the village of

Medea, when exhausted after completing a piece of work and walking for hours across the treeless plain, I came to the edge of a forest and saw two ducks, a deer, and a hare lying together in the grass. Catching sight of me, they seemed about to take flight, but then resumed their even rhythm; pulling up grass, browsing, waddling about. On the road near the Poblet monastery in Catalonia I fell in with two dogs, a big one and a small one, who may have been father and son. They joined up with me, sometimes following me, sometimes running on ahead. I was so tired that I forgot my usual fear of dogs, and besides, or so I imagined, my long wanderings in the region must have steeped me in its smell, so the dogs took me for granted. True enough, they began to play, the "father" describing circles around me and the "son" chasing him between my legs. Great, I thought. Here I have an image of true human tiredness: it creates openings, making room for an epic that will encompass all beings, now including the animals. Here perhaps a digression may be in order. In the chamomile-scented rubble outside Linares, where I go for a walk each day, I have observed very different interactions among human beings and animals. I can speak of them only in shorthand. Those scattered forms apparently resting in the shadows of the ruins or stone blocks but actually lying in ambush, within gunshot of the little cages fastened to flexible poles planted in the rubble. Cages so tiny that the fluttering of the inmates makes them sway, thus offering larger birds an alluring mobile bait. (But the shadow of the eagle is far away, sweeping across my paper as I sit in my eerily quiet eucalyptus grove hard by the ruins of the lead mine, my open-air studio during the ecstatic bellowing and trumpeting of the Spanish Easter Week); —or those excited children running out of the gypsy encampment on the heath, a sleek noble-headed dog frolicking around them, yelping with eagerness at the sight of the spectacle organized by a boy-almost-man: hare let loose on the savanna, dog speeding in pursuit, hare twisting, turning, and doubling back, but soon caught, dropped, caught again more quickly than before, flung this way and that in the dog's jaws. Dog racing across field, hare squeaking interminably, show ending with return of children to camp, dog jumping up, ringleader boy holding out hand, grabbing hare by ears; the hare wet with blood, still twitching a little, its paws go limp; its little face, seen in profile, held high above the children's heads, utterly helpless and forlorn, more sublime than the face of any animal or human being, leads the procession into the sunset. —Or only the other day, as I was on my way home to town from writing in the eucalyptus grove, a crowd of teenagers by the stone wall around the olive field, brandishing olive branches and reeds, shouting, running forward and back, pushing and kicking at a pile of stones, and from under the stones, now visible in the sunlight, a long, thick, coiled snake, at first barely moving, just the twitching of the head and the darting of the tongue—still heavy with winter sleep? Reeds raining down from all sides, splintering yet lethal; the assailants, hardly more than children, myself among them as I remember it, still howling and rushing back and forth; at last the snake rearing to full height yet cutting a pathetic figure, in no position to attack, not even threatening, just mechanically executing the hereditary gesture of the snake, and thus upraised in profile, with head crushed and blood flowing from its mouth, suddenly, just before collapsing under the shower of stones like the hare, a third figure, something like the one that appears for a moment at the back of the stage while the curtain, painted with the usual human and animal forms, rises. But why do I persist in telling and retelling such horrors, which communicate no story but at the most lend confirmation, while what my unifying tirednesses have to tell me calls forth again and again a natural stretching out which induces an epic breathing.

That's all very well, but don't you realize that those horrors were not mere horrors. Look at it this way. You were just going to record them, but in spite of yourself you were very nearly drawn into storytelling, and if in the end you avoided its verb form, the historical past, it was only by a deliberate trick. And besides, your horror stories are more colorful, or in any case more suggestive, than the infinitely peaceful incidents of your epic tiredness?

But I'm not interested in suggestiveness. I have no desire to persuade, not even with images. I only want to remind each one of you of his own very narrative tiredness. And its visual quality will soon become apparent, at the end of this essay—right now if I've become tired enough in the meantime.

But quite aside from your anecdotes and fragmentary glimpses, what is the essence of the ultimate tiredness? How does it work? What good is it? Does it enable a tired person to act?

It is itself the best action, because it is in itself a beginning, a doing, a getting under way, so to speak. This getting under way is a lesson. Tiredness provides teachings that can be applied. What, you may ask, does it teach? The history of ideas used to operate with the concept of the "Thing in itself"; no longer, for an object can never be manifested "in itself," but only in relation to me. But the tirednesses that I have in mind renew the old concept and give it meaning for me. What's more: they give me the idea along with the concept. And better still, with the idea of the thing, I possess, almost palpably, a law: The thing not only is, but *should* be just as it appears at the moment. And furthermore: in such fundamental tiredness, the thing is never manifested alone but always in conjunction with other things, and even if there are not very many, they will all be together in the end. "And now even the dog with its barking says: All together!" And in conclusion: such tirednesses demand to be shared.

Why so philosophical all of a sudden?

Right—maybe I'm not tired enough. In the hour of the ultimate tiredness, there's no room for philosophical questions. Time is also space, and space-time is also history. Being is also becoming. The other becomes I. Those two children down there before my tired eyes are also I. And the way the older sister is dragging her little brother through the room has a meaning and a value, and nothing is worth more than anything else—the rain falling on the tired man's wrist is worth as much as his view of the people walking on the other side of the river, both are good and beautiful, and that is as it should be, now and forever—and above all it is true. How the sister-I grabs me, the brother, by the waist—that is true. And in the tired look, the relative is seen as absolute and the part as the whole.

What becomes of perception?

I have an image for the "all in one": those seventeenth-century, for the most part Dutch floral, still lifes, in which a beetle, a snail, a bee, or a butterfly sits true to life, in the flowers, and although none of these may suspect the presence of the others, they are all there together at the moment, *my* moment.

Couldn't you try to express yourself concretely and not indirectly through historical images?

Very well; then sit down—I hope you've become tired enough by now—with me on that stone wall at the edge of the dirt road, or better still, because we'll be closer to the ground, squat down with me on the strip of grass in the middle of the road. See how all at once, with the help of this colored reflection, the world-map of the "all together" is revealed. Close to the earth, we are at the same time far enough away to see the rearing caterpillar, the beetle boring into the sand, and the ant hobbling over an olive at the same time as the strip of bark rolled into a figure eight before our eyes.

Not an illustrated report; tell me a story.

A few days ago the dead body of a mole was making its way through the dust of this Andalusian road as slowly and solemnly as the statues of sorrow that are carried about on stands during Easter Week here in Andalusia; under it, when I turned it over, there was a procession of glittering-gold carrion beetles. And last winter, on a similar dirt road in the Pyrenees, I squatted down in the exact same way as we are squatting now, and watched the snow falling in small grainy flakes, but, once it lay on the ground, indistinguishable from grains of light-colored sand; in melting, however, it left strange puddles, dark spots very different from those made by raindrops, much larger and more irregular as they trickled away into the dust. And as a child, at just the same distance from the ground as we are now, I was walking in the first morning light with my grandfather, on just such a dirt road in Austria, barefoot, just as close to the ground and just as infinitely far from the dispersed craters in the dust, where the raindrops had struck—my first image, one that will let itself be repeated forever.

At last your metaphors for the effects of tiredness introduce not only small-sized objects but also human measure. But why is the tired individual always you and no one else?

It always seemed to me that my greatest tirednesses were also ours. Late one night in Dutovlje in the Karst, the old men were standing at the bar. I had been at odds with them. Tiredness tells its story through the other, even if I've never heard of him. Those two over there with the slicked-down hair, the gaunt faces, the split nails, and fresh shirts are farmworkers, *labradores*, who have worked hard all day in the wilds and have come a long way on foot to the town bar, unlike all the others who are standing around here; the one over there, for instance, wolfing down his meal all alone, is a stranger to the region, whose home office has sent him to the Land Rover assembly plant in Linares far from his family, and the old man who can be seen day after day standing at the edge of the olive field, a little dog at his feet, his elbows propped on a fork of the tree, grieving for his dead wife. "Fantasy" comes to the ideally tired man but is different from the fantasy of the sleepers in the Bible or the *Odyssey*, who have visions: without visions his fantasy shows him what is. And now, though not tired, I have the gall to tell you my fantasy of the last stage of tiredness. In this stage the tired god sat tired and feeble in his tiredness, but—just a notch tireder than a tired human had ever been—all-seeing, with a gaze that, if acknowledged and accepted by those seen, regardless of where in the cosmos, would exert a kind of power.

That's enough about stages! Speak to me for once about the tiredness you're thinking of, just as your thoughts come to you, in confusion.

Thanks! Such confusion is at present just the thing for me and my problem. So let's have a Pindaric ode, not to a victor but to a tired man. I conceive of the Pentecostal company that received the Holy Ghost as tired to a man. The inspiration of tiredness tells them not so much what should, as what need not, be. Tiredness is the angel who touches the fingers of the one dreaming king, while the other kings go on sleeping dreamlessly. Healthy tiredness is in itself recovery. A certain tired man can be seen as a new Orpheus; the wildest beasts gather around him and are at last able to join in his tiredness. Tiredness gives dispersed individuals the keynote. The more sleepless nights he lived, though, the more brilliantly the private eye Philip Marlowe succeeded in solving his cases. The tired Odysseus won the love of Nausicaä. Tiredness makes you younger than you ever have been. Tiredness is greater than the self. Everything becomes extraordinary in the tranquility of tiredness—how extraordinary, for instance, is the bundle of paper that the astonishingly easygoing man over there is carrying across the astonishingly quiet Calle Cervantes. Epitome of tiredness. On Easter Eve long ago, at the commemoration of the Resurrection, the old men of the village used to lie prone before the tomb, wearing red brocade cloaks instead of their blue work clothes, the sunburned skin of their necks split into a polygonal design by their lifelong exertions; the dying grandmother in her quiet tiredness appeased the whole household, even her incorrigibly choleric husband; and every evening here in Linares I watched the growing tiredness of the many small children who had been dragged to the bars: no more greed, no grabbing hold of things, only playfulness. And with all that, is there still any need to say that even in low-level images of tiredness distinctions are preserved?

All very well and good; undeniably, your problem is concrete enough (despite the typically mystical stammering in your way of expressing it). But how are such tirednesses to be induced? By artificially keeping yourself awake? By means of long-distance flights? Forced marches? Herculean labors? By experimenting with dying? Have you a recipe for your utopia? Pep pills for the entire population? Or powders to be added to the drinking water in the Land of the Untired?

I know of no recipe, not even for myself. All I know is this: Such tiredness cannot be planned, cannot be taken as an aim. But I also know that it never sets in without a cause, but always after a hardship, a difficulty needed to be surmounted. And now let us rise and go out into the streets, among people, to see whether a little shared tiredness may not be waiting for us and what it may have to tell us?

But does real tiredness, or real asking for that matter, imply standing rather than sitting? Remember that gnarled old woman, harassed as usual by her son, who was always in a rush in spite of his gray hair, and how she pleaded: "Oh, let's just *sit* here a little longer."

Yes, let's sit, but not here in this lonely place, amid the rustling eucalyptus leaves, but on the edge of the boulevards, the *avenidas*, looking on, perhaps with a jukebox within reach.

You won't find a jukebox in all Spain.

There's one right here in Linares, a very strange one.

Tell me about it.

No. Another time. In an essay on the jukebox. Perhaps.

But before we go out into the street, one last image of tiredness.

All right. It is also my last image of mankind, reconciled in its very last moments, in cosmic tiredness.

Postscript

Those little birdcages in the savanna were not put there to attract eagles. In answer to my question, a man sitting at some distance from one of these rectangles told me he moved them out into the rubble field because he wanted to hear the little birds singing; and the olive branches thrust into the ground beside the cages were not intended to lure the eagles out of the sky, but to make the siskins *sing*.

Second postscript

Or do the siskins hop for the eagle up there in the sky—which the people would like to see swooping down for a change?

—LINARES, ANDALUSIA,
MARCH 1989

ESSAY ON THE JUKEBOX

Translated by Krishna Winston

Dar tiempo al tiempo.
—*Spanish saying*

And I saw her standing there.
—*Lennon/McCartney*

INTENDING TO MAKE A START AT LAST ON A LONG-PLANNED essay on the jukebox, he bought a ticket to Soria at the bus station in Burgos. The departure gates were in a roofed inner courtyard; that morning, when several buses were leaving at the same time for Madrid, Barcelona, and Bilbao, they had been thronged; now, in early afternoon, only the bus for Soria was parked there in the semicircle with a couple of passengers, presumably traveling alone, its baggage compartment open and almost empty. When he turned over his suitcase to the driver—or was it the conductor?—standing outside, the man said "Soria!" and touched him lightly on the shoulder. The traveler wanted to take in a bit more of the locale, and walked back and forth on the platform until the engine was started. The woman selling lottery tickets, who that morning had been working the crowd like a gypsy, was no longer to be seen in the deserted station. He pictured her having a meal somewhere near the indoor market of Burgos, on the table a glass of dark red wine and the bundle of tickets for the Christmas lottery. On the asphalt of the platform was a large sooty spot; the tailpipe of a since vanished bus must have puffed exhaust there for a long time, so thick was the black layer crisscrossed by the prints of many different shoe soles and suitcase wheels. He, too, now crossed this spot, for the specific purpose of adding his own shoe prints to the others, as if by so doing he could produce a good omen for his proposed undertaking. The strange thing was that on the one hand he was trying to convince himself that this "Essay on the Jukebox" was something inconsequential or casual, while on the other hand he was feeling the usual apprehension that overcame him before writing, and involuntarily sought refuge in favorable signs and portents—even though he did not trust them for a moment, but rather, as now, promptly forbade himself to do so, reminding himself of a comment on superstition in the *Characters* of Theophrastus, which he was reading on this trip: superstition was a sort of cowardice in the face of the divine. But, even so, the prints of these many and different shoes, including their various trademarks, layered on top of each other, white on black, and disappearing outside the circle of soot, were an image he could take with him as he continued his journey.

That he would buckle down to the "Essay on the Jukebox" in Soria had been planned for some time. It was now the beginning of December, and the previous spring, while flying over Spain, he had come upon an article in the airline magazine that featured this remote town in the Castilian highlands. Because of its location, far from any major routes, and almost bypassed by history for nearly a millennium, Soria was the quietest and most secluded town on the entire peninsula; in the center of town and also outside of town, standing by themselves in a desolate area, were several Romanesque structures, complete with well-preserved sculptures. Despite its smallness, the town of Soria was the capital of the province of the same name. In the early twentieth century Soria had been home to a man who, as a French teacher, then as a young husband, then almost immediately as a widower, had captured the region in his poems with a wealth of precise detail, the poet Antonio Machado. Soria, at an altitude of more than a thousand meters above sea level, was lapped at its foundations by the headwaters of the Duero, here very slow-moving, along whose banks—past the poplars that Machado called "singing" (*álamos cantadores*) because of the nightingales, *ruiseñores*, in their dense branches, and between cliffs that repeatedly narrowed to form canyons—according to the appropriately illustrated article, paths led far out into the untouched countryside . . .

With this "Essay on the Jukebox" he intended to articulate the significance this object had had in the different phases of his life, now that he was no longer young. Yet hardly any of his acquaintances had had anything to say when, in the last few months, he had embarked on a sort of playful market research and had asked them what they knew about this piece of machinery. Some, including, to be sure, a priest, had merely shrugged their shoulders and shaken their heads at the suggestion that such a thing could be of any interest. Others thought the jukebox was a kind of pinball machine, while still others were not even familiar with the word and had no idea what was meant until it was described as a "music box" or "music cabinet." Precisely such ignorance, such indifference stimulated him all the more—after the initial disappointment at finding, yet again, that not everyone shared his experiences—to take on this object, or this subject matter, especially since it seemed that in most countries and places the time of jukeboxes was pretty much past (he, too, was perhaps gradually getting beyond the age for standing in front of these machines and pushing the buttons).

Of course he had also read the so-called literature on jukeboxes, though intending to forget most of it on the spot; what would count when he began writing was primarily his own observations. In any case, there was little written on the topic. The authoritative work, at least up to now, was probably the *Complete Identification Guide to the Wurlitzer Jukeboxes*, published in 1984 in Des Moines, far off in the American Midwest. Author: Rick Botts. This is more or less what the reader recalled of the history of the jukebox: it was during Prohibition in the United States, in the twenties, that in the back-door taverns, the "speakeasies," automatic music players were first installed. The derivation of the term "jukebox" was uncertain, whether from *jute* or from the verb *jook*, which was supposed to be African in origin and meant "to dance." At any rate, the blacks used to gather after working in the jute fields of the South at so-called jute joints or juke joints, where they could put a nickel in the slot of the automatic music player and hear Billie Holiday, Jelly Roll Morton, or Louis Armstrong, musicians whom the radio stations, all owned by whites, did not play. The golden age of the jukebox began when Prohibition was lifted in the thirties, and bars sprang up everywhere; even in establishments like tobacco stores and beauty parlors there were automatic record players, because of space limitations no larger than the cash register and located next to it on the counter. This flowering ended, for the time being, with the Second World War, when the materials used to make jukeboxes were rationed—primarily plastic and steel. Wood replaced the metal parts, and then, in the middle of the war, all production was converted to armaments. The leading manufacturers of jukeboxes, Wurlitzer and Seeburg, now produced deicing units for airplanes and electromechanical components.

The form of the music boxes was a story in itself. Through

its form, the jukebox was supposed to stand out "from its not always very colorful surroundings." The most important man in the company was therefore the designer; while the basic structure for a Wurlitzer was a rounded arch, Seeburg as a rule used rectangular cases with domes on top. The principle seemed to be that each new model could deviate from the previous one only so much, so that it was still recognizable. This principle was so firmly established that a particularly innovative jukebox, shaped like an obelisk, topped not by a head or a flame but by a dish containing the speaker, which propelled the music up toward the ceiling, proved a complete failure. Accordingly, variation was confined almost exclusively to the lighting effects or to components of the frame: a peacock in the middle of the box, in constantly changing colors; plastic surfaces, previously simply colored, now marbled; decorative moldings, once fake bronze, now chromed; arched frames, now in the form of transparent neon tubes, filled with large and small bubbles in constant motion, "signed Paul Fuller"—at this point the reader and observer of this history of design finally learned the name of its main hero and realized that he had always unconsciously wanted to know it, ever since he had first been overcome with amazement at encountering one of these mighty objects glowing in all the colors of the rainbow in some dim back room.

The bus ride from Burgos to Soria went east across the almost deserted *meseta*. Even with all the empty seats, it seemed as though there were more people together on the bus than anywhere outside in those barren highlands. The sky was gray and drizzly, the few fields between cliffs and clay lay fallow. With a solemn face and dreamy, wide-open eyes, a young girl ceaselessly cracked and chewed sunflower seeds, something often seen in Spanish movie theaters or on promenades; the husks rained to the floor. A group of boys with sports bags kept bringing new cassettes to the driver, who willingly broadcast their music over the loudspeakers mounted above every pair of seats, instead of the afternoon radio program. The one elderly couple on the bus sat silent and motionless. The husband seemed not to notice when one of the boys unintentionally jostled him every time he went up front; he put up with it even when one of the young fellows stood up while talking and stepped into the aisle, leaned on the back of the old man's seat, and gesticulated right in his face. He did not stir, did not even shift his newspaper to one side when the edges of the pages curled in the breeze created by the boy's gestures. The girl got off the bus and set out alone over a bleak knoll, her coat drawn close around her as she headed across a seemingly trackless steppe without a house in sight; on the floor beneath her vacated seat lay a heap of husks, not as big as one would have expected.

Later the plateau was punctuated by sparse oak groves, the trees small like shrubs, the withered leaves trembling grayish in the branches, and, after an almost unnoticeable pass—in Spanish the word was the same as for harbor, as the traveler learned from his pocket dictionary—which formed the border between the provinces of Burgos and Soria, came plantations of gleaming brown pines rooted atop cliffs, many of the trees also torn from their bit of soil and split, as after a storm, whereupon this closeness on either side of the road immediately gave way again to the prevailing barren landscape. At intervals the road was crossed by the rusted tracks of the abandoned rail line between the two cities, in many places tarred over, the ties overgrown or completely invisible. In one of the villages, out of sight of the road beyond rocky outcroppings—which the bus turned onto and from which, now even emptier, it had to return to the road—a loose street sign banged against the wall of a house; through the window of the village bar, the only thing visible, the hands of cardplayers.

In Soria it was cold, even colder than in Burgos, and bitter cold in comparison with San Sebastián down there by the sea, where he had come into Spain the previous day. But the snow he had been hoping for as a sort of companion to his undertaking did not fall; there was drizzle instead. In the drafty bus station he immediately noted down the times of departure for Madrid, or at least Zaragoza. Outside, on the main road at the edge of the town, between smaller tumbledown houses, shells of high-rises, and the rock-strewn steppe (which otherwise appealed to him), tractor-trailer trucks that seemed coupled together, all with Spanish license plates, thundered past, their wheels splattering a film of mud. When he caught sight of a British marker among them, and then the slogan on the canvas cover that he could understand at a glance, without having to translate it first, he felt for a moment almost at home. Similarly, during a longish stay in just such a foreign Spanish town, where no one knew any other language and there were no foreign newspapers, he had sometimes taken refuge in the only Chinese restaurant, where he actually understood even less of the language but felt safe from all that concentrated Spanish.

It was beginning to get dark, and outlines were blurring. The only highway signs pointed to distant capitals such as Barcelona and Valladolid. So he set out down the street with his heavy suitcase—he had been traveling a long time and had intended to stay in Soria into the New Year. He had found several times that the centers of these Spanish towns, which at first glance seemed almost invisible, were somewhere down below, beyond steppe-like stretches without houses, hidden in the valleys of dried-up rivers. He would stay here at least for the night; this once—he actually felt it as a sort of obligation—he had to get to know the place, now that he was here, and also do it justice (although at the moment, shifting his suitcase from one hand to the other every few steps and trying to avoid bumping into the natives, just beginning their evening ritual of strutting along, straight ahead, he did not succeed), and besides, as far as his "Essay on the Jukebox" was concerned, and in general, he had time, as he told himself now, as often before, in this instance using a verb from the Greek, borrowed from his reading of Theophrastus: *s-cholazo, s-cholazo.*

Yet all he could think of was running away. For his project, one friend or another had offered him, who for some years now had been roaming about without a home, his second apartment or third house, standing empty as winter came on, with silence all around, at the same time in a familiar culture, above all with the language of his childhood, which stimulated (and at the same time soothed) him right there on the horizon, to be reached at any time on foot. Yet his thought of running away did not include going back to where he came from. German-speaking surroundings were out of the question for him now, as was, for example, La Rochelle, with French, which was like second nature to him, where a few days ago he had felt like a stranger in the face of the wide Atlantic, the squat, pastel houses, the many movie theaters, the depopulated side streets, the clock tower by the old harbor that reminded him of Georges Simenon and those of his books that were set there. Not even San Sebastián with its much warmer air and clearly visible semicircular bay on the often turbulent Bay of Biscay, where just a short while ago, before his eyes, the floodwaters had surged upstream at night along the banks of the Basque Urumea River—while in the middle the current had flowed toward the sea—and in a bar, unlit and cold, as if it had been out of operation for years, stood a jukebox, made in Spain, clumsy, almost without design. Perhaps it was a compulsion in him that he forbade himself to run away, to retrace any of his steps, permitting himself only to move on, ever onward across the continent—and perhaps also a compulsion that now that he found himself without obligations and commitments, after a period of being much in demand, he felt that to get started on writing he had to subject himself, if writing was to have any justification at all, to barely tolerable, inhospitable conditions, to a marginal situation that threatened the very basis of daily life, with the added factor that, along with the project of writing, a second project had to be essayed: a sort of investigation or sounding-out of each foreign place, and exposure of himself, alone, without benefit of teachers, to a language that at first had to be as unfamiliar as possible.

Yet now he wanted to run away, not only from this town but also from his topic. The closer he had come to Soria, the intended site for writing, the more insignificant his subject, the "jukebox," had appeared. The year 1989 was just coming to an end, a year in which in Europe, from day to day and from country to country, so many things seemed to be changing, and with such miraculous ease, that he imagined that someone who had gone for a while without hearing the news, for instance voluntarily shut up in a research station or having spent months in a coma after an accident, would, upon reading his first newspaper, think it was a special joke edition pretending that the wish dreams of the subjugated and separated peoples of the continent had overnight become reality. This year, even for him, who had a background devoid of history and a childhood and youth scarcely enlivened, at most hindered, by historic events (and their neck-craning celebrations), was the year of history: suddenly it seemed as if history, in addition to all its other forms, could be a self-narrating fairy tale, the most real and realistic, the most heavenly and earthly of fairy tales. A few weeks earlier, in Germany, an acquaintance, about to set out to see the Wall, now suddenly open, where he was "determined to be a witness to history," had urged him to come along so that these events could be "witnessed by a person good with imagery and language." And he? He had used the excuse of "work, gathering material, preparations"–immediately, instinctively, actually shrinking from the experience, without thinking (though picturing how the very next morning the leading national newspaper would carry, properly framed, the first batch of poems produced by the poetic witnesses to history, and the following morning, likewise, the first song lyrics). And now that history was apparently moving along, day after day, in the guise of the great fairy tale of the world, of humanity, weaving its magic (or was it merely a variation on the old ghost story?), he wanted to be here, far away, in this city surrounded by steppe and bleak cliffs and deaf to history, where, in front of the televisions that blared everywhere, all the people fell silent only once, during a local news item about a man killed by collapsing scaffolding—and here he wanted to essay the unworldly topic of the jukebox, suitable for "refugees from the world," as he told himself now; a mere plaything, according to the literature, to be sure, "the Americans' favorite," but only for the short span of that "Saturday-night fever" after the end of the war. Was there anyone in the present time, when every day was a new historic date, more ridiculous, more perverse than himself?

He did not really take this thought seriously. Of far greater concern was the realization that his little project seemed to contradict what was occurring, more and more powerfully and urgently with the passing years, in the deepest of his nocturnal dreams. There, in the dream depths, his inner pattern revealed itself to him as an image, as image upon image: this he experienced with great force in his sleep, and he continued to dwell on it after awakening. Those dreams insistently told him a story; they told, though only in monumental fragments, which often degenerated into the usual dream nonsense, a world-encompassing epic of war and peace, heaven and earth, West and East, bloody murder, oppression, rebellion and reconciliation, castles and hovels, jungles and sports arenas, going astray and coming home, triumphal unions between total strangers and sacramental marital love, with innumerable, sharply delineated characters: familiar strangers, neighbors who came and went over the decades, distant siblings, film stars and politicians, saints and sinners, ancestors who lived on in these dreams transformed (as they had been in reality), and always new to the children, to the child of the children, who was one of the main characters.

As a rule he himself did not appear, was merely a spectator and listener. As forceful as the images were the feelings this person had; some of them he never experienced while awake, for instance reverence for a simple human face, or ecstasy at the dream blue of a mountain, or even piety (this, too, a feeling) in the face of nothing but the realization "I'm here"; he was acquainted with other feelings as well, but they did not become pure and incarnate to him except in the sensuous intensity of his epic dreaming, where he now experienced not gratitude but the very essence of gratitude, likewise the essence of compassion, the essence of childlikeness, the essence of hatred, the essence of amazement, the essence of friendship, of grief, of abandonment, of fear in the face of death.

Awakening, as if aired out and leavened by such dreams, he felt spreading in waves far beyond him the rhythm he would have to follow with his writing. And again, not for the first time, he was postponing this task, in favor of something inconsequential? (It was those dreams that engendered such thoughts; no one else had authority over him.) And his habit of thinking that, transient as he was, he could commit himself only to occasional pieces—after all, Simenon's short novels, most of them written abroad, in hotel rooms, could hardly be said to have epic breadth—wasn't that again, as his dream reproached him, one of those excuses he had been using for too long now? Why didn't he settle down, no matter where? Didn't he notice that his travels were more and more just a kind of aimless wandering?

When "Essay on the Jukebox" had been merely a glimmer, he had had in mind as a possible motto something Picasso had said: One made pictures the way princes made their children—with shepherdesses. One never portrayed the Pantheon, one never painted a Louis XV fauteuil, but one made pictures with a cottage in the Midi, with a packet of tobacco, with an old chair. But the closer he came to carrying out his plan, the less applicable this painter's saying seemed to a writer's subject matter. The epic dreams manifested themselves too powerfully, too exclusively, and also too contagiously (infecting him with a yearning to translate them into the appropriate language). He was familiar with the phenomenon from his youth, yet always amazed at how, toward the winter solstice, night after night these dreams turned up, predictably, so to speak; with the first image of half sleep the gate to narrative swung open, and narrative chanted to him all night long. And besides: What did an object like the jukebox, made of plastic, colored glass, and chromed metal, have to do with a chair or a cottage? Nothing. Or perhaps something, after all?

He knew of no painter in whose work there was a jukebox, even as an accessory. Not even the Pop artists, with their magnifying view of everything mass-produced, non-original, derivative, seemed to find the jukebox worth bringing into focus. Standing in front of a few paintings by Edward Hopper, with isolated figures in the dim bars of an urban no-man's-land, he almost had a hallucination, as if the objects were there, but painted over, as it were, an empty, glowing spot. Only one singer came to mind, Van Morrison, to whom the "roar of the jukebox" had remained significant forever, but that was "long gone," a folk expression for "long ago."

And besides: Why did his picture of what there was to say of this object immediately take the form of a book, even if only a very small one? After all, wasn't this thing called a book intended, as he conceived it, for the reflection, sentence by sentence, of natural light, of the sun, above all, but not for the description of the dimming artificial light produced by the revolving cylinders of an electrical device. (At least this was the traditional image of a book that he could not shake off.) So wasn't a small piece of writing like this more suitable for a newspaper, preferably for the weekend magazine, on the nostalgia pages, with color photographs of jukebox models from the earliest times to the present?

Having reached this point in his ruminations, ready simply to drop everything toward which his thoughts had pointed in recent months ("Be silent about what is dear to you, and write about what angers and provokes you!"), resolved to enjoy his time for a while, doing nothing and continuing to be a sightseer on the Continent, he suddenly experienced a remarkable pleasure in the possible meaninglessness of his project—freedom!—and at the same time the energy to get to work on this little nothing, though if possible somewhere other than in this world-forsaken town of Soria.

For the night he found a room in a hotel named after a medieval Spanish king. Almost every strange place he had encountered on his travels that had seemed at first sight insignificant and isolated had revealed itself to him, when he set out to walk it, as unexpectedly spread out, as part of the world; "What a big city!" he had marveled again and again, and even

"What a big town!" But Soria, to whose narrow streets he entrusted himself on that rainy evening, did not expand, even when he groped his way in the dark out of town and uphill to where the ruined citadel stood; no glittering *avenida*; the town, nothing but a few faded boxlike walls along bends in the narrow streets, revealed itself to him, as he then wandered from bar to bar, all of them almost empty already, enlivened now by the repetitious siren songs of the slot machines, as an all-too-familiar Central European town, only with more blackness within the city limits—the winter-deserted circle of the bullfighting ring—and surrounded by blackness. He had already concluded that nothing remained to be discovered and generated there. But for now it was nice to be walking without luggage. The front row of a bookstore's display consisted exclusively of books by Harold Robbins—and why not? And in a small square toward midnight the damp, jagged leaves of the plane trees glittered and beckoned. And the ticket booths of the two movie houses, the Rex and the Avenida, had their windows, almost invisible, as only in Spain, next to the wide entrances, looking directly out on the street, and inside, half cut off by the frames, showed the face of what seemed the identical old woman. And the wine did not have a small-town taste. And the pattern on the sidewalk tiles in the town of Soria consisted of interlocking squares, rounded at the edges, while the corresponding pattern in the city of Burgos had been battlements? And the Spanish word for "equanimity" was *ecuanimidad*. He made up a litany with this word, alternating it with that Greek word for having time.

In his dream, a hundred people appeared. A general, at the same time an epigone of Shakespeare, shot himself out of sorrow at the state of the world. A hare fled across a field, a duck swam downriver. A child disappeared without a trace, before everyone's eyes. The villagers, according to hearsay, were dying from one hour to the next, and the priest was completely taken up with burials. (Strange, the role of hearsay in dreams—it was neither said nor heard, but simply moved silently through the air.) Grandfather's nosebleeds smelled of damp dog hair. Another child had the first name Soul. Someone proclaimed, loudly this time, the importance of hearing in these times.

The next day—it remained rainy, and according to the newspaper, Soria was again the coldest province in Spain—he set out for a farewell stroll through town. Without having intended it, he suddenly found himself standing before the façade of Santo Domingo, its age immediately revealed by its dimensions and the light sandstone, worn smooth in many places by the wind. What a jolt he always received from Romanesque structures; he at once felt their proportions in himself, in his shoulders, his hips, the soles of his feet, like his actual, hidden body. Yes, corporeality: that was the sensation with which he now approached, as slowly as possible, this church shaped like a grain box, in a wide arc. In the very first moment, taking in the delicacy of the surface with its rounded arches and figures, he had thought of a phrase used by Borges, "the brotherliness of the beautiful," yet at the same time he was overcome with reluctance to absorb the whole thing at once, and he decided to postpone until evening departing for who knows where, and before leaving to come back again, when the daylight on the stone carvings would have changed. For the time being, he merely tried to identify variations in the groups of figures, already dear and familiar to him. And variations there were (without his having to look for them very long), as always in Romanesque sculpture, and they appeared to him again as the secret emblems of the place. Here in Soria they were visible as far as the eye could see: the solicitous way

God the Father bent at the hips as he helped the newly created Adam to his feet; the blanket, almost smooth in one representation, in other portrayals consistently lumpy, under which the Three Kings slumbered; the acanthus leaf, shell-shaped, the size of a tree, that rose behind the empty tomb after the Resurrection; in a semicircle above the portal (in almond form the outline of the smiling father with the likewise smiling son on his knees, balancing the thick stone book), the allegorical animals representing the Evangelists, crouching not on the ground but on the laps of angels, and not just the apparently newborn lion cub and the bull calf, but even the mighty eagle . . .

As he hurried away, he looked back over his shoulder and saw the delicately carved housing—all the more clearly its emptiness—standing, in the expression used by the cabaret artist Karl Valentin, "out in the open": from this vantage point, the structure, as broad as it was squat (all the apartment buildings around it were taller), with the sky above, in spite of the trucks roaring by, offered a positively ideal image: the building, so utterly different from the rigid façades surrounding it, appeared playful, active precisely in its tranquility—it was playing. And the thought came to him that back then, eight hundred years ago, at least in Europe, for the duration of one stylistic period, human history, individual as well as collective, had been wonderfully clear. Or was that only the illusion conveyed by this absolutely consistent form (not a mere style)? But how had such a form, at once majestic and childlike, and so readily comprehended, emerged?

Soria, as became apparent now by day, lay between two hills, one wooded and one bare, in a valley sloping down to the Duero. The river flowed past the last, scattered houses, on the other side a vast expanse of craggy land. A stone bridge spanned the river, bearing the road to Zaragoza. At the same time as the arches, the newly arrived observer noted their number. A gentle wind was blowing, and the clouds were in motion. Down there, among the leafless poplars along the bank, an excited dog was chasing the leaves that swirled up now here, now there. The reeds were flattened into the dark water; only a few cattails stuck out. The stranger—strange?—given access here by the locale—struck out in the opposite direction toward the well-known promenade of the poet Machado and went upriver, following a dirt path crisscrossed by the roots of the pines. Silence; a current of air at his temples (he had once imagined that one of the manufacturers responsible for such things might offer for these parts of the face a special moisturizer, so that even the slightest puff of air would be felt by the skin, as the epitome of—what should one call it?—the here-and-now).

Back from the wide-open spaces, he had a cup of coffee in a bar down by the river called Río, a young gypsy behind the counter. A few retired men—the Spanish word, according to the dictionary, was *jubilados*—were without exception watching the morning TV program with utter concentration and enthusiasm. From the incessant traffic passing on the highway, glasses and cups shook in the hands of all those present. In one corner stood a barely knee-high cylindrical cast-iron stove, tapered toward the top, with vertical fluting and in the middle an ornament like a scallop shell; in the grate down below the fire glowed red-hot. From the tiled floor rose the scent of the fresh sawdust that had been strewn that morning.

Out on the street, as he was climbing the hill, he came upon an elder, its trunk as thick as a sequoia, its short, bright branches forming a myriad of interwoven and crisscrossed arches. No superstition, even without such signs and portents: he would stay in Soria and, as planned, get to work on his "essay." In between he intended to soak up as much as possible of the mornings and evenings of this easily read little city. "No, I'm not leaving until the thing is done!" In Soria he would watch the last leaves sail off the plane trees. And now the landscape was bathed in that dark, clear light, as if streaming from the earth below, that had always encouraged him to go off at once and write, write, write—without a subject, or for that matter on something like the jukebox. And out into the wide-open spaces, with which here, scarcely out of town, one was promptly surrounded—in which major cities was that the case?—was where he would go every day before sitting down to work, to find the peace and quiet his head required more and more as he got older; once tuned to the silence, the sentences were supposed to take shape on their own; but afterward he would expose himself to the racket, as well as the quieter corners, of the city; no passageway, no cemetery, no bar, no playing field could be left unnoticed in its respective uniqueness.

But it turned out that just now several Spanish holidays fell at the same time—travel time—and so there would be no rooms available in Soria until the beginning of the following week. That was all right with him; it meant he could again postpone getting started, his usual pattern. And besides, forced to decamp temporarily to another city, he could, upon his departure and return, form a picture of Soria's location, remote on the high plateau, also from other directions, not only the westerly one from Burgos; he imagined that would be useful for what lay ahead. So he had two days, and he decided to spend the first in the north, the second in the south, both in places that lay outside Castile, first Logroño in the wine-growing region of La Rioja, then in Zaragoza in Aragon; this plan emerged mainly from his study of the bus schedules. But for the time being he sat down in one of those Spanish back-room restaurants where he felt sheltered because there one could be by oneself and yet, through walls no thicker than planks and the frequently open sliding door, follow what was going on out in the bar, where, what with a television set and pinball machines, things were almost always pretty lively.

In mid-afternoon a nun was the only other passenger on the bus to Logroño. It was raining, and in the mountain pass between the two provinces the route seemed to lead through the middle of the main rain cloud; other than its billowing grayness, there was nothing to be seen through the windows. From the bus's radio came "Satisfaction" by the Rolling Stones, a song that more than any other stood for that "roar of the jukebox," and was one of very few that had held their own in jukeboxes all over the world (had not been replaced), a "classic," one of the passengers thought to himself—while the other, in her black monastic garb, talked with the driver, to the accompaniment of the space-filling sonority of Bill Wyman's bass, which seemed to command respect, about the construction accident that had occurred in a side street nearby while he was eating in his sheltered back-room restaurant: two men crushed under reinforcing rods and freshly poured concrete. Next came Jacques Brel's "Ne me quitte pas" on the radio, that song pleading with the beloved not to leave him, another of those few songs that constituted what might be called the classics of the jukebox, at least according to his inquiries in French-speaking countries, and listed as a rule on the far right in the sacrosanct column (where in Austrian music boxes, for example, one found so-called folk music, and in Italian ones operatic arias and choruses, above all "Celeste Aïda" and the prisoners' chorus from *Nabucco*). But it was strange, the traveler thought, that the Belgian singer's psalm, rising out of the depths, the human voice almost alone, holding nothing back, searingly personal—"I tell you this, and you alone!"—did not seem at all suitable for an automatic record player set up in a public place, coin-operated, yet did seem suitable here, in this almost empty bus taking the curves of a pass almost two thousand meters above sea level, crossing a gray no-man's-land of dreary drizzle and fog.

The pattern of the sidewalk tiles in Logroño was bunches of grapes and grape leaves, and the town had an official chronicler with a daily page to himself in the newspaper, *La Rioja*. Instead of the Duero, the river here was the headwaters of the Ebro, and instead of being on the edge of town, it ran straight through the middle, with the newer part of the city as usual on the opposite bank. High snowbanks lined the wide river; on closer inspection, they turned out to be industrial effluent rocking in the current, and against the façades of the tall buildings on both sides of the river, laundry flapped in the dusky rain. Although he had observed a similar sight in Soria, and although Logroño, down here in the wine-growing plains with a noticeably milder climate, showed itself in its holiday illumination to be an expansive, elegant city with *avenidas* and arcades, he felt something like the tug of homesickness at the prospect of settling in for the winter up there on the *meseta*, where he had spent barely a night and half a day.

Zaragoza on the following day, to the southeast and even farther down in the broad Ebro Valley, had its sidewalks decorated with looping serpentines, which, he thought, represented the meanders of the river, and in fact the town appeared to him, after his first fruitless wanderings in search of the center, a pattern by now familiar to him in Spain, as a royal city, as indicated by the name of the soccer club. Here he could have read foreign newspapers every day, seen all the latest films in the original language, as only in a metropolis, and been there on the weekends when one royal team played against another from Madrid, with Emilio Butragueño himself on the ball—he had a pair of small binoculars in his luggage. Butragueño's uniform was always clean, even in the mud, and one felt one could believe him when he once replied to a reporter who asked whether soccer was an art form: "Yes, for seconds at a time." In the city's theater Beckett was being performed, and people were buying tickets as they did at movie box offices, and in the art museum, looking at the paintings of Goya, who had served his apprenticeship here in Zaragoza, he could have acquired the same receptivity of the senses for work as out there in the stillness around Soria, as well as the agreeable impertinence with which this painter infected one. Yet now only the other town could be considered, where, on the rock-strewn slopes adjacent to the new construction, flocks of sheep had already worn paths and where, despite the altitude, sparrows flew straight up in the wind—he would have missed them. (Someone had once observed that something you could always count on seeing on the television news, in an on-location report, whether from Tokyo or Johannesburg, was the sparrows: in the foreground a group of statesmen lined up for the camera, or smoking ruins; in the background the sparrows.)

What he undertook to do instead in these two cities was to look casually for a jukebox; there had to be at least one in Logroño as in Zaragoza, from earlier times and still in operation (a newly installed one was unlikely; in the Spanish bars the least bit of free space belonged to the slot machines that were squeezed in, one on top of the other). He thought that in the course of time he had developed a sort of instinct for possible jukebox locations. There was little hope downtown, or in urban renewal areas, or near historic monuments, churches, parks, avenues (not to mention the fancy residential sections). He had almost never come upon a music box in a spa or winter resort (although the usually unknown, out-of-the-way neighboring communities were under suspicion, so to speak—O Samedan near Saint Moritz), almost never in yacht harbors or seaside resorts (but certainly in fishing harbors and, even more frequently, in ferry stations: O Dover, O Ostende, O Reggio di Calabria, O Piraeus, O Kyle of Lochalsh with the ferry across to the Inner Hebrides, O Aomori far in the north of the Japanese main island of Honshu, with the meanwhile discontinued ferry over to Hokkaido), less frequently in bars on the mainland and in the interior than on islands and near borders. In his experience, the following locations were especially hot: housing developments along highways, too sprawling to be villages, yet without a downtown, off the beaten track for any kind of tourist traffic, in almost uncontoured plains without lakes nearby (and if there was a river, far outside of town and dried up during most of the year), inhabited by unusual numbers of foreigners, foreign workers and/or soldiers (garrisons), and even there jukeboxes could be ferreted out neither in the middle—this often marked by nothing more than a larger rain puddle—nor on the outskirts (there, or even farther out, along the highways, one found at most a discotheque), but in between, most likely next to the barracks, by the railroad station, in the gas-station bar, or in an isolated saloon along a canal (of course in a bad neighborhood, "on the other side of the freight tracks," for instance, the face of the most faceless conglomerations). Such a prime location for a jukebox, aside from the one of his birth, he had once found on the Friuli plain, in Casarza, which has given itself the epithet "della Delizia" because of the type of grapes harvested in the region. From the pleasant, wealthy, jukebox-purged capital of Udine he had arrived there one summer evening, "behind the Tagliamento," going on only six words from a poem by Pasolini, who had spent part of his youth in this small town and later had castigated the jukeboxes of Rome, together with the pinball machines, as an American continuation of the war by other means: "in the desperate void of Casarza." After an attempted walking tour that would include the outskirts of town, soon broken off because of the traffic on all the arterial roads, he turned around, went at random into the bars, of which there were not a few, and in almost every one he could see from the entrance a jukebox glowing at him (one fancy one had a VCR with a screen above it, from which the sound also emanated). And all these variously shaped old and new boxes were in operation, playing not background music, as was often the case elsewhere, but loud, insistent music; they were blaring. It was a Sunday evening, and in the bars—the closer he got to the railroad station, the more so—farewells were taking place or recruits were already waiting out the last hours before having to report for duty at midnight, most of them apparently having just returned by train from a short furlough. As it got later, most of them no longer formed groups but sat there by themselves. They gathered around a Wurlitzer, a reproduction of the classic rainbow-shaped type, with bubbles pulsing around the rainbow. The soldiers were clustered so thickly that the blinking lights of the machine peeked through their bodies here and there, and their faces and necks, bent toward the record arm, were bathed alternately in blue, red, and yellow. The street across from the station formed a wide curve behind them and immediately disappeared into the darkness. In the station bar itself, the surfaces were already being washed down. But a couple of the fellows in gray-and-brown uniforms were still hovering near the jukebox, some of them with their duffel bags already on their shoulders. Here, to match the neon lighting, the jukebox was a newer, no-nonsense model in bright metal. Each man stood there by himself, and at the same time as if in formation around the apparatus, which, in the otherwise empty room, with the tables shoved against the wall and a chair here and there, boomed out at a higher volume over the damp tiled floor. While one of the soldiers stepped aside as the mop approached, his eyes, wide open, unblinking, remained fixed in one direction; another lingered, his head turned back over his shoulder, on the threshold. It was full moon, in the glass door the shaking, rattling, pounding, long-drawn-out, of a dark freight train passing, which blocked the cornfields beyond the tracks. At the bar the young woman with even, fine features and a gap between her teeth.

But in these Spanish towns his instinct betrayed him every time. Even in bars in the poorer parts of town, behind piles of debris, at the end of a cul-de-sac, with that dim lighting that here and there made him hasten his steps even at a distance, he did not find so much as the coldest trail, even in the form of a paler outline on a sooty wall, of the object he sought. The music played there came—standing outside, he sometimes let himself be deceived through the walls—from radios, cassette players, or, in special cases, from a record player. The Spanish street bars, and there seemed to be more of them in every town than anywhere else in the world, were perhaps either too new for such an almost ancient object (and all lacked the back rooms suitable for it), or too old, and intended mainly for old people, who sat there seriously playing cards—jukebox and cardplaying, yes, but only in the less serious establishments—or sat with their heads propped in their hands, alone. And he imagined that in their heyday jukeboxes had been banned by the dictatorship here, and after that had simply not been in demand. To be sure, he made not a few discoveries in the course of his futile searching, taking a certain pleasure in the almost sure fruitlessness of it, about the special corners, the variations in the seemingly so similar cities.

Back from Zaragoza in Soria, in the east of whose province he had seen hardly anything, traveling at night on a railroad line that ran far from any roads, he now needed a room suitable for his essay; he wanted to get started—finally—the very next day. Up high on one of the two hills, or down below in the midst of the town? Up high, and by definition outside of town, he would perhaps feel too cut off again, and surrounded by streets and houses too confined. A room looking out on an inner courtyard made him too melancholy, one looking out on a square distracted him too much, one facing north would have too little sun for writing, in one facing south the paper would blind him when the sun was shining, on the bare hill the wind would blow in, on the wooded one dogs being walked would be barking all day, in the pensions—he checked out all of them—the other guests would be too near, in the hotels, which he also circled, he would probably be alone too much in winter for a good writing mood. For the night he took a room in the hotel on the bare hill. The street leading up to it ended in front of the stone building in a muddy square; the footpath into town—he tried it out at once—led through a steppe covered with moss and thistles, then past the façade of Santo Domingo, its very existence stimulating when he looked at it, and straight to the small squares, whose dimensions included plane trees, evocative of the mountains, the remaining leaves swaying in the breeze, curiously full at the tips of the highest branches, glittering star-shaped against the night-black sky. The room up there appealed to him also: not too confining and not too spacious—as a rule, he did not feel as if he was in the right place when there was too much space. The city, not too close and not too far, also not too far below, shone into the neither too large-paned nor too small-paned window, toward which he shoved the table, away from the mirror, experimenting further: a tiny table, to be sure, but enough of a surface for a piece of paper, pencils, and an eraser. He felt well taken care of here; this was his place for the time being.

When the next morning came, he experimented with sitting at the right hour, testing the light as it would really be, the temperature as it should be for the essay: now the room was too noisy for him (yet he should have known that precisely in so-called quiet locations the noises posed far more of a risk to collecting one's thoughts than on the loudest streets, for they came abruptly instead of steadily—suddenly the radio, laughter, echoes, a chair scraping, something popping, hissing, and, to make it worse, from close by and inside the building, from corridors, neighboring rooms, the ceiling; once the writer's concentration was lost, the image got away from him, and without that, no language). Then it was strange that the next room was not only too cold for sitting hour after hour (didn't he know that only luxury hotels kept the heat on during the day, and that, besides, when the writing was going well, he involuntarily always breathed in such a way that he didn't feel the cold?), but this time also too quiet, as if the enclosed spaces meant being locked in and a sense of openness were available only outdoors in nature, and how to let this kind of quiet in the window in December?

The third room had two beds—one too many for him. The fourth room had only one door separating it from the next room—at least one too few for him . . . In this way he learned the Spanish word for "too," a rather long word, *demasiado.* Wasn't one of Theophrastus's "characters" or types that man "dissatisfied with the given," who, upon being kissed by his sweetheart, says he wonders whether she also loves him with her soul, and who is angry with Zeus, not because he makes it rain but because the rain comes too late, and who, finding a money purse on the path, says, "But I've never found a treasure!"? And a child's rhyme also came to mind, about someone who was never happy anywhere, and he changed the words a little: "A little man I knew was puzzled what to do. / At home it was too cold, so he went into the wood. / In the wood it was too moist—soft grass was his next choice. / Finding the grass too green, he went next to Berlin. / Berlin was far too large, so he bought himself a barge. / The barge proved far too small, so he went home after all. / At home . . ." Wasn't this the recognition that he wasn't in the right place anywhere? On the contrary, he had always been in the right place somewhere—for instance?—in locations where he had got down to writing—or where a jukebox stood (though not in private dwellings!). So he had been in the right place wherever, in any case and from the outset, it was clear that in the long run he couldn't stay?

Finally he took the room that turned up next, and it was good; whatever challenges came his way—he would accept them. "Who will win out—the noise or us?" He sharpened his bundle of pencils out the window, pencils he had bought in all different countries during his years of traveling, and then again often German brands: how small one of them had become since that January in Edinburgh—was it already that long ago? As the pencil curls swirled away in the wind, they mixed with ash from the smoke of a wood fire, as down below, in front of the building, by the kitchen door, which gave directly on the thistle, rock, and moss steppe, an apprentice with a knife as long as his arm was cleaning a pile of even longer fish, the gleaming scales of the fish shooting sparkling into the air. "A good sign or not?" But now, after all this, it was too late in the day to get started. Accustomed to postponing his form of play, he felt once again actually relieved and used the delay for a walk out onto the steppe, in order to check out a few possible paths for the quality of the soil—not too hard, not too soft—and for the atmospheric conditions: not too exposed to westerly storms, but also not too sheltered.

Meanwhile something was happening to him. When he first had the inspiration—that's what it was—which at once made sense to him—of writing an essay on the jukebox, he had pictured it as a dialogue onstage: this object, and what it could mean to an individual, was for most people so bizarre that an idea presented itself: having one person, a sort of audience representative, assume the role of interrogator, and a second appear as an "expert" on the subject, in contrast to Platonic dialogues, where the one who asked the questions, Socrates, secretly knew more about the problem than the other, who, puffed up with preconceptions, at least at the beginning, claimed to know the answer; perhaps it would be most effective if the expert, too, discovered only when he had to field the other's questions what the relative "place value" of these props had been in the drama of his life. In the course of time the stage dialogue faded from his mind, and the "essay" hovered before him as an unconnected composite of many different forms of writing, corresponding to the—what should he call it—uneven? arrhythmic? ways in which he had experienced a jukebox and remembered it: momentary images should alternate with blow-by-blow narratives, suddenly broken off; mere jottings would be followed by a detailed reportage about a single music box, together with a specific locale; from a pad of notes would come, without transition, a leap to one with quotations, which, again without transition, without harmonizing linkage, would make way perhaps to a litany-like recitation of the titles and singers listed on a particular find—he pictured, as the underlying form that would give the whole thing a sort of coherence, the question-and-answer play recurring periodically, though in fragmentary fashion, and receding again, joined by similarly fragmentary filmed scenes, each organized around a different jukebox, from which would emanate all sorts of happenings or a still life, in ever-widening circles—which could extend as far as a different country, or only to the beech at the end of a railroad platform. He hoped he could have his "essay" fade out with a "Ballad of the Jukebox," a singable, so to speak "rounded" song about this thing, though only if, after all the leaps in imagery, it emerged on its own.

It had seemed to him that such a writing process was appropriate not merely to the particular subject matter but also to the times themselves. Didn't the narrative forms of previous eras—their consistency, their gestures of conjuring up and mastering (strangers' destinies), their claim to totality, as amateurish as it was naïve—when employed in modern books strike him nowadays as mere bluster? Varied approximations, some minor, some major, and in permeable forms, instead of the standard imprisoning forms, were what he felt books should be now, precisely because of his most complete, intense, unifying experiences with objects: preserving distance; circumscribing; sketching in; flirting around—giving your subject a protective escort from the sidelines. And now, as he aimlessly checked out trails in the savanna, suddenly an entirely new rhythm sprang up in him, not an alternating, sporadic one, but a single, steady one, and, above all, one that, instead of circling and flirting around, went straight and with complete seriousness in medias res: the rhythm of narrative. At first he experienced everything he encountered as he went along as a component of the narrative; whatever he took in was promptly narrated inside him; moments in the present took place in the narrative past, and not as in dreams but, without any fuss, as mere assertions, short and sweet as the moment itself: "Thistles had blown into the wire fence. An older man with a plastic bag bent down for a mushroom. A dog hopped by on three legs and made one think of a deer; its coat was yellow, its face white; gray-blue smoke wafted over the scene from a stone cottage. The seedpods rustling in the only tree standing sounded like matchboxes being shaken. From the Duero leaped fish, the wind-blown waves upstream had caps of foam, and on the other bank the water lapped the foot of the cliffs. In the train from Zaragoza the lights were already lit, and a handful of people sat in the carriages . . ."

But then this quiet narration of the present also carried over into his impending "essay," conceived as varied and playful; it became transformed, even before the first sentence was written, into a narrative so compelling and powerful that all other forms promptly faded to insignificance. That did not seem terrible to him, but overwhelmingly splendid; for in the rhythm of this narration he heard the voice of warmth-giving imagination, in which he had continued to believe, though it all too seldom touched his inner heart: he believed in it precisely because of the stillness it brought, even in the midst of deafening racket; the stillness of nature, however far outside, was then nothing by comparison. And the characteristic feature of imagination was that in conjunction with its images the place and the locale where he would write his narrative appeared. True, there had been times in the past when he had felt a similar urge, but at such times he had relocated a birch in Cologne to Indianapolis as a cypress, or a cow path in Salzburg to Yugoslavia, or the place where he was writing had been consigned to the background as something unimportant; but this time Soria was to appear as Soria (perhaps also with Burgos, and also with Vitoria, where an old native had greeted him before he said anything), and would be as much the subject matter of the narrative as the jukebox.

Until far into the night he continued his observations in narrative form, though by now it had become a form of torture—literally every petty detail (the passerby with a toothpick in his mouth, the name Benita Soria Verde on a gravestone, the poet's elm, weighted with stones and concrete in honor of Antonio Machado, the missing letters in the HOTEL sign) imposed itself on him and wanted to be narrated. This was no longer the compelling, warming power of imagery carrying him along, but clearly a cold compulsion, ascending from his heart to his head, a senseless, repeated hurling of himself against a gate long since closed, and he wondered whether narration, which had first seemed divine, hadn't been a snare and a delusion—an expression of his fear in the face of all the isolated, unconnected phenomena? An escape? The result of cowardice? But was a man walking along with a toothpick between his lips, in the winter, on the *meseta* of Castile, his nodded response to a greeting, really so insignificant? Be that as it might: he did not want to know in advance the first sentence with which he would begin on the morrow; in the past, whenever he had hammered out the first sentence, he had promptly found himself blocked when it came to the second. On the other hand: away with all such patterns! And so on . . .

The morning of the following day. The table at the window of the hotel room. Empty plastic bags blowing across the rock-strewn landscape, catching here and there on the thistles. On the horizon, an escarpment shaped like a ski jump, with a rain-bearing mushroom cloud over the approach ramp. Closing his eyes. Jamming a wad of paper into the cracks around the window through which the wind whistles its worst. Closing his eyes again. Pulling out the table drawer whose handle rattles as soon as he begins to write. Closing his eyes for the third time. Howls of distress. Opening the window: a small black dog right beneath it, hitched to the foundation, drenched with rain as only a dog can be drenched; its wails, which briefly fall silent now and then, accompanied by clouds of breath visibly puffed out into the steppe. *Aullar* was the Spanish word for "howl." Closing his eyes for the fourth time.

On the ride from Logroño to Zaragoza he had seen the stone cubes of the vintners' huts out in the winter-deserted vineyards of the Ebro Valley. In the region he came from, one could also see such huts along the paths that led through the grain fields, though built of wood, and the size of a plank shed. On the inside they also looked like a shed, with the light coming only through the chinks between the boards and the knotholes, clumps of grass on the floor, stinging nettles in the corners, growing luxuriantly between the harvest tools leaning there. And yet each of the huts on the few acres his grandfather tenant-farmed felt to him like a realm unto itself. As a rule, an elderberry grew nearby, its crown providing shade for this thing set out in the middle of the field, and its arching branches forcing their way into the interior of the hut. And there was just room enough for a small table and a bench, which could also be set outside by the elderberry. Wrapped in cloths to keep fresh and be protected from insects, the jug of cider and some cake for a snack. In the domain of these sheds he had felt more at home than ever in solidly built houses. (In such houses, a comparable sense of being in the right place had come over him most when he glanced into a windowless storage room or stood on the threshold between inside and outside, where one was still safe indoors while snow and rain from outside blew lightly against one.) Yet he viewed the field huts less as refuges than as places of rest or peace. Later it was enough simply to glimpse in his region a light gray, weathered storage shed, blown crooked by the wind, off in the distance by a fallow field, in passing; he would feel his heart leap up and dash to it and be at home in the hut for a moment, along with the flies of summer, the wasps of autumn, and the coldness of rusting chains in winter.

The huts back home had been gone for a long time. Only the much larger barns, used exclusively for hay storage, still existed. But long ago, at a time when the huts were still there, the domestic or localized magic they held for him had been transferred to jukeboxes. Even as an adolescent, with his parents, he didn't go to the inn or to have a soda, but to the "Wurlitzer" ("Wurlitzer is Jukebox" was the advertising slogan), to listen to records. What he had described as his sense of having arrived and feeling sheltered, each time only fleetingly, in the realm of the field huts was literally true of the music boxes as well. Yet the external form of the various devices and even the selections they offered meant at first less than the particular sound emanating from them. This sound did not come from above, as from the radio that stood at home in the corner with the shrine, but from underground, and also, although the volume might be the same, instead of from the usual tinny box, from an inner space whose vibrations filled the room. It was as if it were not an automatic device but rather an additional instrument that imbued the music—though only a certain kind of music, as he realized in retrospect—with its underlying sound, comparable perhaps to the rattling of a train, when it suddenly becomes, as the train passes over an iron bridge, a primeval thunder. Much later, a child was standing one time by such a jukebox (it was playing Madonna's "Like a Prayer," his own selection), the child still so small that the entire force of the loudspeaker down below was directed at his body. The child was listening, all ears, all solemn, all absorbed, while his parents had already reached the door, were ready to leave, calling to the child again and again, in between smiling at his behavior, as if to apologize for their offspring to the other patrons, until the song had died away and the child, still solemn and reverent, walked past his father and mother onto the street. (Did this suggest that the obelisk-shaped jukeboxes' lack of success had less to do with their unusual appearance than with the fact that the music was directed upward, toward the ceiling?)

Unlike with the field huts, he was not satisfied to have the jukeboxes simply stand there; they had to be ready to play, quietly humming—even better than having just been set in motion by a stranger's hand—lit up as brightly as possible, as if from their inner depths; there was nothing more mournful than a dark, cold, obsolete metal box, possibly even shamefacedly hidden from view under a crocheted Alpine throw. Yet that did not quite correspond to the facts, for he now recalled a defective jukebox in the Japanese temple site of Nikko, the first one encountered in that country after a long journey between south and north, hidden under bundles of magazines, the coin slot covered over with a strip of tape and promptly uncovered by him—but at any rate there, at last. To celebrate this find he had drunk another sake and let the train to Tokyo out there in the darkness depart without him. Before that, at an abandoned temple site way up in the woods, he had passed a still smoldering peat fire, next to it a birch broom and a mound of snow, and farther along in the mountainous terrain a boulder had poked out of a brook, and as the water shot over it, it had sounded just like the water in a certain other rocky-mountain brook—as if one were receiving, if one's ears were open to it, the broadcast of a half-sung, half-drummed speech before the plenary session of the united nations of a planet far off in the universe. Then, at night in Tokyo, people had stepped over others lying every which way on the railroad steps, and even later, again in a temple precinct, a drunk had stopped before the incense burner, had prayed, and then staggered off into the darkness.

It was not only the belly resonance: the "American hits" had also sounded entirely different to him back then on the jukeboxes of his native land than on the radio in his house. He always wanted the radio volume turned up when Paul Anka sang his "Diana," Dion his "Sweet Little Sheila," and Ricky

Nelson his "Gypsy Woman," but at the same time he felt guilty that such nonmusic appealed to him (later, when he was at the university and finally had a record player in his room, with the radio as an amplifier, for the first few years it was reserved for what was conventionally felt to deserve the name of music). But from the jukebox he boldly unleashed the trills, howls, shouts, rattling, and booming that not merely gave him pleasure but filled him with shudders of rapture, warmth, and fellowship. In the reverberating-steel guitar ride of "Apache," the cold, stale, and belch-filled Espresso Bar on the highway from the "City of the Plebiscite of 1920" to the "City of the Popular Uprising of 1938" got plugged into an entirely different kind of electricity, with which one could choose, on the glowing scale at hip level, numbers from "Memphis, Tennessee," felt oneself turning into the mysterious "handsome stranger," and heard the rumbling and squeaking of the trucks outside transformed into the steady roar of a convoy on "Route 66," with the thought: No matter where to—just out of here!

Although back home the music boxes had also been a gathering point for Saturday-night dances—a large semicircle around them was usually left clear—he himself would never have thought of joining in. He did enjoy watching the dancers, who in the dimness of the cafés became mere outlines around the massive illuminated case whose rumble seemed to come out of the ground—but for him a jukebox, like the field huts earlier, was a source of peace, or something that made one feel peaceful, made one sit still, in relative motionlessness or breathlessness, interrupted only by the measured, positively ceremonial act of "going to push the buttons." And in listening to a jukebox he was never beside himself, or feverish, or dreamy, as he otherwise was with music that affected him—even strictly classical music, and the seemingly rapturous music of earlier, preceding eras. The dangerous part about listening to music, someone had once told him, was the propensity it had to make one perceive something that remained to be done as already done. The jukebox sound of his early years, on the other hand, literally caused him to collect himself, and awakened, or activated, his images of what might be possible and encouraged him to contemplate them.

The places where one could mull things over as nowhere else sometimes became, during his years at the university, places of evasion, comparable to movie theaters; yet, while he tended to sneak into the latter, he would enter his various jukebox cafés in a more carefree manner, telling himself that these proven places of self-reflection were also the right places for studying. This turned out to be a delusion, for once he was alone again, for instance before bedtime, and tried to review the material he had gone over in such a public setting, as a rule he had not retained much. What he owed to those niches or hideouts during the cold years of his university studies were experiences that he now, in the process of writing about them, could only characterize as "wonderful." One evening in late winter he was sitting in one of his trusty jukebox cafés, underlining a text all the more heavily the less he was taking it in. This café was in a rather untypical location for such places, at the edge of the city park, and its glass display cases with pastries and its marble-topped tables were also incongruous. The box was playing, but he was waiting as usual for the songs he had selected; only then was it right. Suddenly, after the pause between records, which, along with those noises—clicking, a whirring sound of searching back and forth through the belly of the device, snapping, swinging into place, a crackle before the first measure—constituted the essence of the jukebox, as it were, a kind of music came swelling out of the depths that made him experience, for the first time in his life, as later only in moments of love, what is technically referred to as "levitation," and which he himself, more than a quarter of a century later, would call—what? "epiphany"? "ecstasy"? "fusing with the world"? Or thus: "That—this song, this sound—is now me; with these voices; these harmonies, I have become, as never before in life, who I am: as this song is, so am I, complete!"? (As usual there was an expression for it, but as usual it was not quite the same thing: "He became one with the music.")

Without at first wanting to know the identity of the group whose voices, carried by the guitars, streamed forth singly, in counterpoint, and finally in unison—previously he had preferred soloists on jukeboxes—he was simply filled with amazement. In the following weeks, too, when he went to the place every day for hours, to sit surrounded by this big yet so frivolous sound that he let the other patrons offer him, he remained in a state of amazement devoid of name-curiosity. (Imperceptibly the music box had become the hub of the Park Café, where previously the most prominent sound had been the rattle of newspaper holders, and the only records that were played, over and over, were the two by that no-name group.) But then, when he discovered one day, during his now infrequent listening to the radio, what that choir of sassy angelic tongues was called, who, with their devil-may-care bellowing of "I Want to Hold Your Hand," "Love Me Do," "Roll Over, Beethoven," lifted all the weight in the world from his shoulders, these became the first "nonserious" records he bought (subsequently he bought hardly any other kind), and then in the café with columns he was the one who kept pushing the same buttons for "I Saw Her Standing There" (on the jukebox, of course) and "Things We Said Today" (by now without looking, the numbers and letters more firmly fixed in his head than the Ten Commandments), until one day the wrong songs, spurious voices, came nattering out: the management had left the old label and slipped in the "current hit," in German . . . And to this day, he thought, with the sound of the early Beatles in his ear, coming from that Wurlitzer surrounded by the trees in the park: When would the world experience such loveliness again?

In the years that followed, jukeboxes lost some of their magnetic attraction for him—perhaps less because he now was more likely to listen to music at home, and surely not because he was getting older, but—as he thought he recognized when he got down to work on the "essay"—because he had meanwhile been living abroad. Of course he always popped in a coin whenever he encountered—in Düsseldorf, Amsterdam, Cockfosters, Santa Teresa Gallura—one of these old friends, eager to be of service, humming and sparkling with color, but it was more out of habit or tradition, and he tended to listen with only half an ear. But its significance promptly returned during his brief stopovers in what should have been his ancestral region. Whereas some people on a trip home go first "to the cemetery," "down to the lake," or "to their favorite café," he not infrequently made his way straight from the bus station to a music box, in hopes that, properly permeated with its roar, he could set out on his other visits, seeming less foreign and maladroit.

Yet there were also stories to tell of jukeboxes abroad that had played not only their records but also a role at the heart of larger events. Each of these events had occurred not just abroad but at a border: at the end of a familiar sort of world. If America was, so to speak, the "home of the jukebox," when he was there none had made much of an impression on him—except, and there time and again, in Alaska. But: did he consider Alaska part of the "United States"? One Christmas Eve he had arrived in Anchorage, and after midnight Mass, when outside the door of the little wooden church, amid all the strangers, him included, a rare cheerfulness had taken hold, he had gone to a bar. There, in the dimness and confusion of the drunken patrons, he saw, by the glowing jukebox, the only calm figure, an Indian woman. She had turned toward him, a large, proud yet mocking face, and this would be the only time he ever danced with someone to the pounding of a jukebox. Even those patrons who were looking for a fight made way for them, as if this woman, young, or rather ageless, as she was, were the elder in that setting. Later the two of them had gone out together through a back door, where, in an icy lot, her Land Cruiser was parked, the side windows painted with Alaska pines silhouetted on the shores of an empty lake. It was snowing. From a distance, without their having touched each other except in the light-handedness of dancing, she invited him to come with her; she and her parents had a fishing business in a village beyond Cook Inlet. And in this moment it became clear to him that for once in his life there was a decision imagined not by him alone but by someone else; and at once he could imagine moving with the strange woman beyond the border out there in the snow, in complete seriousness, for good, without return, and giving up his name, his type of work, every one of his habits; those eyes there, that place, often dreamed of, far from all that was familiar—it was the moment when Percival hovered on the verge of the question that would prove his salvation, and he? on the verge of the corresponding Yes. And like Percival, and not because he was uncertain—he had that image, after all—but as if it were innate and quite proper, he hesitated, and in the next moment the image, the woman, had literally vanished into the snowy night. For the next few evenings he kept going back to the place again and again, and waited for her by the jukebox, then even made inquiries and tried to track her down, but although many remembered her, no one could tell him where she lived. Even a decade later, this experience was one of the reasons he made a point of standing in line all morning for an American visa before flying back from Japan, then actually got off the plane in the wintry darkness of Anchorage and spent several days wandering through the blowing snow in this city to whose clear air and broad horizons his heart was attached. In the meantime, nouvelle cuisine had even reached Alaska, and the "saloon" had turned into a "bistro," with the appropriate menu, a rise in status that naturally, and this was to be observed not only in Anchorage, left no room for a heavy, old-fashioned music machine amid all the bright, light furniture. But an indication that one might be present were the figures—of all races—staggering onto the sidewalk from a tubelike barracks, as if from its most remote corner, or outside, among hunks of ice, a person surrounded by a police patrol and flailing around—as a rule, a white male—who then, lying on his stomach on the ground, his shoulders and his shins, bent back against his thighs, tightly tied, his hands cuffed behind his back, was slid like a sled along the ice and snow to the waiting police van. Inside the barracks, one could count on being greeted right up front at the bar, on which rested the heads of dribbling and vomiting sleepers (men and women, mostly Eskimos), by a classic jukebox, dominating the long tube of a room, with the corresponding old faithfuls—one would find all the singles of Creedence Clearwater Revival, and then hear John Fogerty's piercing, gloomy laments cut through the clouds of smoke—somewhere in the course of his minstrel's wandering, he had "lost the connection," and "If I at least had a dollar for every song I've sung!" while from down at the railroad station, open in winter only for freight, the whistle of a locomotive, with the odd name for the far north of Southern Pacific Railway, sends its single, prolonged organ note through the whole city, and from a wire in front of the bridge to the boat harbor, open only in summer, dangles a strangled crow.

Did this suggest that music boxes were something for idlers, for those who loafed around cities, and, in their more modern form, around the world? No. He, at any rate, sought out jukeboxes less in times of idleness than when he had work, or plans, and particularly after returning from all sorts of foreign parts to the place he came from. The equivalent of walking out to find silence before the hours spent writing was, afterward, almost as regularly, going to a jukebox. For distraction? No. When he was on the track of something, the last thing in the world he wanted was to be distracted from it. Over time, his house had in fact become a house without music, without a record player and the like; whenever the news on the radio was followed by music, of whatever kind, he would turn it off; also, when time hung heavy, in hours of emptiness and dulled senses, he had only to imagine sitting in front of the television instead of alone, and he would prefer his present state. Even movie theaters, which in earlier days had been a sort of shelter after work, he now avoided more and more. By now he was too often overcome, especially in them, by a sense of being lost to the world, from which he feared he would never emerge and never find his way back to his own concerns, and that he left in the middle of the film was simply running away from such afternoon nightmares. So he went to jukeboxes in order to collect himself, as at the beginning? That wasn't it anymore, either. Perhaps he, who in the course of the weeks in Soria had tried to puzzle out the writings of Teresa of Avila, could explain "going to sit" with these objects after sitting at his desk by a somewhat cocky comparison: the saint had been influenced by a religious controversy of her times, at the beginning of the sixteenth century, between two groups, having to do with the best way to move closer to God. One group—the so-called *recogidos*—believed they were supposed to "collect" themselves by contracting their muscles and such, and the others—*dejados*, "leavers," or "relaxers"—simply opened themselves up passively to whatever God wanted to work in their soul, their *alma*. And Teresa of Avila seemed to be closer to the leavers than to the collectors, for she said that when someone set out to give himself more to God, he could be overwhelmed by the evil spirit—and so he sat by his jukeboxes, so to speak, not to gather concentration for going back to work, but to relax for it. Without his doing anything but keeping an ear open for the special jukebox chords—"special," too, because here, in a public place, he was not exposed to them but had chosen them, was "playing" them himself, as it were—the continuation took shape in him, as he let himself go: images that had long since become lifeless now began to move, needed only to be written down, as next to (in Spanish *junto*, attached to) the music box he was listening to Bob Marley's "Redemption Song." And from Alice's "Una notte speciale," played day after day, among other things, an entirely unplanned woman character entered the story on which he was working, and developed in all directions. And unlike after having too much to drink, the things he noted down after such listening still had substance the next day. So in those periods of reflection (which never proved fertile at home, when he tried, at his desk, to force them; he was acquainted with intentional thinking only in the form of making comparisons and distinctions), he would set out not only to walk as far as possible but also out to the jukebox joints. When he was sitting in the pimps' hangout, whose box had once been shot at, or in the café of the unemployed, with its table for patients out on passes from the nearby mental hospital—silent, expressionless palefaces, in motion only for swallowing pills with beer—no one wanted to believe him that he had come not for the atmosphere but to hear "Hey Joe" and "Me and Bobby McGee" again. But didn't that mean that he sought out jukeboxes in order to, as people said, sneak away from the present? Perhaps. Yet as a rule the opposite was true: with his favorite object there, anything else around acquired a presentness all its own. Whenever possible, he would find a seat in such joints from which he could see the entire room and a bit of the outside. Here he would often achieve, in consort with the jukebox, along with letting his imagination roam, and without engaging in the observing he found so distasteful, a strengthening of himself, or an immersion in the present, which applied to the other sights as well. And what became present about them was not so much their striking features or their particular attractions as their ordinary aspects, even just the familiar forms or colors, and such enhanced presentness seemed valuable to him—nothing more precious or more worthy of being passed on than this; a sort of heightened awareness such as otherwise occurs only with a book that stimulates reflection. So it *meant* something, quite simply, when a man left, a branch stirred, the bus was yellow and turned off at the station, the intersection formed a triangle, the chalk was lying at the edge of the pool table, it was raining, and, and, and. Yes, that was it: the present was equipped with flexible joints! Thus, even the little habits of "us jukebox players" deserved attention, along with the few variations. While he himself usually propped one hand on his hip while he pushed the buttons, and leaned forward a little, almost touching the thing, another person stood some distance away, legs spread, arms outstretched like a technician; and a third let his fingers rebound from the buttons like a pianist, then immediately went away, sure of the result, or remained, as if waiting for the outcome of an experiment, until the sound came (and then perhaps disappeared without listening to any more, out onto the street), or as a matter of principle had all his songs selected by others, to whom he called out from his table the codes, which he knew by heart. What they all had in common was that they seemed to see the jukebox as a sort of living thing, a pet: "Since yesterday she hasn't been quite right." "I dunno what's wrong with her today; she's acting crazy." So was one of these devices just like any other, as far as he was concerned? No. There were telling differences, ranging from clear aversion to downright tenderness or actual reverence. Toward a mass-produced object? Toward the human touches in it. The form of the device itself mattered less and less for him as time went on. As far as he was concerned, the jukebox could be a wartime product made of wood, or could be called—instead of Wurlitzer—Music Chest, or Symphony, or Fanfare, and such a product of the German economic miracle could look like a small box, even have no lights at all, be made of dark, opaque glass, silent and to all appearances out of commission, but then the list of selections would light up once you put the coin in, and after you pushed the buttons that internal whirring would begin, accompanied by the selector light on the black glass front. Not even the characteristic jukebox sound was so decisive for him anymore, emanating from the depths as from under many soundless layers, the unique roaring that could often be heard only if one listened for it, similar, he thought one time, to the way the "river" in William Faulkner's story can be heard far below the silent, standing ocean waters in the land the river has flooded from horizon to horizon, as the "roaring of the Mississippi." In a pinch, he could make do with a wall box, where the sound came out flatter, or more tinny, than it ever had from a transistor radio, and if absolutely necessary, if there was so much noise in the place that the actual sound of the music became inaudible, even a certain rhythmic vibration sufficed; he could then make out the chorus or even just one measure—his only requirement—of the music he had selected, from which the whole song would play in his ear, from vibration to vibration. But he disliked those music boxes where the choice of songs, instead of being unique and "personally" put together at that location, was itself mass-produced, the same from one place to the next throughout an entire country, without variation, and made available to the individual establishments, indeed forced on them, by an anonymous central authority, which he could picture as a sort of Mafia, the jukebox Mafia. Such unvarying, lockstep programs, with choices among only current hits, even in a fine old Wurlitzer—by now there was hardly anything else in all countries—could be recognized by the fact that there was no longer a typed list; it was printed, completely covering the slots for individual song titles and performers' names. But, strangely enough, he also avoided those jukeboxes whose list of offerings, like the menu in certain restaurants, was done in a uniform handwriting from top to bottom, from left to right, although, as a rule, precisely there every single record seemed intended for him alone; he did not like a jukebox's program to embody any plan, no matter how noble, any connoisseurship, any secret knowledge, any harmony; he wanted it to represent confusion, with an admixture of the unfamiliar (more and more as the years went by), and also plenty of pieces for escape, among them, to be sure, and all the more precious, the very songs (just a few, to be hunted down among all the chaotic possibilities, were enough) that met his needs at the moment. Such music boxes also made themselves known in their menu of choices; with a hodgepodge of machine- and handwritten notations, and, above all, handwriting that changed from title to title, one in block letters, in ink, the next in flowing, almost stenographic secretary style, but most, even with the most dissimilar loops and slants of the letters, showing signs of particular care and seriousness, some, like children's handwriting, as if painted, and, time and again, among all the mistakes, correctly written ones (with proper accents and hyphens), song titles that must have struck the waitress in question as very foreign, the paper here and there already yellowed, the writing faded and hard to make out, perhaps also taped over with freshly written labels with different titles, but where it showed through, even if illegible, still powerfully suggestive. In time, his first glance more and more sought out those records in a jukebox's table of choices that were indicated in such handwriting, rather than "his" records, even if there was only one such. And sometimes that was the only one he listened to, even if it had been unfamiliar or completely unknown to him beforehand. Thus, in a North African bar in a Paris suburb, standing in front of a jukebox (whose list of exclusively French selections immediately made it recognizable as a Mafia product), he had discovered on the edge a label, handwritten, in very large, irregular letters, each as emphatic as an exclamation point, and had selected that smuggled-in Arab song, then again and again, and even now he was still haunted by that far-resonating SIDI MANSUR, which the bartender, rousing himself from his silence, told him was the name of "a special, out-of-the-ordinary place" ("You can't just go there!").

Was that supposed to mean that he regretted the disappearance of his jukeboxes, these objects of yesteryear, unlikely to have a second future?

No. He merely wanted to capture and acknowledge, before even he lost sight of it, what an object could mean to a person, above all what could emanate from a mere object. An eating place by a playing field on the outskirts of Salzburg. Outdoors. A bright summer evening. The jukebox is outside, next to the open door. On the terrace, different patrons at every table, Dutch, English, Spanish, speaking their own languages, for the place also serves the adjacent campgrounds, by the airfield. It is the early eighties, the airfield has not yet become "Salzburg Airport," the last plane lands at sundown. The trees between the terrace and the playing field are birches and poplars, in the warm air constant fluttering of leaves against the deep yellow sky. At one table the locals are sitting, members of the Maxglan Working Man's Athletic Club with their wives. The soccer team, at that time still a second-division club, has just lost another game that afternoon, and will probably be dropped from the league. But now, in the evening, those affected are talking about the trees for a change, while there is a constant coming and going at the window where beer is dispensed—from the tents and back. They look at the trees: how big they've gotten and how straight they've grown, since they, the club members, went out and with their own hands dug them up as seedlings from the black mossy soil and planted them here in rows in the brown clay! The song the jukebox sends out again and again that evening into the gradually oncoming darkness, in the pauses between the rustling and rasping of the leaves and the even buzz of voices, is sung in an enterprising voice by Helene Schneider, and is called "Hot Summer Nites." The place is completely empty, and the white curtains billow in at the open windows. Then at some point someone is sitting inside, in a corner, a young woman, silently weeping.

Years later. A restaurant, a *gostilna*, on the crown of the Yugoslavian Karst, at some remove from the highway from Stanjel (or San Daniele del Carso). Indoors. A mighty old-fashioned jukebox next to a cupboard, on the way to the restroom. Visible behind ornamental glass, the record carousel and turntable. To operate it, one uses tokens instead of coins, and then it is not enough to push a button, of which there is only one; first, one has to turn a dial until the desired selection lines up with the indicator arrow. The mechanical arm then places the record on the turntable with an elegance comparable to the elbow flourish with which an impeccably trained waiter presents a dish. The *gostilna* is large, with several dining rooms, which on this evening in early fall—while outside the *burja*, or *bora*, blasts without relief over the high land, coming from the mountains in the north—are full, mostly with young people: an end-of-term party for several classes from all the republics of Yugoslavia; they have met one another for the first time here, over several days. Once the wind carries the distinctive signal of the Karst train down from the cliffs, with the dark sound of a mountain ferry. On the wall, across from the customary picture of Tito, hangs an equally colorful but much larger portrait of an unknown: it is the former proprietor, who took his own life. His wife says he was not from around here (even if only from the village in the next valley). The song, selected this evening by one student after another, that wafts through the dining rooms over and over again is sung in a self-conscious and at the same time childishly merry unison, even, as an expression of a people, danceable, and has one word as its refrain: "Jugoslavija!"

Again years later. Again a summer evening, before dusk, this time on the Italian side of the Karst, or, to be precise, the border of the limestone base, once heaved out of the sea, of the cliffless lowlands, here marked by the tracks of the railroad station of Monfalcone. Just beyond it, the desert of stones that rises toward the plateau, concealed along this section of track by a small pine forest—on this side the station, surrounded by the abruptly different vegetation of cedars, palms, plane trees, rhododendrons, along with the requisite water, pouring plentifully from the station fountain, whose spigot no one has bothered to turn off. The jukebox stands in the bar, under the window, which is wide open after the heat of the day; likewise open, the door leading out to the tracks. Otherwise, the place is almost entirely without furniture; what little there is has been shoved to one side, and they are mopping up already. The lights of the jukebox are reflected in the wet terrazzo floor, a glow that gradually disappears as the floor dries. The face of the barmaid appears very pale at the window, in contrast to those of the few passengers waiting outside, which are tanned. After the departure of the Trieste-Venice Express, the building appears empty, except that on a bench two adolescent boys are tussling, yelling at the top of their voices; the railroad station is their playground at the moment. From the darkness of the pines of the Karst, swarms of moths are issuing forth. A long, sealed freight train rattle-pounds by, the only bright spot against the outside of the cars being the little lead seals blowing behind on their cords. In the stillness that follows—it is the time between the last swallows and the first bats—the sound of the jukebox is heard. The boys tussle a bit longer. Not to listen, but probably quite by chance, two railroad officials come out of their offices to the platform, and from the waiting room comes a cleaning woman. Suddenly figures, previously overlooked, appear all over the scene. On the bench by the beech, a man is sleeping. On the grass behind the restrooms, soldiers are stretched out, a whole group, without a trace of luggage. On the platform to Udine, leaning against a pillar, a huge black man, likewise without luggage, just in shirt and pants, engrossed in a book. From the thicket of pines behind the station swoop again and again, one following close upon the other, a pair of doves. It is as if all of them were not travelers but inhabitants or settlers in the area around the railroad station. Its midpoint is the fountain, with its foaming drinking water, blown and spattered by the breeze, and tracks on the asphalt from many wet soles, to which the last drinker now intentionally adds his own. A bit farther down the tracks, accessible on foot, the subterranean Karst river, the Timavo, comes to the surface, with three branches, which in Virgil's time, according to the *Æneid*, were still nine; it immediately broadens out and empties into the Mediterranean. The song the jukebox is playing tells of a letter written by a young woman who has ended up far away from her home and from everything she ever knew or dreamed of, and is now full of brave and perhaps also sorrowful astonishment; it floats out into the dusky railroad land of Monfalcone in the friendly voice of Michelle Shocked, and is called "Anchorage, Alaska."

During the weeks in Soria he sometimes managed to think this about what he was doing: "I'm doing my work. It agrees with me." Once he found himself thinking, "I have time," without the usual ulterior motives, just that one, big thought. It rained and stormed over the Castilian highlands almost every day, and he used his pencils to jam the curtain into the cracks around the window. The noise still bothered him more. The fish-scaling down below, outside the kitchen door, became a daily dismembering, with a meat ax, of altogether different animals, and the agreeably looping paths on the steppe turned out to be a motocross course. (Soria was even competing, he discovered, for the European championship.) Seen on television, this sport, with its heroes bouncing into the air like video-game figures, had something admirable about it, but now, sitting at his table, he found the buzzing of a hornet around his head a blessing by comparison. Again and again he came back from his walk filled with strength—his own kind of strength—for work, and promptly lost it in the racket. The noise destroyed something not only for the moment but for good. The worrisome thing was that it put him at risk of disparaging an activity like his conjuring up of images and then putting them into words, which required so much solitude. On the other hand, in silence he had in fact occasionally gone astray, and now actually drew strength precisely from his weakness—his doubts, even more his hopelessness—going to work in defiance of his surroundings. Every day he traced his arc past the façade of Santo Domingo—no, in contrast to the new buildings behind it, that was no façade. Peace emanated from it; all he had to do was take it in. Amazing how the sculptures told their stories: Eve, being led to Adam by God, was already standing back-to-back with her husband in the next scene, where he gazed up at the Tree of Knowledge, and word of Christ's Resurrection, given by one of the women to the first in the long line of Apostles, was immediately passed down the row to the end, as one could see from the body language; only the last in line, motionless, seemed not to have heard yet.

Before work he walked with short steps, afterward with longer ones, not out of a sense of triumph, but because he was dizzy. Going up the mountainside made him breathe more deeply and think more clearly, but it could not be too steep, or his thoughts would grow too agitated. Likewise, he preferred going upstream to the other direction; there was an element of forging one's way, with the energy that produced. If he wanted to keep from brooding, he walked along the ties of the abandoned rail line that had linked Soria and Burgos, or went even farther out of town into the darkness, where he had to watch where he put his feet. When he returned from the darkness of the steppe to town, he was so tense from groping his way along that he felt like having the playful figures of Santo Domingo loosen him up and smooth the tightness from his face. He repeated the same routes, just adding a variation every day; yet it seemed to him as if all the other paths were waiting to be taken. Along Antonio Machado's promenade lay years' worth of tissues and condoms. During the day there were, besides him, almost exclusively old men out on the steppe, usually alone, with worn shoes; before they blew their noses, they ceremoniously pulled out their handkerchiefs and shook them. Before work he made a point of saying hello to at least one of them, intending to be greeted in turn; he did not want to go back to his room without having experienced this moment of smiling; sometimes he even stopped just for that purpose and let one of them catch up with him, so as to get in the "*Hola!*" and the jerk of the head. Before that he read the paper every day, by a large window in Soria's Central Bar, with the help of a dictionary. *Llavero* meant a "bunch of keys": with a raised bunch of keys a woman took part in a demonstration in Prague; *dedo pulgar* meant "thumb": the American president gave the thumbs-up sign to indicate the successful bloodletting in Panama; *puerta giratoria* meant a "revolving door" (through which Samuel Beckett in his time had entered the Closerie des Lilas in Paris). The news of the execution of the Ceauçescu couple he read not with satisfaction but with an old, newly reawakened horror of history. When time allowed, he continued to decipher the characters of Theophrastus, and came to feel fond of many of them, or at least some of their traits—which he perhaps recognized as his own. It seemed to him that their weaknesses and foolishness were indications of lonely people who could not fit in with society, in this case the Greek polis, and in order to be part of it in some way played their ludicrous game with the courage born of desperation; if they were overzealous, unsuitably youthful, boastful, or, more revealingly, always "in the wrong place at the wrong time," the explanation was often simply that they could not find their niche among the others, even their children and slaves. Occasionally he would look up and gaze out the window at a plane tree—still with its withered foliage—and next to it an already completely bare mountain maple, in which, almost predictably, except in a violent storm, the sparrows would be perched like buds, so quiet that the whipping, flapping, swirling jagged leaves next to them were more like birds than they were. He experienced his most powerful sense of place down by the bridge that spanned the river, less at the sight of the stone arches and the dark winter water flowing past than of the sign at the highest point of the bridge: RIO DUERO. One of the bars down by the water was called Alegría del Puente, "Joy of the Bridge," and when he read the sign he immediately took the detour, the *rodeo*, to go in. Along the riverbanks, where they were not sheer cliffs, smooth-polished glacial boulders protruded from the earth, and on the remains of the city walls, far out in the steppe, the wind of the centuries had ridged, striped, pitted, patterned the yellow sandstone, and he saw several old palaces on the Plaza Mayor built on foundations of pebbles naturally cemented at the bottom of glacial lakes. To be able to read the landscape a little in passing grounded one, and he learned that in Spain geography had always been subservient to history, to conquests and border drawings, and only now was more attention being paid to the "messages of places." Sometimes colors were particularly alive in winter. While the sky looked sulfurous, a fallow field down below was greening up, and the paths through the rock-strewn fields also showed mossy green. Where everything else had long since faded, a rosebush covered with hips formed a glowing red arch. A pair of magpies fluttered up, their wings brightening the air like rapidly turning wheels. On a day when it was not raining, little puffs of dust sprang up around the town, and he got a feel for summer in these parts. The shadows of clouds passed over the bare highlands, as if pulled from underground—as if there were cloud shadows everywhere, but their home was here in Castile. One morning there was an hour without wind for a change, and in the clear sun both the northern and the eastern sierra could be seen with snow cover for the first time, and although both mountain chains were a small airplane journey away, he saw the sparkling slopes checkered by cloud shadows, motionless, for the duration of that hour without wind. In his thoughts he was so preoccupied with the snow that he involuntarily stamped it off his shoes when he reached his door. A few times, when he was groping his way across the deserted area outside town (he sent himself there for this very purpose), the night sky cleared up briefly, and the effect was all the more amazing when Castor and Pollux showed their fraternal distance, Venus glittered, Aldebaran sparkled in Arabic fashion, the W of Cassiopeia formed wide thighs, the Big Dipper bent its handle, and Lepus, the hare, in flight from the hunter Orion, dashed horizontally across the firmament. The Milky Way with its numerous Delta branches was a pale reflection of the universe's initial explosion. Strange, the feeling of having a "long time" during this December in Soria: already, after the first day spent writing, when he caught sight of the river down there, he found himself thinking, "There he is, the good old Duero!" When one weekend he had not made his rounds past the Río Bar, he felt, back by its little cast-iron stove, as if he had not visited this gray cylinder "in ages." Scarcely a week after his arrival, he thought, as he wandered past the bus station: "This is where I stepped out into the rain with my suitcase that time!" In the midst of a roaring gale, a toad lurching through the steppe grass. Before the plane trees' leaves dropped, their stems broke, became fringed, spun on the fringes. When the cock was in the muddy garden where the unripe tomatoes were left as feed, did his tail feathers move of their own accord, or was that the wind? But his true heraldic animals were those dogs he saw wandering around in the evening, limping on three legs: at the end of his day's journey, one of his knees usually gave out, too. Once, when according to the paper Soria was not the coldest town in Spain, he felt disappointed. Once, on the main street, a pot with a red poinsettia was carried along, beneath the green, still not fallen, always wet leaves of the plane trees; not once in those weeks did the puddles in the hollows around the roots evaporate. The fog was dark gray, and against that background the many white cocoons of the needle-eating processionary moths stood out all the more menacingly in the mountain pines. On Christmas Day it rained so hard that, during his usual walk through town, besides him only a solitary sparrow seemed to be on the street. Then, from the county jail, without an umbrella, a very small woman and her big son emerged and crossed the sea of mud to a temporary barracks set up there, and he imagined that behind the high walls they had just visited a relative, one of the Basques on a hunger strike, and were camping out here until he was freed. In the evening there was a sudden flash of light between torrents of rain, and something hit him on his forehead and chin, and when he looked around, he saw a car with its roof all white coming from out of town, and way up in the black of night a few flakes began to float as they fell: "*Nieve!*" he thought, his first spontaneous word in Spanish. In a bar they struck up a flamenco song, for once without the usual gypsy-like note of futility, but cheerful, confident, with the air of a herald, and a notion ran through his mind: here, finally, was the appropriate way to sing for—not Christmas, but *Navidad*, the birth; this was how one of the shepherds would describe what he had seen in that holy night, and his description was of course also a dance. Here, as everywhere in the world, he saw passersby who, at the first drops of rain, put up the umbrellas they always had with them, and even here on the *meseta* it was the fashion for young girls, when they entered a restaurant, to blow their bangs off their foreheads. Thunderous wind, like an airplane taking off (actually, something one almost never heard over the city), in the poplars along the

Duero. A large hen tenderly groomed the comb of a little rooster, standing on one leg in the muck. In a bare almond tree there was already one branch with white flower buds. Most of the evils with which he was familiar from his accustomed surroundings, including those within him, remained at a distance here, housed as he was once again by his work, and yet, in the long run, a sense of life—this he recognized in Soria—could not come from what was absent. Hoarfrost lay on the tree roots that terraced steps into a path. One time, as he sat at his table, something outside detonated and he heard it as a temple bell.

In the end he believed he had explored almost every corner of the city (he memorized these *rincones* as if they were vocabulary words). He entered almost a hundred buildings, for, as he discovered in the course of his conscientious wanderings, little Soria had well over a hundred bars, off the beaten track, in alleys between buildings, often without signs, hidden, like so many things in Spanish towns, from casual glances and known only to those who lived there—as if reserved for them alone. Again and again he found on walls, along with the announcements about hunting times and the pictures of toreros, poems by Antonio Machado, also as wall calendars, some with graffiti on them, one even with a swastika, yet, it seemed to him, not for the usual reasons, but because the poems, at least those chosen as wall decorations, had to do with nature. Amazing how in many establishments there were only young people, and how there were even more bars for older people exclusively and explicitly closed to anyone else (with a table in the corner for the old women): to all appearances, a stricter separation than any political one. Most of the retirees in the province spent their "golden" years here in the capital, and when they were not playing cards in their bars, they sat quietly by themselves at a table or fumbled and poked around incessantly, searching for something. Young and old and he, the stranger in the land, in addition: all their wintry hands lay equally pale on the counters, while the glow of the streetlights outside showed up, for example, the scars on a concrete wall left by a falling metal scaffolding that had killed two pedestrians back when he arrived.

Besides his pleasure in the variations in these places that appeared so similar, he also felt particularly driven to find a jukebox in Soria, first probably out of the old compulsion, but later more and more because this would have been the proper time for it: work, winter, the evenings after the long walks in the pouring rain. Once, already far out along the *carretera* to Valladolid, he heard from a bar along the highway a deep sound that then turned out to belong to a pinball machine decorated like a chamber of horrors; in a gas-station bar he saw the sign WURLITZER—on a cigarette machine; in a building being torn down in the *casco*, the center of Soria, surrounded by craters of rubble, he caught sight, in the Andalusian-style tiled bar there, of the selection chart from an ancient Marconi apparatus, a forerunner of the jukebox, used as wall decoration. The only time he laid eyes on his object in Soria was in the Rex movie theater, in an English film set in the early sixties: there it stood, in a back room, waiting for the moment when the hero went by on his way to the men's room. The only living jukebox in Spain, so to speak, remained for him the one from Linares, in Andalusia. At that time, too, in the spring, he had needed it: work, the commotion of Easter Week. That jukebox, which he had come upon only shortly before leaving, the search long since abandoned, greeted him in a cellar off a side street. A place the size of a storeroom, no windows, only the door. Open at irregular times, and, when open, only in the evening, but then the sign was often not lit—you had to try the door to see if anything was going on there. The proprietor, an old man (turning on the ceiling light only when a guest arrived), usually alone with the jukebox. This one had the unusual feature that all the selection tabs were blank, like nameplates in a high-rise apartment house with all the names missing; like the entire place, it seemed to be out of service; only the alphanumeric codes at the beginning of the blank tabs. But all over the wall, in every direction, up to the ceiling, record covers were tacked, with the proper codes written on them by hand, and thus, after the machine had been switched on, each time only on request, the desired record—the belly of the seemingly disemboweled object turned out to be chockfull of them—could be set in motion. Suddenly there was so much space in that little hovel from the monotonous thumping deep inside the steel, so much peace emanated from that place, in the midst of the hectic Spanish pace and his own. That was on Calle Cervantes in Linares, with the abandoned movie theater across the street, with remains of a sign reading *Estreno*, premiere, and bundles of newspapers and rats in the barred lobby, at a time when on the steppe outside the city the hardheaded steppe chamomile was in bloom, and more than thirty years after Manuel Rodriguez, called Manolete, was gored to death by a bull in the arena at Linares. A few steps below the bar, which was called El Escudo, "The Escutcheon," was Linares's Chinese restaurant, sometimes a place of peace for a person from elsewhere, like the jukebox. In Soria, too, he discovered, to his surprise, a seemingly hidden Chinese restaurant; it looked closed, yet the door sprang open, and when he stepped inside, the large paper lanterns were switched on. He remained the only diner that evening. In town he had never seen the Asian family that ate here at the long table in the corner and then disappeared into the kitchen. Only the girl stayed behind and served him in silence. On the walls, pictures of the Great Wall, from which the place took its name. Strange, how when he dipped his porcelain spoon into the bowl with the dark soup, the bright heads of the bean sprouts popped up, here in the Castilian highlands, like figures in an animated cartoon, while in the nightly storm outside the window the poplar branches clicked. The young girl, otherwise idle, was painting Chinese letters into a notebook at the next table, one close to the other, in a writing far more even than his own during these weeks (not only the storm gusts, the rain, and the darkness when he took notes outdoors, since he had been at work, had ruined it), and as he kept watching her, a girl who had to feel incomparably more foreign than he did in this area, in this Spain, he sensed with amazement that he had only now really set out from the place he came from.

ESSAY ON THE SUCCESSFUL DAY

Translated by Ralph Manheim

A SELF-PORTRAIT BY WILLIAM HOGARTH, AN EIGHTEENTH-CENTURY moment, showing a palette divided approximately in the middle by a gently curving line, the so-called Line of Beauty and Grace. And on my desk a flat, rounded stone found on the shore of Lake Constance, dark granite, traversed diagonally by a vein of chalky white, with a subtle, almost playful bend, deviating from the straight line at exactly the right moment and dividing the stone into two halves, while at the same time holding it together. And that trip in a suburban train through the hills to the west of Paris, at the afternoon hour when as a rule the fresh air and clean light of certain early-morning departures are vitiated, when nothing is natural any longer and it seems likely that only the coming of darkness can bring relief from the closeness of the day, then suddenly the tracks swing out in a wide arc, strangely, breathtakingly high above the city, which unexpectedly, along with the crazy reality of its enigmatic structures, opens out into the fluvial plain—there on the heights of Saint-Cloud or Suresnes, with that unforeseen curve, an instant transition changed the course of my day, and my almost abandoned idea of a "successful day" was back again, accompanied by a heartwarming impulse to describe, list, or discuss the elements of such a day and the problems it raises. The Line of Beauty and Grace on Hogarth's palette seems literally to force its way through the formless masses of paint, seems to cut between them and yet to cast a shadow.

Who has ever experienced a successful day? Most people will say without thinking that they have. But then it will be necessary to ask: Do you mean "successful" or only "happy"? Are you thinking of a successful day or only of a "carefree" one, which admittedly is just as unusual. If a day goes by without confronting you with problems, does that, in your opinion, suffice to make it a successful day? Do you see a distinction between a happy day and a successful one? Is it essentially different to speak of some successful day in the past, with the help of memory, and right now after the day, which no intervening time has transfigured, to say not that a day has been "dealt with" or "got out of the way," but that it has been "successful"? To your mind, is a successful day basically different from a carefree or happy day, from a full or busy day, a day struggled through, or a day transfigured by the distant past—one particular suffices, and a whole day rises up in glory—perhaps even some Great Day for Science, your country, our people, the peoples of the earth, mankind? (And that reminds me: Look—look up—the outline of that bird up there in the tree; translated literally, the Greek verb for "read," used in the Pauline epistles, would signify a "looking up," even a "perceiving *upward*" or "recognizing upward," a verb without special imperative form, but in itself a summons, an appeal; and then those hummingbirds in the jungles of South America, which in leaving their sheltering tree imitate the wavering of a falling leaf to mislead the hawk . . .) —Yes, to me a successful day is not the same as any other; it means more. A successful day is more. It is more than a "successful remark," more than a "successful chess move" (or even a whole successful game), more than a "successful first winter ascent," than a "successful *flight*," a "successful operation," a "successful relationship," or any "successful piece of business"; it is independent of a successful brushstroke or sentence, nor should it be confused with some "poem, which after a lifetime of waiting achieved success in a single hour." The successful day is incomparable. It is unique.

It is symptomatic of our particular epoch that the success of a single day can become a "subject" (or a reproach). Consider that in times gone by more importance was attached to faith in a correctly chosen moment, which could indeed stand for the whole of life. Faith? Belief? Idea? In the remote past, at all events, regardless of whether you were herding sheep on the slopes of the Pindus, strolling about below the Acropolis, or building a wall on the stony plateau of Arcadia, you had to reckon with a god of the right moment or time-atom, a god in any case. And in its day, no doubt, this god of the moment was more powerful than all seemingly immutable embodiments of gods—always present, always here, always valid. But in the end he, too, was dethroned—or, who knows?—mightn't it have been your god of "now!" (*and* of the eyes that meet, and of the sky which, formless only a moment ago, suddenly took on form, *and* of the water-smooth stone, which suddenly showed the play of its colors, *and*, *and*) that was dethroned by the faith that came after—no longer image or idea, but faith "born of love" in a new Creation, in which all moments and epochs are fulfilled through the Incarnation, death, and Resurrection of the Son of God, and thus in so-called eternity, a gospel whose missionaries proclaimed first that it was not made to the measure of man, and second that those who believed in it would transcend the mere moments of philosophy and enjoy the aeons, or, rather, the eternities of religion. There then followed, distinct from both the god of the moment and the God of eternity, though without sufficient zeal to demolish the one or the other, a period of purely immanent, or, to state it plainly, secular power, which put its reliance—your kairos-cult, your Greeks, your heavenly beatitude, your Christians and Muslims mean nothing to me—on something intermediary, on the success of my here-and-now, of the successful individual lifetime. Faith? Dream? Vision? Most likely—at least at the start of this period—a vision: the vision of people who have been disillusioned with all faith of any kind; a sort of defiant daydream. Since nothing outside me is thinkable, I will make the utmost of my life. Thus the era of this third power was superlative in word and deed: labors of Hercules, world movements. "Was"? Does it follow that this era is past? No, the idea of a whole life made successful by activity is of course still in force and will always remain fruitful. But apparently there is little more to be said about it, for the epics and romances of adventure of the pioneers, who resolutely lived the original dream of the active life, have already been told and provide the models for today's successful lives—each one a variant of the well-known formula: Plant a tree, get a child, write a book—and all that's left to talk about are strange little variations or glosses, tossed off at random, something for example about a young man of thirty, married to a woman whom he was confident of loving to the end, a teacher at a small suburban school, to whose monthly magazine he contributed occasional theater or movie notes, who had no further plans for the future (no tree, no book, no child), telling friends, not only since the completion of his thirtieth year, but on his last few birthdays as well, with festively lit-up eyes, of his certainty that his life had been successful (the words sound even weirder in the French original, "j'ai réussi ma vie"—"I've made a good thing of my life"?). Was the epochal vision of the successful life still at work in this man of today? Was his statement still an expression of faith? It is a long time since those words were spoken, but in my imagination, regardless of what may have happened to the man since, I feel sure that if anyone asks him he will still automatically give the same reply. So it must be faith. What sort of faith? –What can have become of that young "successful life"?

Do you mean to imply that, unlike successful lives, your so-called successful day is more meaningful today than any mere glosses or copies or travesties? Is it so very different from the motto from the Golden Age of Rome, *carpe diem*, which today, two thousand years later, can serve equally well as a brand of wine, an inscription on a T-shirt, or the name of a nightclub. (Once again it all depends on how you translate it: "Make the best of your day"—as it was understood in the century of action—? "Gather the day"—whereby the day becomes one great favorable moment—? or "Let the day bear fruit"—whereby Horace's famous dictum suddenly comes close to my today-problem—?) And what is a successful day anyway—because thus far you have only been trying to make clear what it is not? But with all your digressions, complications, and tergiversations, your way of breaking off every time you gain a bit of momentum, what becomes of your Line of Beauty and Grace, which, as you've hinted, stands for a successful day and, as you went on to assure us, would introduce your essay on the subject. When will you abandon your irresolute peripheral zigzags, your timorous attempt to define a concept that seems to be growing emptier than ever, and at last, with the help of coherent sentences, make the light, sharp incision that will carry us through the present muddle and in medias res, in the hope that this obscure "successful day" of yours may take on clarity and universal form. How do you conceive of such a day? Give me a rough sketch of it, show me a picture of it. Tell me about this successful day. Show me the dance of the successful day. Sing me the song of the successful day!

There really is a song that might have been called "A

Successful Day." It was sung by Van Morrison, my favorite singer (or one of them), and it actually has a different title, the name of a small American town that is otherwise of no interest. It tells the story in pictures of a car ride on a Sunday—when a successful day seems even more unlikely than on any other day of the week—for two, a man and a woman, no doubt, in the we-form (in which the success of a day seems an even greater event than for one person alone): fishing in the mountains, driving on, buying the Sunday paper, driving on, a snack, driving on, the shimmer of your hair, arriving in the evening, with roughly this last line: "Why can't every day be like this?" It's a very short song, maybe the shortest ballad ever, it hardly takes a minute, and the man who sings it is almost elderly, with a few last strands of hair, and it talks more than it sings about that day, without tune or resonance, in a kind of casual murmur, but out of a broad, powerful chest, suddenly breaking off just as it swells its widest.

Nowadays, the Line of Beauty and Grace might be unlikely to take the same gentle curve as in Hogarth's eighteenth century, which, at least in prosperous, self-sufficient England, conceived of itself as a very earthly epoch. Isn't it typical of people like us that this sort of song keeps breaking off, lapsing into stuttering, babbling, and silence, starting up again, going off on a sidetrack—yet in the end, as throughout, aiming at unity and wholeness? And isn't it equally typical of us late-twentieth-century people that we think about a single successful day rather than some sort of eternity or an entire successful life—no, not only in the sense of "Live in the present," and certainly not of "Gather ye rosebuds," but also in the urgent, needful hope that by investigating the elements of this one period of time one might devise a model for a greater, still greater, if not the greatest possible period, because now that all the old ideas of time have gone up in smoke, this drifting from day to day without rule or precept (except perhaps with reference to what one should *not* do in one's lifetime), devoid of ties (with you, with that passerby) or the slightest certainty (that the present moment of joy will be repeated tomorrow if ever), though bearable in youth, when it may even be accompanied or encouraged by carefreeness, gives way in time to more frequent dissatisfaction and, with advancing age, to indignation. And since age, unlike youth, cannot rebel against heaven, against present conditions on earth, or anything else, my indignation turns against myself. Damn it, why aren't we together anymore? Why at three o'clock this afternoon has the light in the country lane, or the clatter of the train wheels, or your face ceased to be the event it was this morning and promised to remain forever and ever. Damn it, why, quite unlike what is supposed to happen as one grows older, am I less able than ever to remember, hold fast, and treasure the moments of my life? Damn it, why am I so scatterbrained? Damn, damn, damn. (And while we're at it, look at those gym shoes drying on the windowsill of the gabled house across the street; they belong to the neighbor kid we saw last night in the floodlight of the makeshift football field, plucking at the seam of his jersey while running to intercept a pass.)

So, to judge by what you say about the successful moment, the successful life, whether eternal or individual, you regard the idea of the successful day as a kind of fourth power. And that leads you to endow this successful day with a fragrance that will never evaporate but, regardless of what may happen to you tomorrow, will somehow linger on. Thus it is time to ask once again: "How precisely do you envision a successful day?" I can give you no precise picture of a successful day. I have only the idea, and I almost despair of showing you a recognizable contour, bringing out the design, or tracing the original light trail of my day, or disclosing it in simple purity, as I longed to do at the start. Since there is nothing but the idea, the idea is all I can tell you about. "I'd like to tell you an idea." But how can an idea be told? There came a jolt (the "ugliness" of this word has often been held up to me, but once again there is no other way of saying it). It grew light? It widened? It took hold of me? It vibrated? It blew warm? It cleared? It was day again at the end of the day? No, the idea resists my narrative urge. It provides me with no picture to serve as an excuse. And yet it was corporeal, more corporeal than any image or representation has ever been; it synthesized all the body's dispersed senses into energy. Idea means this: It provided no picture, only light. This idea was not recollection of well-spent childhood days; it cast its beam exclusively forward, on the future. If it can be told, then only in the future form, a future story, such as "On a successful day, day will dawn again at noon. It will give me a jolt, two jolts: one pressing me onward, the other reaching deep inside me. At the end of the successful day, I shall have the effrontery to say that for once I had lived as one should live—with an effrontery corresponding to my innate reserve." No, the idea was not about childhood days, the days of yore; it was about a grownup day, a future day, and the idea was in reality an action, it acted, intervened beyond the simple future, as a hortative form, with the help of which, for example, Van Morrison's song might be rendered more or less as follows: "On the successful day, the Catskill Mountains should be the Catskills, the turn-off to the rest area should be the turn-off to the rest area, the Sunday paper should be the Sunday paper, nightfall should be nightfall, your radiance beside me should . . ." Of course, but how is that sort of thing to be brought about? Will my own dance be enough? Or should it be "Anmut" or "Grazia" or "Gnade" instead of "Grace"? And what does it signify that the time when the idea of the successful day first crossed my mind was not a long period of near-despair? The monster of speechlessness has given way to silence. In broad daylight his dream about the bird's nest made of hay, flat on the ground, with the naked, cheeping chicks in it, recurred. The particles of mica in the stone sidewalk glittered close to my eyes. His memory of his mother's warmth that day when she gave him all the money she had for a new watch strap, and his memory of the maxim: "God loveth a cheerful giver." The flying blackbird's wing that grazed the hedge far down the road grazed him at the same time. On the asphalt platform of the Issy-Plaine station the overlapping marks of a thousand different shoe soles imprinted by yesterday's rain have now dried into a lighter color. As he passed the unknown child, the child's cowlick repeated itself in his mind. The steeple of Saint-Germain-des-Prés, across from the cafés, the bookshop, the salon de coiffure, and the pharmacy, was simultaneously translated to another day, removed from the "current date" and its moods. Last night's deadly fear was what it was. The splintered shop window was what it was. The disorders beyond the Caucasus were what they were. My hand and her hip—they were. It was the warmth of earth colors from the path along the railroad to Versailles. A dream of the all-encompassing, all-absorbing book, long gone from the world, long dreamed to an end—was back again all of a sudden; or renewed? here in the daytime world, and needed only to be written down. A Mongoloid woman, or perhaps a saint, with a knapsack on her back ran across the pedestrian crossing in an ecstasy of terror. And that night there was only one customer in the bar of another small-town station; while the *patron* was drying glasses, the house cat was playing with a billiard ball between the tables, the jagged shadows of the plane-tree leaves were dancing over the dusty windowpane, and the urgent need arose to find a different word from *blinking* for the lights of a moving train seen through a curtain of foliage—as though the discovery of a single appropriate word could make this entire day successful in the sense that "all phenomena (or, in contemporary, secular terms: all forms) are light."

Then at last, in disregard of logic or timeliness, a third voice, obscure, dim of outline, stuttering-stammering, a storytelling voice that seemed to come from below, from the underbrush, from far away, butted into our essay on the successful day. —At last? Or unfortunately? To its detriment?

Fortunately or not, an "unfortunately" is in order, for a while at least; for in the following a relapse into hairsplitting cannot be avoided. Does Van Morrison's song tell of a successful day, or only of a happy one? Because in the present context a "successful day" was dangerous, fraught with obstacles, narrow escapes, ambushes, perils, tempests, comparable to the days of Odysseus on his homeward wanderings, a story of days that can end only in eating, drinking, reveling, and the "godlike bedding of a woman." But the dangers of my present day are neither the boulder from the giant's sling nor any of the other well-known perils; the dangerous part of my day is the day itself. Most likely this has always been the case, especially in epochs and parts of the world where wars and other catastrophes seemed far behind (how many diaries from how many so-called Golden Ages begin in the morning with resolutions for that one day and in the evening record their failure)—but when was such a day, yours or mine, ever seen before? And in an even more golden future mightn't its problem be even more timely and acute? At least for people like you and me, here and now in our halfway peaceful regions, the "specific demands of the day," quite apart from its duties, struggles, distractions—days as such, available days, each moment of which offers possibilities to be grasped at—have become a challenge, a potential friend, a potential enemy, a game of chance. But if such an adventure, or duel, or mere contest between you and the day, is to be withstood, conquered, made to bear fruit, it is essential that you receive no decisive help from any third factor, neither a piece of work nor the most delightful pastime, nor even from Van Morrison's bumpy ride; indeed, even such a distraction as "a short walk" would seem to be incompatible with a successful day—as though the day itself were the undertaking to be accomplished and brought home folded and packaged by me, preferably right here on the spot, while lying, sitting, standing, or at the most taking a few steps back and forth, doing nothing but looking and listening, or perhaps just breathing, but that involuntarily—with no effort on my part, as in every other segment of life on such a day—as though total involuntariness were prerequisite to this success. And would it thus give rise to a dance?

And now two fundamentally different versions of the individual's adventure with this day can be plotted. In the first he succeeds, the moment he wakes up, in casting off those dreams that are mere ballast that would encumber him on his course, and taking with him those that will form a counterweight to world events and the happenings of his day; in the morning air the earth's continents merge; at the same time a crackling is heard in the leaves of a bush in Tierra del Fuego; the alien light of the afternoon, unbewitched from one moment to the next through knowledge of a fata morgana emanating from yourself; and from then on what's needed for success is just to let night fall without losing your eyes for the dusk. And then, though nothing has happened, you must have it in you to go on interminably about your day. Ah, the moment when at last there was nothing but the old man in the blue apron in the front garden! And the opposite version? It must be short—preferably something like this: Paralyzed by the gray of dawn, a bundle of misery is cast adrift; his ship, named *The Adventure of the Day*, capsizes in the waters of the forenoon, so he never gets to know the silence of midday, let alone the hours after that—and ends up deep in the night at the exact same place from which our hero should have started out at the crack of dawn. To tell the truth, the words and images with which to relate the failure of his day do not exist, except for such worn-out allegories as we have just been using.

Thus it would seem that, before you can regard a day as successful, every moment from waking to falling asleep at night must count, or, more specifically, represent a trial (or danger) faced. But aren't you struck by the fact that for most other people a single moment counts as a successful day (and that there is something smug about your conception so different from the prevailing view)? "When I stood at the window in the dawning light, a little bird darted by and let out a sound which seemed to be meant for me—that in itself was a successful day" (Narrator A). —"The day became successful at the moment when the phone—though you had no other plan than to go on reading the book—communicated to me the Wanderlust of your voice" (Narrator B). —"To be able to tell myself that the day is successful, I had no need of a particular moment—all I needed on waking was a mere breath, *un souffle*, or something of the sort" (a third narrator). And hasn't it occurred to you that as a rule the question of whether a day is to be successful has been decided before the day has properly begun?

Here at least we shall not count a single moment, however glorious, as a successful day. (We shall count only the whole day.) Nevertheless, the moments I have mentioned, especially the first moments of full consciousness after the night's sleep, may well provide the starting point for the Line of Beauty and Grace. And once the starting point for the day is set, let the day proceed point by point in a high arc. As I listen for a tone, the tonality of the whole day's journey reveals itself to me. The tone does not have to be a full sound, it can be indifferent, as often as not a mere noise; the essential is that I make myself all ears for it. Didn't the clicking of the buttons, when I stripped my shirt off the chair this morning, provide me with a kind of diapason for my day? And when yesterday morning, instead of reaching blindly and heedlessly for the first thing I needed, I did so carefully, with open eyes, didn't that supply me with the right rhythm for taking hold of things all the rest of the day? And mightn't the continual sensation of wind and water in the new morning—or, instead of "sensation," wouldn't it be preferable to say "awareness," or simply "feeling" in my eyes, my temples, and wrists—mightn't this sensation attune me to the coming elements of the day, prepare me to dissolve into them and let them work on me? (Answer reserved for the present.) Such a successful moment: Viaticum? Impulse? Nourishment with breath as spirit for the rest of this one day; for such a moment gives strength, and in telling about the next moment one might, drawing on another literal translation of "moment" again from a Pauline epistle, begin with "And with one casting of the eye . . .": With one casting of the eye the sky turned blue, and with the next casting of the eye the green of the grass became a greening, and . . . Who has ever experienced a successful day? But who has ever experienced a successful day? Not to mention the difficulty of tracing the curve of that line!

The clouds of the still invisible dog's breath came puffing through the cracks in the fence. The few remaining leaves on the trees trembled in the foggy wind. The forest began just behind the village railroad station. Two men were washing the telephone booth; the one outside was white, the one inside was black.

And if I fail to seize a moment of this kind, does it mean

that my whole day has failed? If this last apple, instead of being carefully picked, were torn blindly from the branch—would all the preceding consonances between the day and me be nullified? If I were insensitive to the glance of a child, evaded the beggar's glance, were unable to face the glance of that woman (or even of that drunk)—would that mean a break in my rhythm, a fall from my day? And would it be impossible to make a fresh start that same day? Would that day's failure be irrevocable? With the consequence that for me the daylight would not only diminish as it does for most other people, but also, and this is where the danger lies, that brightness of form might degenerate into the hell of formlessness? Thus, for example, if the musical clicking of the buttons against the wood were repeated on such an unsuccessful day, I should be condemned to hear it as noise. Or if in a moment of carelessness I were to reach out "blindly" for a glass and drop it, causing it to shatter into smithereens, wouldn't that be a catastrophe and far more than a mere mishap, though of course everyone else in the room would deny it: —the incursion of death into the current day? And would I be condemned—and rightly so—as the most presumptuous of beings, because in aspiring to live a successful day I had wanted to be like a god? For the idea of such a day—to move onward and ever onward on the same level while carrying light—is, after all, a project fit only for our ill-fated Lucifer. Does this mean that my attempt at a successful day is in danger of degenerating at any moment into a story of murder and mayhem, of running amok, devastation, annihilation, and suicide?

You are confusing a successful day with a perfect day. (No need to say anything about the latter or its god.) At the end of a thoroughly imperfect day, you might cry out in spite of yourself: "A successful day!" Conceivable, too, is a day during which you have been painfully aware of unsuccessful moments, and yet at the end of which you report at length to your friends on "a striking success." Your leaving the book that, as you sensed in reading the first line, started the day off right, in the train, needn't mean that you've lost your fight with the angel of the day; even if you never find the book again, your reading that began so full of promise may well continue in a different manner—perhaps more freely, more spontaneously. The success of my days seems to depend on how I evaluate (another ugly word, but the brooding writer finds no better—*appraise*? *estimate*?) deviations from the line, my own as well as those imposed by Madame World. The success of our "successful day" expedition seems to presuppose a certain indulgence toward myself, my nature, my incorrigibilities, as well as an insight into the hazards of daily life even under favorable circumstances: the insidiousness of objects, evil eye, that one word spoken at the wrong moment (even if only overheard by someone in a crowd). Thus in my undertaking, everything hinges on the handicap I allow myself. How much mucking around, how much carelessness or absentmindedness I tolerate in myself. How much incomprehension, impatience, unfairness, how much clumsiness, how many heartless remarks, spoken without thinking (or not even spoken), how many newspaper headlines, or advertisements that catch my eye or ear, how many stitches in my side will it take before I lose my openness to the shimmering that corresponds to the episodic greening and bluing of grass and sky, and the occasional "graying" of stone, signifying that on a certain day the "coming of day" carries over to me and to space. I am too hard on myself, not indifferent enough about my mishaps with things, too full of demands on the times, too convinced that everything is going to the dogs: I have no standard for the success of a day. Indeed, what with myself and the kinds of things that happen regularly or irregularly, the situation would seem to call for a special kind of irony—the affectionate kind—and of humor, of the sort named after the gallows. Who has ever experienced a successful day?

His day began promisingly. A few lance-shaped pencils lay on the windowsill along with a handful of oval hazelnuts. Even the numbers of both sets of objects contributed to his sense of well-being. He had dreamed about a child lying on the bare floor in a bare room, who said when he bent down to him: "You're a good father." On the street the postman whistled as he did every morning. The old woman in the house next door was already closing her dormer window for the rest of the day. The sand in the columns of trucks en route to the building site was as yellow as the drifting sand that made up the hills of the region. By letting the water in the hollow of his hand act on his face, he had gained awareness not only of the water in the village here but also of the "water of Ioannia on the far slope of the Pindus," of the "water of Bitola in Macedonia," of the water that morning in Santander, where the rain seemed to be pelting down, but when he went out proved to be so fine a curtain that he hardly got wet when passing through it. With the sound of a turning book page in his ears, he heard from far beyond the gardens the clanking of the local train slowing down in the station and at the same time, amid the squawking of the crows and the whining of the magpies, the lone cheeping of a sparrow. Then he looked up, never before had he seen the bare, solitary tree high up on the edge of the wooded hill, through whose branches as they shifted in the wind the brightness of the plateau shone down into the house, while on the table at which he sat reading, the letter *S*, sewn into the tablecloth, revealed a picture of an apple and of a smooth, black, rounded stone. When he looked up again—"work can wait, I can wait, it and I, we can both wait"—the day was literally whirring, and he noticed now, without having looked for the words, he was thinking to himself: "Sacred world!" He went out into the forest to chop wood for a fire in the fireplace, which it seemed to him would be better suited to such a day rather than to the evening. As he was sawing the thick, tough tree, the blade stuck, breaking his rhythm; he tugged violently, but it refused to budge; he could only give up, pull—or better, "wrench"—the saw out and start in a different place. The whole comedy repeated itself—the blade stuck in the heartwood, he pushed and shook until he had almost reached the point of no return . . . and then with stunning force the log, more mangled than sawed, fell on the foot of the would-be hero of the day. Finally, after a first flaring and a subdued hissing, his fire collapsed, and he cursed the holy day in the exact same words for which his rustic grandfather had been known throughout the village: Shut up, blasted birds, beat it, sun. Later, it sufficed for his pencil point to break, and not only the day, but the future as well, was compromised. By the time he realized that these very mishaps might have made something of the day, it had long since become a different day. If he had observed it with care, he would have recognized that this vain attempt to light a fire—hadn't the smothering and blackening of the flame represented a mysterious moment of community?—was the quintessence of all futilities, and not only those of a personal nature. If he had recognized this, he would have stopped trying and exercised patience. And similarly, the blow of the log on his toes had given him something more than pain. It had also touched something else in him, at the same place; something like the friendly muzzle of an animal. And that again was an image—an image in which all the logs from his childhood down to the present moment united to fall—or rather, to roll, bounce, dance, or rain down on all his different shoes, socks, and variously sized child or adult feet; for that other contact was so miraculously gentle that if he had merely taken note of it for a moment he would have been all amazement. And similarly, as he realized later on when he looked back at a distance, his setbacks while sawing wood provided him with a complete parable, or fable?, for the success of his day. The main thing was to begin with a jolt and find the right starting point for the saw's teeth, a groove in which the saw could continue to function. After that, the sawing took on a rhythm. For a time it went easily and gave him pleasure; one thing led to another; sawdust sprayed from both sides, the tiny leaves of the nearby box tree curled, the crackling of the foliage caught in it mingled with the squeaking of the saw; the rumble of a garbage can was followed by the droning of a jet plane high in the sky. And then, gradually as a rule and, provided he kept his mind on what he was doing, perceptible in advance, the saw entered into a different layer of the wood. Here it became necessary to change his rhythm—to slow down, but that was the risky part of it—to do so without halting or skipping a beat; even when the rhythm changed, the general sawing movement had to maintain its regularity; otherwise, the saw would be sure to stick. Then, if at all possible, one had to pull it out and reapply it, preferably, as the fable taught, not in the same place or in one too close to it, but in a totally different place, because . . . If the change of place was successful at the second try, and the sawing was finally successful in the lower half of the tree trunk—long after the exhilarated sawyer had lost sight of the saw's teeth—already he was elsewhere in his thoughts, making plans for the evening or sawing a human enemy in two instead of the tree—then a new danger threatened, if not a forking branch he had overlooked, then (usually no more than a finger's breadth from the point where the piece of wood, having been cut through that far, would fall of its own accord) that narrow but extremely tough layer in which steel would strike against stone, nail, and bone all in one, and just before the finale, so to speak, the undertaking would come to grief. For a brief moment, music to the ears of a stranger but to the sawyer himself caterwauling—and that was the end of it. And yet he had been so close to success that sawing for its own sake, just being with the wood, its roundness, its smell, its grain, just traversing the material, while studying its special characteristics and resistances, became the ideal embodiment of his dream of disinterested pleasure. And likewise the breaking pencil point . . . and so forth and so on, all day. Thus, he reflected later, in an attempt at a successful day, everything, at least in moments of misfortune, of pain, of failure, when things were going wrong—the essential was to summon up the presence of mind needed for a different variety of this moment and thus to transform it, by a liberating act of awareness or reflection, whereby the day—as though this were the prerequisite for its success—would acquire its élan and its wings.

You make it sound as though your successful day were child's play.

No answer.

By then it was noon. The night's hoarfrost had thawed even in the shaded corners of the garden, and as the bowed, stiff blades of grass straightened up, a soft breeze blew through them. A stillness arose, became a picture when he walked in the sunlight on the untraveled noonday road, with those pairs of varicolored butterflies which, emerging unexpectedly out of the void, seemed to be moving backward and came so close to the wayfarer that he seemed to feel in his outer ears the vibration of their wings, which instantly communicated itself to his steps. For the first time he heard, in the interior of the almost uninhabited house, the midday bells of the village church mingling with those of the next village (which, as usual in this part of the country, began without transition or interval, on the other side of the street) ring out with a palpable message: a call in all directions to all isolated beings. The city of Paris lay deep at the bottom of a bowl, surrounded by stony desert mountains, and in the soundless dusk the fervid calls of the muezzins poured down upon it from every peak and slope round about. Involuntarily he looked up from the line he was reading and went out with the cat, crossing the garden in a long, curving diagonal; it passed through his mind how long ago another cat had announced the onset of rain by galloping to shelter under the overhanging roof the moment the first drop from the distant horizon fell on its fur. He looked around, noted, as he had done for weeks, how the garden's last fruit, one enormous pear, still hung on the otherwise empty tree, and hefted it for a moment in the hollow of his hand, while across the street, in the neighboring village, a black-haired Chinese girl carrying a varicolored back satchel kept stroking a blue-eyed Alaskan dog through the fence (though he could not hear it, the dog's whimpering was all the more prolonged in his imagination), and a little farther on, in the gap between the houses at the distant junction of two streets, the sun's reflection on a passing train lit up the grass of the embankment for a moment, the length as it were of a word, a monosyllable, during which he glimpsed an empty seat in one compartment, slashed with a knife and mended with fairy-tale care, cross-stitch after cross-stitch in the stiff plastic fabric, and he felt himself gripped by the faraway hand that was pulling the thread tight. Thus his forehead grazed his dead; he watched them just as they watched him, he who was doing nothing but sitting there, sympathetically, not at all as in their lifetime. What more was there to do, to discover, to recognize, to discover in a day? Behold: no king of eternity, no king of life (and if so only a "secret" one) —No, here stands the king of the day! The only odd part of it was that at this point a trifle sufficed to topple him from his imperious throne. At the sight of the passerby who came sauntering out of the side street, with his coat over his arm, stopped, patted his pockets, and quickly turned back, my sympathy turned to desperation. Stop! But once in ecstasy I could no longer find the way back into myself: There, the blackbird's yellow bill. And, at the end of the avenue, the brownish edge of the one mallow still in bloom. And that leaf—tugging at an invisible thread as it falls, and apparently rising back into the sun—it looks like a bright-colored kite. And the horizon, black with a swarm of monumental, meaningless words! Stop! Leave me in peace! (To him ecstasy meant panic.) But enough! Stop! —No more reading, gazing, being-in-the-picture, no more day—this couldn't go on. What now? And unexpectedly, after the procession of leaping forms and ecstatic colors, long before nightfall, death barred the passage through this day. At one stroke, its sting punctured the whole extravaganza. After that, could anything be more crackbrained than the idea of a successful day? Mustn't his essay on it start all over again, with a radically new attitude, that of gallows humor? Is it impossible to lay down a line for the success of a day, not even a labyrinthine line? But must one not infer that this constant starting the essay from scratch is itself a possibility, the possibility specific to the project? The essay must be. Quite possibly the day (the object named "day") had now become my mortal enemy, an enemy that cannot be transformed into a helpful living-and-traveling companion, a luminous model, a lasting fragrance, quite possibly the "successful day" project is diabolical, an invention of the devil, the disrupter, a veil dance with nothing behind it, a maddening tongue play, followed directly by a devouring, a road pointer that, if you follow it, closes into a noose; that may be, but I fail to see why, in view of all the failures I have met with in my quest for a successful day, I am still unable to *say* that the idea of a successful day is a snare and a delusion, and consequently that cannot be the case. I can say, however, that the idea is indeed an idea, for I didn't think it up or get it from my reading; it came to me in a time of distress, and it came with a power that for me has always carried credibility—the power of the imagination. Imagination is my faith, the idea of a successful day was conceived in its most ardent moment, and after each one of my countless shipwrecks, on the following morning (or afternoon) it lit the way for me anew, just as in Mörike's poem a rose "*vorleuchtet*" (shone before), and I was able with its help to make a fresh start. The success of the day was something that had to be attempted—even if in the end the fruit turned out to be hollow or dry: thus this vain labor of love was superfluous at least for the foreseeable future, and then the road would be open for something different. And another dependable insight was that a "nothing" day (a day marked not even by changing lights, a day without wind or weather) gave promise of the utmost richness. Nothing was, and again there was nothing, and again there was nothing. And what did this nothing and again nothing do? It signified. More was possible with nothing but the day, far, far more both for you and for me. And that was the crux: the main thing was to let the nothing fructify from morning to night (or even midnight). And I repeat: the day was light. The day is light.

The blackness of the nameless pond in the woods. Snow clouds above the Île-de-France horizon. The smell of pencils. The ginkgo leaf on the boulder in the garden of La Pagode cinema. The carpet in the topmost window of the Vélizy railroad station. A school, a pair of children's glasses, a book, a hand. The whirring in my temples. For the first time this winter, the powerful cracking of the ice under the soles of my shoes. In the railroad underpass, he acquired eyes for the substance of light. Reading in a crouch, close to the grass. While I was breaking off leaves, suddenly a whiff in my nostrils resembling the essence of the declining year. The word for the sound of the train pulling into the station had to be *thumping*, not *clanking*. And the last leaf falling from the tree didn't "crackle," it "clicked." And a stranger involuntarily exchanged greetings with him. And again the old woman hauled her pushcart to the weekly village market. And the usual disorientation of a foreign car driver in this out-of-the-way place. And then in the forest, the greening of the path where he used to take a walk with his father whenever there was something to talk over, a path that even had a name in his language, *zelena pot*, "the green path." And then in the bar near the church of the next village, the pensioner, whose grandfather's watch chain extended in a curved line from his belly to his trouser pocket. And for once he overlooked the evil eye cast by one of the old inhabitants. And the proverbial "Thanks [instead of disgruntlement] for your trouble"; for once the transformation was successful. But why then in the middle of the enjoyable afternoon, fear of the rest of the day, of nothing but the day? As though there were no getting through the coming hours ("This day will be the end of me")—no way out. The ladder leaning against the early-winter tree. So what? The blue of the flowers deep in the grass of the railroad embankment—so what? Paralysis, consternation, a kind of horror, and the serene silence shattered by more and more speechlessness. Eden is burning. And, on the other hand, it becomes evident that there is no formula for the success of a day. "O morning!" The exclamation doesn't work. No more reading, no more day? No more possession of words? No more day? And such muteness excludes prayer, all but such impossible prayers as "Morning me," "Early me," "Begin me again." Who knows whether certain mysterious suicides were the secret consequences of such a quest for the successful day, begun energetically on the so-called ideal line. But, on the other hand, doesn't my failure to stand up to the day tell me something? That my internal order is wrong? That I'm not made for a whole day? That I shouldn't look for morning at nightfall? Or perhaps I should?

And he made it start again. The day when the idea of the successful day had come to live in him on the tangent of the suburban train high above gigantic Paris—how had it been as a whole? What was before that flare-up? What came after it? ("*Ausculta, o filii*, listen, my son," said the angel in the church on Lake Constance, where the chalky vein had copied Hogarth's Line of Beauty and Grace for him on the black stone.) —What had gone before, he remembered, was a nightmarish night spent on a mattress in an otherwise totally deserted house in a southern suburb of Paris. This dream had consisted of nothing, or so it had seemed, but a night-long motionless image, in which, amid unchanging twilight and soundless air, he was exposed to the elements on a bare, towering cliff, alone for the rest of his life. And only one thing happened, but that happened perpetually, heartbeat after heartbeat, utter forlornness—the planet was congealed, but in his heart tempestuous fever. When he finally awoke, it was as though his night-long fever had consumed his forlornness—for a time at least. Over the half-parched garden the sky was blue, for the first time in a long while. He helped himself out of his feeling of dizziness with a dance step, "the dizzy man's dance." The world went green before his eyes, that was the cypresses along the garden wall. Under the sign of grief and of this green he began his day. What would I be without a garden? he thought. I never want to be without a garden again. And still there was pain in his breast, a dragon devouring him. Sparrows landed in the bushes, once again the birds of the right moment. I saw a ladder and wanted to climb it. A mason's straightedge was floating in the gutter, and farther down the street the young postwoman was pushing her bicycle with the yellow saddlebags. Instead of PROPRIÉTÉ PRIVÉE, DÉFENSE D'ENTRER, he read . . . DÉFENSE D'AIMER. It was late morning, and as he walked he let the quietness of the place blow through his parted fingers. Temples, inflated sails. He was supposed that day to finish an article on translation, and at last he had an image for that sort of activity: "The translator felt himself gently taken by the elbow." Work or love? Get to work, that's the way to rediscover love. The man behind the counter in the North African bar was just starting up: "*O rage! O désespoir . . .*" and a woman on her way in remarked, "It doesn't smell of couscous here. It smells of ragout, that's because the sun is back again—*merci pour le soleil.*" Give me the day, give me to the day. After a long bus ride through the southern and then the western suburbs and a hike through the forests of Clamart and Meudon, he sat down at a table in the open beside a pond, finished his piece about translation, an activity that he abjured in his last sentence: "Not the confident, lowered glance at the existing book, but an eye-level glance into the uncertain!" The wild strawberries at the edge of the path seemed to look on and blush. "The wind took him over." He thought of the raven that bellowed "like a bazooka" into his dream of forlornness. By the pond of the next forest he ate a sandwich on the terrace of the fishermen's bar. A fine rain was falling in spirals, as though enjoying itself. And then, in the middle of the afternoon, that train ride circling around above Paris, first eastward, then northward in an arc, then back in an eastward arc—so that in a single day he had almost circled the entire metropolis—during which the idea of the successful day recurred, no, *recurred* was not the right word, it should have been "was transformed": during which the idea of the successful day was transformed from a "life idea" to a "writing idea." His heart, which still ached from his nightmare, expanded when he saw the "Heights of the Seine" at his feet. (Suddenly he understood the name of the department, Les Hauts-de-Seine.) Illusion? No. The true element of life. And then what? Now, half a year later, in the late autumn, he remembered how after the excessively bright life of the "casting of the eye," he had positively welcomed the dark, underground stretch near La Défense. Exhilarated, he let himself be jostled by the after-work crowd in the hall of the Gare Saint-Lazare, which in French is known as the Hall of the Lost Steps. At the American Express Company near the Opéra he provided himself with as much cash as possible after waiting in a long line with rare, and in his own opinion rather alarming, patience. Amazed at the size and emptiness of the toilets, he stayed there longer than necessary, looking around, as though there were something to be discovered in such a place. One of a crowd, he stood watching television in a bar on the rue Saint-Denis; a World Cup soccer match was on, and to this day he remembers his annoyance at not having quite succeeded in repressing all side glances at the streetwalkers who were overflowing from every doorway and back court of that street—as though the ability to overlook were a part of such a day. And then what? He seemed to have lost consciousness of everything else, except for a moment later in the evening when he sat with a child on his lap at a kind of school desk, putting the finishing touches to his sketch about translation—in his memory, a strange picture of juggling with two hands—and for some time late at night when in a garden café I found myself unintentionally exchanging stories with the man sitting across from you—which had the effect in the gentlest possible way of breaking you open and sharing you with myself. Then as now the day seemed marked by that gigantic S-curve of the railroad line, which can be seen only in bird's-eye view, but can be felt deep down inside to be the most beautiful of all meanders, parallel to that of the Seine below but swinging much wider, rediscovered a month later in a quiet corner of the Tate Gallery in the furrow in Hogarth's palette, and yet another month later in the white vein in the stone found on the shore of the stormy, autumnal Lake Constance, at the present moment running in the same direction as the pencils here on my table: that is the enduring outline of the day. And its color is chiaroscuro. And its adjective, like that of the idea which it gave me, is, as it should be, *fantastic*, and its noun, after my solitary night of peril, the word *with*.

So your idea of writing an essay about a successful day was itself a successful day?

That was before the summer. Over the garden the swallows were flying "so high!" I shared a young woman's pleasure in smoothing out the curved brim of a straw hat; the Pentecost fête was lively in the night wind of our village, the cherry tree stood fruit-red beside the railroad tracks, the workaday garden came to be called the Garden of the Step Taken—and now it was winter, as, for example, it revealed itself on the railroad curve repeated yesterday for my reassurance as I could see by the handrail and the gray flowering of the clumps of wild grapes against the misty network of the Eiffel Tower, the snowberries whishing past the distant towers of La Défense, the acacia thorn jerking past the barely discernible hazy whiteness of the domes of the Sacré-Coeur.

Once again: In the light of all this, was that a successful day?

No answer.

I think, no, thanks to my imagination, I know it was. How much more could be done with that day, with nothing but that day. And now its momentum is in my life, in your life, in our epoch. ("We lost our momentum," said the captain of a baseball team that had been about to win the game.) The day is in my power, for my time. If I don't give the day a try now, then I've missed my chance of enduring; more and more often, I realize, all the while growing angrier at myself, how as time goes on more and more moments speak to me and how I understand, and above all appreciate, less and less of what they say. I must repeat, I am furious with myself, over my inability to maintain the morning light on the horizon, which just now made me look up and come to rest (*into* rest, we read in the Pauline epistle), so that, when I start reading, the blue of the heather still occupies the middle ground, a few pages farther on it is a vague spot in the Nowhere, and by the onset of dusk the motionless form of the blackbird in the bush is still "the outline of Evening Island after a day on the open sea," and a tick of the watch later is nothing more—meaningless, forgotten, betrayed. Yes, that's how it is: more and more as the years go by—the richer the moments seem to me, the louder they denounce me to high heaven—I see myself as a traitor to my day, day after day, forgetful of the day, forgetful of the world. Again and again I resolve to remain faithful to the day, with the help, led "by the hand" (*maintenant*, "hand-holding," that's your word for "now") of those moments. I would like to hold them, think about them, preserve them, and day after day, no sooner have I turned away from them than they literally "fall" from my hands, as though to punish me for my infidelity, for, it can't be denied, I had turned away from them. Fewer and fewer of the increasingly frequent significant moments of the day *ripen*, yes, that's the word, ripen anything for me. The moment of the children's voices this morning in the lane ripened nothing; now in the afternoon, with clouds drifting eastward, it produces no aftereffect—though at the time they seemed to rejuvenate the wintry forest . . . Should that be taken to mean that the time for my essay on the successful day is past? Have I let the moment slip by? Should I have gotten up earlier? And rather than an essay, mightn't the psalm form—a supplication presumed in advance to be in vain—have been more conducive to the idea of such a day? Day, let everything in you ripen something for me. Ripen the ticking of the lanceolate willow leaves as they fall through the air, the left-handed ticket agent deep in his book, who once again makes me wait for my ticket, the sun on the door handle. Ripen me. I've become my own enemy, I destroy the light of my day, destroy my love, destroy my book. The more often individual moments resound as pure vowels—*vowel* is another word for such a moment—the more seldom I find the consonant to go with it, to carry me through the day. The glow at the end of the sandy path to the nameless pond: Ah! but a moment later it has faded, as though it had never been. Divine Being, or "Thou, the more-than-I" that once spoke through the Prophets and later on "through the Son," dost thou also speak in the present, purely through the day? And why am I unable to hold, grasp, pass on what thus speaks through the day, and, I believe, or rather, thanks to my imagination, know, starts speaking anew at every moment? "He who is and who was and who will be": Why can what once was said of "the god" not be said of my present day?

On a successful day—attempt at a chronicle of this day—globules of dew on a raven feather. As usual, the old woman, though perhaps not the same one as yesterday, stood around in the newspaper shop long after completing her purchase, and spoke her mind. The ladder in the garden—embodiment of his need to get out of himself—had seven rungs. The sand in the trucks moving through the village was the same color as the façade of Saint-Germain-des-Prés. The chin of a young girl in the library touched her neck. A tin bucket took its shape. A mailbox turned yellow. The market woman wrote the bill on the palm of her hand. On a successful day it happens that a cigarette butt rolls in the gutter, that a cup smokes on a tree stump, and that a row of seats within the dark church is bright in the sunshine. It happens that the few men in the café, even the loudmouth, keep silent together for a long moment, and that the stranger to the village keeps silent with them. It happens that my sharpened hearing for my work also opens me up to the sounds in the house. It happens that one of your eyes is smaller than the other, that the blackbird hops under the bush, and that when the lower branches rise I think "updraft." Finally, it even happens that nothing happens. On the successful day, a habit will be discontinued, an opinion vanish, and I shall be surprised by him, by you, by myself. And along with *with*, a second word form will dominate; namely, *and*. In the house I shall discover a corner that has hitherto been overlooked, where "someone could live!" As I turn into a side street, "Where am I? I've never been here before" will be a sensational moment; when I see the light-dark space in a hedge, the "New World explorer" feeling will set in, and when I walk a little farther than usual and look back, a cry of "I never saw that before" will escape me. Your repose, as sometimes happens in children, will also be amazement. On the successful day, I shall simply have been its medium, simply have gone along with the day, let the sun shine on me, the wind blow on me, the rain rain on me, my verb will have been *let*. In the course of the day, your inwardness will become as varied as the outside world, and by the end of the day you will have translated Odysseus's epithet, "the much-buffeted," to yourself as "the many-sided," and that many-sidedness will have made you dance inwardly. On a successful day, the hero would have been able to "laugh" at his mishaps (or would at least have started to laugh at the third mishap). He would have been in the company of forms—if only of the various leaves on the ground. His I-day would have opened out into a world-day. Every place would have acquired its moment, and he would have been able to say: "This is it." He would have arrived at an understanding with mortality. ("Never has death spoiled the sport of the day.") His epithet for everything would have been an unchanging "In view of": In view of you, in view of a rose, in view of the asphalt, and matter, or "corporeity"?, would have cried out to him, time and again for creation. He would have put on a show of good cheer and cheerfully done nothing, and from time to time a weight on his back would have kept him warm. For a moment, for a "casting of the eye," the time of a word, he would suddenly have become you. And at the end of the day he would have called out for a book—something more than a mere chronicle: "The fairy tale of the successful day." And at the very end, he would have gloriously forgotten that the day was supposed to be successful . . .

Have you ever experienced a successful day? Everyone I know has experienced one; most people have actually had many. One was satisfied if the day hadn't been too long. Another said something like: "Standing on the bridge, with the sky over me. In the morning, laughed with the children. Just looking, nothing special. There's happiness in looking." And in the opinion of a third, simply the village street through which he had just passed—with the raindrops dripping from the enormous key of the locksmith's sign, with the bamboo shoots cooking in somebody's front garden, with the three bowls on a kitchen windowsill containing tangerines, grapes, and peeled potatoes, with the taxi parked as usual outside the driver's house—was in itself a "successful day." The priest, whose pet word was *longing*, considered a day when he heard a friendly voice successful. And hadn't he himself, who longed time and again for an hour in which nothing had happened, except that a bird turned about on a branch, that a white ball lay at the bottom of a bush, and that schoolchildren were sunning themselves on the station platform, thought in spite of himself: Has this been the whole day? And often in the evening, when he called the events of the past day to mind—yes, it was a kind of "calling"—didn't the things or places of a mere moment occur to him as names for it. "That was the day when the man with the baby carriage went zigzagging through the piles of leaves." "That was the day when the gardener's banknotes were mixed with grass and leaves." "That was the day when the café was empty when the refrigerator rumbled and the light went out . . ." So why not content ourselves with a single successful hour? Why not simply call the moment a day?

Ungaretti's poem "I illuminate myself / with the immeasurable" is entitled "Morning." Couldn't those two lines just as well be about the "afternoon"? Was a fulfilled moment or a fulfilled hour really enough to make you stop asking if you had failed again that day? No use attempting a successful day—why not content ourselves with a "not entirely unsuccessful one"? And if your successful day existed, wasn't your fantasy, however richly and wonderfully it whirred, accompanied by a strange fear of something like an alien planet, and didn't your usual unsuccessful day appear to you as part of Planet Earth, as a kind of—possibly detested—home? As though nothing here below could succeed; except perhaps in grace? in mercy? in grace *and* mercy—if nowadays that didn't imply something improper, undeserved, perhaps even accomplished at someone else's expense? Why now does "successful day" remind me of my dead grandfather, who in his last days did nothing but scratch the wall of his room with his fingernails, lower down from hour to hour. In view of all the general failure and loss, what does a single success amount to?

Not nothing.

The day of which I can say it was "a day," and the day when I was only passing the time. At the crack of dawn. How have people handled their days up to now? How is it that in old stories we often find "Many days were fulfilled," in place of "Many days passed"? Traitor to the day: my own heart. It drives me out of the day, it beats, it hammers me out of it, hunter and hunted in one. Be still! No more secret thoughts. Leaves in my garden shoes. Out of the cage of revolving thought. Be still. Bend down under the apple tree. Go into a crouch. The crouching reader. At knee height, things coalesce to form an environment. And he prepares for the daily injury. Spreads his toes. "The seven days of the garden." That's what the unwritten sequel to *Don Quixote* should be called. To be in the garden, to be on earth. The rate of the earth's rotation is irregular, that's why the days are of unequal length, especially in view of the mountain ranges' resistance to the wind. The success of the day and passivity. Passivity as action. He let the fog drift outside the window; he let the grass blow behind the house. Letting the sun shine on one was an activity; now I'm going to let my forehead be warmed, now my eyeballs, now my knees—and now it's time for teddy-bear warmth between my shoulder blades. The sunflower head does nothing but follow the sun. Compare the successful day with Job's day. Instead of "value the moment," it should be "heed" the moment. The course of the day—thanks precisely to its rough spots, if taken to heart—is in itself a kind of transubstantiation—more than anything else, it can tell me *what I am*. Pause in your endless restlessness, and you will find rest in your flight. And by resting in his flight, he began to hear. Hearing, I am at my peak. Thanks to my keen hearing, I can hear the whirring of a sparrow's wing through the noise. When a leaf falls on the line of the distant horizon, I hear it deep inside me as a ringing. Listening as a safecracker with his jimmy listens for the clicking of the gears. Slowed by flight, the blackbird's hop-skip-jump over the hedge is humming a tune for me. Just as some people hum when reading a book. (But the most you can expect of a newspaper reader is a whistling between the teeth.) "Seeing you are dull of hearing," stormed the zealot in one of his epistles, and in another: "Stop disputing over mere words, it does no good and only bedevils those who listen." A pure tone. If only I could produce a pure tone once for a whole day. Perhaps more important than hearing is pure presence—Picasso's last wife, for example, is said to have done nothing, just to have been present in his studio. A successful day, a hard day. Suddenly, as I was raking the garden leaves, a rooster's foot gleamed candlelight yellow from out of the pile of brownish leaves. Colors darken, form brightens. In the shady corner, where the ground is still frozen hard, my footsteps sound as they did that day in the rushes.

When I look up, the sky is a vault. What did "snow cloud" mean? Rich whiteness with a blue cast. Cracking hazelnuts in the palm of my hand, three of them. In Greek there used to be a word for "I am," which was simply a long-drawn-out *O*; it occurred in such sentences as "While I am in the world, I am the light of the world." And the word for what just passed through the cypress tree was: *lightwave*. Look and keep looking with the eyes of the right word. And it began to snow. It is snowing. *Il neige*. To be silent. There was silence. He was silent in the sign of the dead. One should not say: "He (she) blessed the temporal world" (he [she] passed away) but: "He, she, the dead, bless the temporal world for me, provided I leave them alone." And at the same time wanting to stammer: he wanted to stammer. In the suburbs everything is supposedly so "individual" (a suburbanite speaking). The one-legged stance of the garbage collector at the back of his truck. The bumps placed on the roads at regular intervals were called "decelerators." A single day may not have been sufficiently far-reaching as a model; perhaps it was a model only to itself—which gave pleasure? During the lunch break I help the roofers carry slats down from the ridge. Shouldn't I have stayed home all day, doing nothing but "dwelling"? Bring about a successful day by pure dwelling? To dwell, to sit, to look up, to excel in uselessness. What did you do today? I heard. What did you hear? Oh, the house. Ah, beneath the tent of my book. But why are you going out now, instead of staying in the house, where you were in your place with your book? Because what I've read—I want to digest it out of doors. And look at the corner of the house, which is called "Travels": a small suitcase, a dictionary, hiking shoes. The ringing of bells in the belfry of the village church: the pitch is just right for this noon hour, and up here in the dark dormer window all that can be seen of them is a whirring as of bicycle spokes. Deep within the earth, there are occasional tremors, the so-called slow tremors, and for a while, so it is said, the planet reverberates with them: "the bell movement," the ringing of the earth. The silhouettes of a man and a child with a back satchel sway in the railroad underpass, as if the man were riding on a donkey. According to Goethe, life is short but the day is long, and I seem to remember Marilyn Monroe singing a song that went: "One day too long, one life too short . . ." and another: "Morning becomes evening under my body." Let the quick ellipse described by the last of the leaves of the plane tree in falling provide the line for the ending of my attempted successful day—abbreviation! Hogarth's Line of Beauty is not actually engraved in the palette; it is stretched over it like a curved rope or a whiplash. The successful day and succinctness. (And, alongside it, the desire to postpone the end—as though I, I in particular, could learn more from my essay with each passing day.) The successful day and joyful expectation. The successful day and the discoverer's aberrations. Morning a still life—afternoon a muddle: a mere pseudolaw? Don't let yourself be ruled by these daily pseudolaws. And once again St. Paul. For him "the day" is the Day of Judgment—and for you? The day of measurement; it will not judge, but measure you; you are its people. Who here is talking to whom? I'm talking to myself. The dead silence of the afternoon. Nevertheless, the sound of children running, heard through the wind. And high up there the flower heads of the plane trees are still dangling: "his (her) heart is in it" (from the French). And at any moment, in the rustling of the withered dwarf oaks, now, for instance, I become you. What would we be without that rustling? And what word goes with it? The (toneless) yes. Stay with us, rustling. Keep pace with the day—speak in cadence with the day (homology). What became of that day on the curve high above all Paris, between Saint-Cloud and Suresnes, not far from the Val d'Or station. It hung in the balance. The bright-dark shimmer that day when the swallows veered in the summer sky, and the black-white-blue moment now: the magpies and the winter sky. The S-line again, a few days ago, on the shoulder, neck, and throat of John the Evangelist at the Last Supper over the portal of Saint-Germain-des-Prés, his whole trunk lies there on the table next to the Lord Jesus—for, like the other stone figures, he had been beheaded by the Revolution. The successful day and again history's glorious forgetfulness: instead, the endless lozenge pattern of human eyes—on the streets, in the corridors of the Métro, in the trains. The gray of the asphalt, the blue of the evening sky. The shakiness of my day, the solid and enduring? Set your footprint upon the snow of the station platform beside the print of a bird's foot. A hard day once began to teeter when a single raindrop struck my inner ear. The shoe brush on the wooden stairs at sunset. A child writing its name for the first time. Keep going until the first star. Van Morrison in his song doesn't sing about "fishing in the mountains," but "out all day," about bird-watching. He lets his tongue sing, and barely begun, his song is at an end. The moment of the mud-spattered forester's car in the row of clean cars. The doors of the forest open with a creak. Revolving door of a successful day: in it, things as well as people flare up as *beings*. The successful day and the will to divide it. Constant, wild obligation to be fair. Oh, hard day! Successful? Or "saved"? Unexpectedly, still in the dark, the thrust of joy in carrying on. Yes, a modified word—a proof correction that stands for the day: *thrust* instead of your usual *jolt*. Stop on your night walk: the path is brightening—for once you can say "my path"—and increasing awareness of secrecy, "behold, she comes with the clouds," comes with the wind. Triad of the screech owl. Blue moment of the boat in one woodland pond, black moment of the boat in the next pond. For the first time in this suburb, behind the Heights of the Seine that hide the lights of Paris, caught sight of Orion high in the winter night, behind it parallel columns of smoke from factory chimneys, and under it the five stone steps, leading up to a door in a wall, and Ingrid Bergman in *Stromboli*, who collapses after an almost fatal night on the black, rocky slopes of the volcano, revives at sunrise, and can't get over her amazement. "How beautiful! What beauty!" In the 171 night bus a lone passenger, standing. The burned-out telephone booth. Collision between two cars at the Pointe de Chaville: from one of them leaps a man with a pistol. Glaring television lights in the front windows of the avenue Roger Salengro, the house numbers on which go up to over 2000. The thunder of the bombers taking off from the military airfield in Villacoublay, just beyond the wooded hills, more frequently from day to day with the approach of war.

"But now you're losing the line completely. Go home to your book, to writing and reading. To the original texts, in which for example it is said: 'Let the word resound, stand by it—whether the moment be favorable or not.' Have you ever experienced a successful day? With which for once a successful moment, a successful life, perhaps even a successful eternity might coincide?"

"Not yet. Obviously!"

"Obviously"?

"If I had experienced anything even remotely resembling that, I imagine, I should have to fear not only a nightmare for the following night but the cold sweats."

"Then your successful day is not even an idea, but only a dream?"

"Yes, except that instead of *having* it, I've *made* it in this essay. Look at my eraser, so black and small, look at the pile of pencil shavings below my window. Phrases and more phrases in the void, to no good purpose, addressed to a third incomprehensible something, though the two of us are not lost. Time and again in his epistles, not to the congregations, but to individuals, his helpers, Paul, from his prison in Rome, wrote about winter. For example, 'Do try to get here before winter. And when you come, bring the cloak I left with Carpus at Troas . . .'"

"And where is the cloak now? Forget the dream. See how the snow falls past the empty bird's nest. Arise to transubstantiation."

"To the next dream?"

PUBLISHER'S NOTE

Peter Handke and Ralph Manheim had a fruitful, long-standing collaboration and were accustomed to reviewing translations together. Mr. Manheim, who translated works by many internationally acclaimed writers, died shortly after completing his translation of two pieces included in this volume: "Essay on the Successful Day" and "Essay on Tiredness." The final editing of these two essays was done after Mr. Manheim's death, with Mr. Handke's approval.

Printed in the USA
CPSIA information can be obtained
at www.ICGtesting.com
LVHW041157040424
776395LV00002B/368

9 781250 862969